Graphic Standards
Field Guide
to Hardscape

Also available in the Graphic Standards Field Guide series:

Graphic Standards Field Guide to Commercial Interiors
Graphic Standards Field Guide to Softscape
Graphic Standards Field Guide to Hardscape
Graphic Standards Field Guide to Residential Architecture
Graphic Standards Field Guide to Home Inspections
Graphic Standards Field Guide to Residential Construction
Graphic Standards Field Guide to Building Construction

Graphic Standards Field Guide to Hardscape

LEONARD J. HOPPER, RLA FASLA

John Wiley & Sons, Inc.

A special thank you to those who helped develop the Graphic Standards Field Guide series:
Corky Binggeli, ASID
Nina M. Giglio CSI, Assoc. AIA, SCIP
Dennis J. Hall, FCSI,FAIA, SCIP
Leonard J. Hopper, RLA, FASLA

This book is printed on acid-free paper. ∞

Published by John Wiley & Sons, Inc., Hoboken, New Jersey

Published simultaneously in Canada

Limit of Liability/Disclaimer of Warranty: While the publisher and the author have used their best efforts in preparing this book, they make no representations or warranties with respect to the accuracy or completeness of the contents of this book and specifically disclaim any implied warranties of merchantability or fitness for a particular purpose. No warranty may be created or extended by sales representatives or written sales materials. The advice and strategies contained herein may not be suitable for your situation. You should consult with a professional where appropriate. Neither the publisher nor the author shall be liable for any loss of profit or any other commercial damages, including but not limited to special, incidental, consequential, or other damages.

For general information about our other products and services, please contact our Customer Care Department within the United States at (800) 762-2974, outside the United States at (317) 572-3993 or fax (317) 572-4002.

Wiley also publishes its books in a variety of electronic formats. Some content that appears in print may not be available in electronic books. For more information about Wiley products, visit our web site at www.wiley.com.

Library of Congress Cataloging-in-Publication Data
Hopper, Leonard J.
    Graphic standards field guide to hardscape / Leonard J. Hopper.
        p. cm. — (Graphic standards field guide series ; 2)
    Includes index.
  ISBN 978-0-470-42965-5 (pbk. : acid-free paper); ISBN 978-0-470-90070-3 (ebk);
ISBN 978-0-470-90071-0 (ebk); ISBN 978-0-470-90072-7 (ebk)
  1. Landscape construction—Designs and plans—Standards. 2. Garden structures—Designs and plans—Standards. I. Title.
  TH4961.H67 2010
  717—dc22
                                2010016941
Printed in the United States of America
10 9 8 7 6 5 4 3 2 1

Contents

Introduction

Welcome to Wiley's *Graphic Standards Field Guide*

We know that when you're on a jobsite or in a meeting, questions come up. Even the most seasoned professional may wish they could look up just that one piece of information that is just outside their instant recall or just beyond their current experience. There is a real need to make immediate on-site decisions—to access information on the spot, no matter where you are.

Graphic Standards Field Guide to Hardscape is designed to be a quick and portable reference for busy professionals like you. It focuses on just the information you need away from the design desk, no matter where you are.

Who This Book Is For

The connection between what happens in the design office and the project site (before, during, and after construction) is critical. Yet there is a trend toward creating a separation between office and site. This book attempts to bridge that gap and provide a hand field reference that will be a valuable resource on site visits.

If you're a landscape architect, designer, construction inspector or facilities manager involved in site work, this book is for you. This book contains the critical core information you'll need when working away from the office. It's like having the jobsite knowledge of your firm's most experienced professional in your pocket.

How This Book Is Organized

The content of this book is organized chronologically according to the sequence each of the topics would normally occur in a project. Each chapter covers a specific division, and includes topics appropriate to hardscape site design and construction. Use the chapter opening pages to find a specific topic within a division, or refer to the index to find exactly what you need.

Some of the material is geared toward preliminary site visits, assessing existing conditions, and factors to consider during design development. Some information will be valuable as the project moves into the preparation of contract documents. Other information on how the contractor executes the information provided on that contract drawings will be helpful during the construction phase.

Information on specific topics is presented in lists and tables, making it easy to find and reference quickly. Construction details and drawings, coupled with photographs, demonstrate standards and help you evaluate what you may encounter on-site.

Each topic contains the following sections:

Description: A brief overview of the topic, to provide some context.

Assessing Existing Conditions: Key things to look for when you're in the field that will help guide your decisions.

Acceptable Practices: Keys to what constitutes good quality work and references to industry standards.

Practices to Avoid: A quick list of what to look out for.

References: Look to this section for where to find more information about the topic within this book or in other sources.

This symbol ● indicates things you may see in the field that are good rules of thumb or acceptable practices.

How To Use This Book

The Field Guides are meant to go anywhere you go. Take them to meetings and site visits or keep one in the glove compartment just in case—the book is a handy reference to have on hand whenever you are away from the design desk and out of the office.

Use the Field Guides to:

- Help a client evaluate a prospective property or site.
- Develop an existing conditions inventory and analysis.
- Define a project scope with site opportunities and constraints.
- Find information on unexpected on-site conditions.
- Remind yourself of possibilities and alternatives.
- Create a checklist to make sure you asked all the right questions during a site visit.
- Expand your expertise of construction practices.

Ultimately, a good design professional must have an understanding of the relationship that the existing conditions of the site and construction materials and practices have with every phase of the design process. Toward that end, this book attempts to strengthen that understanding.

About the Author

Leonard J. Hopper, FASLA, is a former project administrator for site improvements for the New York City Housing Authority. Currently, Hopper is a Senior Associate with Mark K. Morrison Landscape Architecture, PC in New York City. In the thirty years with NYCHA and the past four with Mark K. Morrison, Len has been responsible for all phases of design development, project management and construction administration across a broad spectrum of the profession. As a participant in the Sustainable Sites Initiative, Len served on a technical subcommittee that established guidelines and performance benchmarks that focus on documenting how sites can use natural elements in designs that provide human benefits as well as benefits to the environment and he continues to serve as a technical advisor to that group's ongoing efforts.

As a faculty member at The City College School of Architecture, Urban Design and Landscape Architecture, Masters in Landscape Architecture Program; at Columbia University, Masters of Science in Landscape Design Program; and at SUNY Farmingdale's Horticultural Technology Management Program, Len teaches the technology course sequence that includes site inventory and analysis, grading, soil science, storm water management, soil erosion and sediment control, construction materials and details.

Len served as Editor-in-Chief of *Landscape Architectural Graphic Standards* and *Landscape Architectural Graphic Standards*, Student Edition and author of *Security and Site Design* (all from Wiley).

Len Hopper is an active member of the American Society of Landscape Architects, serving as National President for 2000–2001. He served as President of the Landscape Architecture Foundation for 2005–2006. In recognition of his accomplishments and contributions, Len received an award for "Outstanding Leadership on Issues Affecting Urban Design, Rehabilitation and Policy" by the Landscape Architecture Foundation in 1993. He was elected to ASLA's Council of Fellows in 1994 and was recipient of the ASLA President's Medal in 2005.

About Graphic Standards

First Published in 1932, *Architectural Graphic Standards* (AGS) is a comprehensive source of architectural and building design data and construction details.

Now in its Eleventh Edition, AGS has sold more than one million copies and has become one of the most influential and indispensable tools of the trade for architects, builders, draftsmen, engineers and students, interior designers, real estate professionals and many others. The entire family of Graphic Standards resources is ready to help you in your work. In recent years the franchise has expanded to include *Interior Graphic Standards*, *Planning and Urban Design Standards*, and the most recent publication, *Landscape Architectural Graphic Standards*. Each of these major references follows in the tradition of *Architectural Graphic Standards* and is the first source of comprehensive design data for any design or construction project. Explore what these products have to offer, and see how quickly they become an essential part of your practice.

Visit www.graphicstandards.com for more information.

Acknowledgments

This book would never have been completed without the patience, support and gentle prodding of my Editor, Kathryn Malm Bourgoine and the help whenever I needed it from her assistant Lauren Poplowski. You could not ask for two better people to work with.

Many thanks to my family who had to share vacation time with me typing away on the computer to meet a deadline. And especially my wife Cindy, who kept the music playing and the beer cold in the most hectic of times. I could not have written this book without their generous sharing of my time and their constant support.

PART I

EXISTING CONDITIONS

Chapter 1

Site Survey

Site Inventory and Observations

Photographic Information

Site Inventory and Observations

Description

A site inventory and observations are integral to the design process. Some of the things they provide are:

- Document and evaluate the condition of existing context and site features as part of the development of a base plan.
- Provide a basis for the development of the site's opportunities and constraints.
- Observe and document any social or cultural factors that should be considered during the design development phase.
- Provide up-to-date site information in order to prepare accurate contract documents.

Assessing Site Conditions

In order to accurately assess existing site conditions, several visits to the site may be necessary throughout the various phases of the project, often with a different focus, depending on what phase the project is currently in. Site visits at various times of the day, days of the week and seasons of the year, and in varying weather conditions, may be required to gain a comprehensive picture of how the site may be used. Take plenty of field notes and document existing conditions with photos (see Photographic Information topic).

Some observations of user behavior and analysis can help to understand a site. An observation should indicate adjacent buildings, their use, entries and views into and from the project area.

Observing a space for visible clues as to what users do—and don't do—which can be done even when no one is present. Clues such as:

- Cigarette butts around a bench;
- A short-cut path worn across a lawn;
- Raised gardening beds full of weeds.

All tell a story. The location of these clues should be included on a site plan.

A systematic observation and recording of actual use should be scheduled at different hours of the day and different days of the week. Times and days might be determined in consultation with staff (at a staffed facility), or by casual observation at a more public facility, to ensure the major use periods are being covered. For each observation period, record all that is happening, as follows:

- Locate on a site plan the exact location of each user
- Number each of the located users
- Record against numbers in a field notebook the age, gender, and activity of each user
- Add arrows to indicate movement. Circle designated users to indicate people in a group

It is important to use a new copy of the site plan for each visit, as these activity maps will be used like stop frames in a movie. When all the observations are completed, the data can be aggregated onto one comprehensive site plan (typical pattern of use), aggregated by different variables (e.g., dot map of male/female use, adult/child use), displayed as bar graphs (e.g., of different activities, overall use by adults/teens/children), or displayed as a line graph (e.g., use throughout day). All the data recorded by this method is quantitative and is much more accurate than asking people.

However, this form of observation provides no information as to what people *feel*—why they come to this place. Interviews with users are essential to learn *why* they come to the space, *how often* they come, what they *like*, what they'd like to *change*, whether they *feel different* after being there (if yes, what it is about the place that helps them feel different). There are two basic ways of wording questions in an interview: multiple choice or open-ended. It is good to use both types.

- An example of a multiple-choice question is: "Do you come here more than once a day/once a day/once every few days/about once a week/less often?" You check the appropriate box corresponding to the response on the interview form; data is quantitative.
- An open-ended question might ask, "How do you feel after spending time in the garden?" Write down all that the respondent says. This provides richer, more qualitative answers.

Acceptable Practices

The physical site features should be inventoried and evaluated. Record quantity, condition (good, fair, poor), location, and any remarks for each of the site elements. Examples of site elements include but are not limited to: adjacent land use; public transportation; recreation equipment; curbs; walls; fence; etc.

Practices to Avoid

- Avoid rushing through a site visit. Well spent time during a site visit is always better than having to make repeat visits to gather information that could be gathered in a single, comprehensive site visit.
- Avoid scheduling too little time for a site visit. Often, a good deal of information can be gathered about how a site is being used, by just spending some time there and observing what takes place during the course of a day.
- Avoid making quick judgments about how a site is used based on one limited visit.

Photographic Information

Description

Photo documentation of every phase of a project, from existing conditions through completion, can save time, money, help answer questions and provide a basis for resolving disputes. With digital photography and the ease of storing photos, it is always better to take more photos than less.

▶ **The hardest photo to take is the existing condition "before" shot, after the project has been completed.**

A systematic approach to site photography will provide an organized catalogue of photos that will be easy to access, as the need arises. An organized library of photos can provide many advantages, some of which include:

- A documentation of existing conditions prior to the start of construction.
- A good reference during the preparation of contract documents that can minimize additional site visits.
- Help respond to requests for information from contractors during the bidding process.
- Help respond to questions during the construction process.
- Confirm construction practices and document conformance or deviations with the contract documents.
- Resolve disputes and provide accountability, such as whether damage to existing site elements to remain occurred during the construction process.
- Documentation of how site elements have been constructed as well as underground utilities that will not be visible after the project has been completed.
- Provide before and after pictures of the project. After a project is completed, it is very easy to quickly forget how the site looked prior to the project being undertaken.

▶ **Do not limit your photos to just your site. Document existing conditions of adjacent sites, sidewalks and streets, in detail, as often issues are raised by other owners during the construction process.**

Figure 1.1 Existing wall on adjacent property documenting condition before the start of construction.

A camera with 6 megapixels or more is sufficient for almost all project photo documentation. An image can be zoomed in on the computer screen to a fairly high level of quality before becoming too pixilated. The highest optical zoom will help with detailed photos and close-ups,

Figure 1.2 Existing sidewalk adjacent to site. Documenting the existing trees, street light and utility pole provides information that can prove helpful throughout all phases of the project.

more so than digital zoom, which provides less digital quality. Most all cameras have variable quality settings that can be adjusted.

▶ With higher megapixel cameras, it is best to shoot most photos at a medium setting, to keep the digital file size manageable for attachments to e-mails, which is often necessary for quick sharing of photos.

Assessing Site Conditions

Photographs taken during an initial site visit, as part of preparing a proposal or starting a design project, should be comprehensive and detailed. Think ahead and take photos that can be used later to create a digital visualization of your proposed design. As the design is not yet developed during these early visits, all design opportunities of the existing site should be photographed.

There can be a tendency to take many overall photos but not many detailed photos. This can lead to trips back to the site to confirm information that could have been contained in the initial photo series. Particularly useful can be photos that document specific details like whether a fence is installed in a curb or individual footings, is a curb or pavement in good shape or poor shape, is the pavement sinking in a particular area, does the drain appear to be clogged, etc. These are all examples of the type of photos that can help inform decisions during the schematic, design development and construction documentation phases.

Detailed photos that document the condition of existing site elements to remain and be protected can be invaluable if a question arises as to whether something was damaged during construction.

Whenever possible or appropriate, notes should accompany photos to explain why a particular photo is being taken. In the field, being able to note important information quickly is key. For specifically taken

Figure 1.3 Photos of existing conditions and proposed design visualizations.
Source: Photos courtesy of Mark K. Morrison Associates.

Figure 1.4 Detailed photos are useful during the design development phase. Here the overview photo shows the corner condition in context with a detailed close-up of the wall condition.

photos, note the date, time, photo number, location, and description or reason the photo is being taken and why it is important. Develop a set of abbreviations to make this process go quickly in the field and expand those notes once back in the office.

Although identifying the location and direction a photo is being taken on a site plan is very helpful, this can be time consuming and not every photo needs that level of detail. Another approach is to take the site photos sequentially as you walk through the site, including enough context to relate the photo back to the plan and identify any close-up detail photos and their location. In this way, you can identify locations and elements on the site plan back at the office, just as if you were walking through the site with the plan in your hand.

Acceptable Practices

A project should be photo documented throughout all phases of a project, including but not limited to:

- Community or scope meetings
- Existing site prior to design or construction
- Existing conditions at time of bid
- Site preparation, access, staging areas, safety and security measures
- Demolition and removals
- Underground or unforeseen conditions
- Materials delivered to the site
- Excavation, compaction, installation of new materials
- Formwork and reinforcing
- Progress photos at regular intervals during the construction phase
- Completed project and any ribbon cutting or opening ceremonies

It is advisable to make sure the time and date stamp feature of your camera is set properly (but not to be displayed on the image). It is also a good idea to note weather-related factors that can be a factor during construction and provide important and comprehensive back-up for the photos. Saving the digital photos in computer folders labeled chronologically and by category can save time when needing to look back for specific photo documentation.

A set of existing site photos, progress photos during construction and completed project photos, all taken from the same vantage point, can be very valuable for comparison purposes. Be aware of where previous photos have been taken from and take subsequent photos from the same location and in the same direction.

Figure 1.5a

Figure 1.5b

Figure 1.5c Photos of existing conditions (Figure 1.5a), during construction (Figure 1.5b), and this photo after completion taken from relatively the same location and in the same direction.

Figure 1.6 Using a ruler to confirm measurements in the field can be very effective, particularly when coupled with the ability to zoom in closer with a digital image.

▶ For detailed photos and close-ups provide a ruler or object (like a pen) for scale and measurement. Photo documentation of specific measurements can provide valuable information and back-up during all phases of the project

Practices to Avoid

- Do not delay downloading your photos, take care of this task as soon as possible.
- Do not just download photos without organizing them into specific folders.
- Do not set the camera to record the date and time on the image, this time stamp can cover important information that you may need to see.

References

OTHER RESOURCES:

- Landscape Architectural Graphic Standards, First Edition, Hoboken, NJ: John Wiley & Sons, 2007.

PART II

TEMPORARY CONSTRUCTION INSTALLATIONS

Chapter 2

Temporary Access Roads and Parking

Temporary Access Roads and Parking Areas

Description

All site construction projects require access to the site for equipment required to build the project. The need for temporary access roads and parking areas will vary based on the size and complexity of the scope of work.

All site construction projects will require a construction entrance. Many site construction projects will require temporary access roads (for construction equipment and detours of roads that are being disrupted by the construction). Many site construction projects will require temporary parking spaces (for construction workers and possibly for those whose parking spaces are displaced during the construction phase).

It is critical that the logistics of these temporary accommodations not be left to chance or the contractor's discretion. They are an important part of the construction process and these temporary routes and areas need to be designated on plans and criteria associated with them included in the specifications.

Any areas designated for temporary access or parking should include the stripping and stockpiling of existing topsoil for restoration or other use as part of the project. An area for the stockpiling of topsoil should be shown on the site plan.

Assessing Site Conditions

The following factors should be considered when assessing existing site conditions related to temporary access and parking for a construction site:

- The location of vehicle access and parking areas should create a minimum of disturbance or inconvenience to existing vehicular traffic patterns, pedestrian circulation and surrounding context of the construction site (local residents, businesses, those working adjacent to the construction site, etc).

- Temporary roads and parking areas need to provide access for the owner's personnel to existing facilities and buildings.
- Temporary roads and parking areas need to provide and maintain access for emergency services and fire hydrants.
- Temporary access roads to the site must be compatible with the regular service and delivery routes.

The assessment should include photographic documentation of the existing conditions as a record to be referenced when the areas damaged or disrupted need to be restored to their previous condition at the completion of all construction activities.

Acceptable Practices

Temporary Construction Access Point

Temporary construction access point(s) should be indicated on the site plans:

- The contractor should provide temporary fencing, barricades and signage to prevent unauthorized access to the project site.
- Signage should indicate that the area is closed to the public during the construction phase of the project as well as directions to alternate temporary routes.
- The contractor should only utilize construction equipment of a size and weight that can be accommodated on existing roads that lead to the site.
- The temporary construction access point should include suitable facilities for cleaning personnel, equipment and vehicles. This should include a means to remove mud and dirt for vehicle wheels before leaving the site. No vehicles should be allowed to track soil off site.

▶ **Where washing is required, the area should be stabilized with aggregate that drains onto an approved sediment-trapping device. All sediment shall be prevented from entering storm drains, ditches, or watercourses.**

Any surface water flowing to a temporary construction entrance that is disrupted during the construction phase, should be piped under the entrance to maintain the existing drainage pattern and positive drainage of the area.

Temporary Access Roads

- Temporary access roads should be indicated on the site plans along with the criteria for the selected routes.
- Interference with existing vehicular and pedestrian circulation should be minimized.
- Temporary pedestrian routes should be hard surfaced and take into consideration drainage, slip resistance, lighting, railings, crosswalks, ADA requirements and any other safety concerns.
- Temporary fencing, tree protection, site preparation, detours and signage related to the temporary access roads should be indicated on the site plans.
- Temporary access roads should provide as direct and efficient a route as possible, which can accommodate the type, size and weight of the types of vehicles and equipment anticipated.
- Temporary access roads should minimally include 6 in. of aggregate on a geotextile fabric. For larger and longer-term projects, the aggregate layer should be topped with an asphaltic concrete wearing course of a minimum of 1-1/2 in.
- Access requirements (times, quantities, special needs) that might conflict with ongoing existing uses, should be coordinated on the site plans and specifications to avoid problems during construction.
- Wherever possible, temporary access routes to the site should try to use existing roads or routes that are proposed roads on the design plan.
- The size of temporary access roads and maneuverability space should be determined by the anticipated types and sizes of equipment required to complete the project, not necessarily the largest equipment available. Smaller equipment that is adequate to perform the necessary work will minimize damage to the site.

▶ A carefully thought out temporary access plan can limit disruption and damage to the site resulting in a more cost-effective approach that minimizes the amount of restoration that will be required.

Temporary Parking Areas

- Temporary parking areas should be designated on the site plans and be of sufficient size to accommodate the number of construction personnel vehicles anticipated or for those whose parking spaces have been displaced by the construction (displaced handicapped accessible parking should be replaced meeting all ADA requirements and as close as possible to the facility or destination as possible unless another reasonable accommodation can be made).

- If temporary parking areas for construction personnel are desig-nated within the contract limit line, these locations should be coor-dinated with ongoing construction work and construction equipment access and movement throughout the site.
- Temporary parking areas that are located on turf or earth should be covered with 6 in. of aggregate over a geotextile fabric to minimize soil compaction and facilitate restoration.

Restoration

After construction is complete, the temporary access roads and park-ing areas should be restored to the previous condition or as indicated in the contract documents. All pavements that have been damaged should be replaced with pavements equal to the original installation and meet the adjacent materials in an appropriate manner.

Any earth or turf areas to be restored should receive a deep tilling to mitigate soil compaction that might have taken place. Existing topsoil that had been stockpiled or new topsoil as necessary should be spread over the disrupted areas, along with any soil amendments that might be specified. The areas should be re-vegetated to restore them to their pre-project condition.

▶ **The contractor should be made responsible for ongoing mainte-nance, care and replacement until the successful establishment of turf or vegetation.**

Practices to Avoid

- Avoid leaving temporary access and parking out of the contact doc-uments. Without clear designations of areas and their use, a contrac-tor's desires and the best interests of the client and protection of the site are likely to come into conflict.
- Do not allow construction equipment or parking vehicles under existing trees. This commonplace practice to benefit from the tree's shade is very damaging to the tree.
- Avoid any pressure to provide more space for temporary access and parking than is reasonably required. Additional space requests should include a justification as to why the space is necessary and the request reasonable.

Staging Areas

Description

Staging areas are designated locations where:

- Construction activities take place.
- Construction equipment is stored.
- Construction trailers are located.
- Dumpsters for debris are located.
- Construction materials are stockpiled.

By designating specific locations for these activities, soil compaction and other construction-related damage to the site is limited rather than spread out throughout the entire site.

Construction staging areas should provide efficient access to materials and operations with minimal negative impacts to the surrounding community and uses. Staging areas should be clearly designated on the site plans.

Figure 2.1   Staging area for materials are stored at one end of an area that requires compaction. The last of the material is to be installed in the location of the staging area. Topsoil is stockpiled for re-distribution onto the site.

Assessing Site Conditions

An initial assessment of existing conditions should be performed to identify potential staging areas to be used during construction and their impacts. Staging areas should provide a safe and large enough work zone for the construction of the project. On large projects with multiple phases it may be necessary to provide a logical sequence of staging areas and access to them as construction progresses. The size of designated staging areas should be based on the anticipated:

- Size and number of trailers that will be required.
- Quantity and types of materials to be stored.
- Type and size of equipment that will be stored.

Try to designate areas that are near the work zone but not within the work zone, so as not to interfere with the construction.

Acceptable Practices

- The staging area should be clearly delineated with high-visibility fencing, barricades and/or signage to prevent the public from entering.
- Existing pavements can make good staging areas as long as the weight of anticipated vehicles and materials will not exceed the pavement's ability to support them. In dense urban areas, the public street is often used as the staging area (with appropriate permits).
- Areas of proposed pavement as part of the new design make good staging areas. Soil compaction in these areas is not a problem.
- Special areas should be designated for storing and mixing chemicals, cutting or drilling of different materials. These activities can contaminate soils affecting plant growth and restoration.
- Areas for parking vehicles, construction equipment, refueling and vehicle and equipment maintenance should be located in one part of the staging area only, away from drainage structures, because of the potential of leaks, drips or spills. Any contamination should be cleaned up immediately and disposed of properly.
- The contractor should try and coordinate delivery of materials as close to possible to when they will be needed. This not only reduces the size of the staging area required but lessens the opportunity for theft or damage of the stored materials.
- Piles of soil or materials stored in the staging area should be covered with plastic sheeting to prevent contact with rainwater.

- Place an adequate number of trash and recycling cans around the staging area to minimize construction litter.
- Clean up spills on dirt areas by digging up and disposing of contaminated soil properly.

Restoration

Staging areas concentrate damage to the site to a limited area. In addition to the leaks and spills that can contaminate soil, soil compaction at a staging area is always a condition that requires remediation.

Soil compaction results from a large singular force or repetitive small forces, both of which are likely to occur at a staging area. These forces collapse the voids between the solid soil particles. Water, air, and roots are unable to penetrate the solid mass, which reduces or destroys capacity to sustain life, requiring additional efforts to restore the staging area to its pre-construction condition.

At the planning stages for locating staging areas and the access to these areas, an eye should be kept toward the ultimate restoration after construction is completed. Activities that could compact the soil should be kept away from trees that are to remain on the site. Tilling and soil amendments to loosen the compacted soil and prepare for re-vegetation should be anticipated and specified.

Practices to Avoid

The size of staging areas should be matched to the equipment that is needed to successfully carry out the proposed construction. This does not necessarily mean the largest equipment available. Larger equipment requires more area for storage, operating, turning and results in greater soil compaction. Smaller equipment generally results in less damage to the site. Therefore, matching the size and power of the equipment needed to the project size and scope of work is an important balancing of needs versus space required for staging.

Staging areas should generally try to avoid being located:

- Near wetlands, streams, ponds, shorelines or other water bodies.
- In areas of steep slope.
- In areas that are susceptible to earth slides or seismic activity.
- In areas that are within the 100-year floodplain.
- In farmlands, or areas that are an integral part of a wildlife network.
- In areas that are designated as parklands or near walking trails.

Avoid runoff problems, practice good storm water management:

- Avoid having storm water runoff enter or leave the site.
- Do not allow storm water to flow into or out from the site. Install barriers around the perimeter of the site to block storm water runoff.
- Identify all storm drains, drainage swales and creeks located near the site and make sure all site users are aware of their locations to prevent pollutants from entering them.
- Do not allow sediment or other materials to flow into storm drain inlets.

▶ Never allow a contractor to hose down pavement or impermeable surfaces where fluids have spilled. Use dry cleanup methods (sweeping and use of absorbent materials) whenever possible, and dispose of used materials properly. Never attempt to wash spills away with water or bury them.

References

OTHER RESOURCES:

- J. William Thompson and Kim Sorvig. Sustainable Landscape Construction. Washington, DC: Island Press, 2000.
- Landscape Architectural Graphic Standards, First Edition, Hoboken, NJ: John Wiley & Sons, 2007.

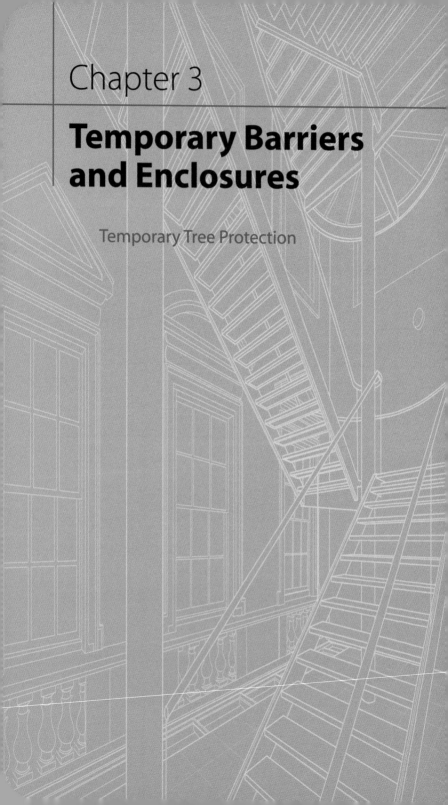

Chapter 3

Temporary Barriers and Enclosures

Temporary Tree Protection

Temporary Tree Protection

Description

Wounding of the aboveground parts of a tree due to construction activities is more than unsightly; it can leave a tree vulnerable to infection by insect vectors or fungal diseases. In contrast, damage to the underground parts of a tree is typically less obvious but usually has a much greater impact on the health of a tree. Whereas a broken limb is relatively easy to address, soil compaction or root destruction is more difficult and takes much longer to remediate.

Trees are damaged during construction in four primary ways:

- The aboveground parts of a tree are subjected to physical damage, for example, broken limbs, scarring of trunks, and mechanical damage to roots protruding above grade.
- A tree's root system can be damaged during excavation.
- Chemical damage can be inflicted on the root system (cement, paint, acid, etc.) when the ground beneath the canopy is used as a washing/rinsing area for tools and other construction equipment.
- The soil is compacted within the critical root zone of a tree.

The root system of an established tree extends to, at minimum, a distance out from its trunk equal to the height of the tree. Most tree roots are located in the top 6 to 18 in. of soil, and the majority of a tree's active root system exists in the top 8 in. of soil in and around the drip line. A change in grade either above or below this natural level can have devastating effects on the health of a tree.

In addition to supporting and anchoring the tree, the main functions roots serve are to extract oxygen, water, and nutrients from the soil and transport them from the root hairs to the stem. All of these ingredients are essential for a tree to survive and are contained in the pore spaces within a soil. Tree roots exist and can survive only in the pore spaces between soil particles.

By understanding the critical function of roots, their relative shallow soil habitat, and how extensive they are in relation to the aboveground parts of the trees (which they support), it becomes obvious just how destructive it is to compact the soil in and around the drip

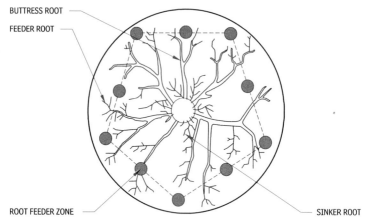

Figure 3.1 Plan view of typical tree root system. The 10 gray dots indicate the general outline of the feeder root zone, which is located close to the drip line of the tree where the majority of absorption and other root/soil interface activity take place.
Source: Hopper, Landscape Architecture Graphic Standards. Copyright 2007, John Wiley & Sons, Inc.

line of any tree. The options for repairing damaged trees as a result of soil compaction are very limited. Therefore, prevention is far better than any attempt to cure.

Assessing Site Conditions

The existing trees on the site should be evaluated using the following criteria:

- Tree value, including: aesthetic, cultural, and ecological value.
- Tree health.

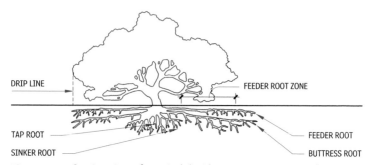

Figure 3.2 Section view of a typical deciduous tree root system showing the far-reaching lateral growth of the tree's winter feeder roots beyond the drip line, which support the tree's nutritional needs.

Figure 3.3 This tree has its trunk protected by vertical wooden slats wired together. The wood barrier protects the critical root zone from compaction by construction equipment and activities.

- Species tolerance to construction and other mechanical disturbance'
- Site suitability (post-construction).

Certified arborists possess a unique body of knowledge and skills that make them the best choice for evaluating trees according to these criteria and should be part of the site assessment team.

After all existing trees have been assessed, the certified arborist will advise whether a tree is suitable for retention. Occasionally, the certified arborist will recommend against retaining healthy trees, which will inevitably be compromised by the impact of construction. If the tree is particularly valuable, the certified arborist may recommend an alternative construction technique and/or a design change. However, this information must be acted on *prior* to drawing the final design plans, in order to avoid costly and time-consuming changes during the actual construction phases.

Once a tree has been earmarked for retention, a tree protection zone (TPZ) must be identified. The TPZ comprises the area around the tree or groups of trees in which no grading or construction activities should occur. The tree and its protection zone should be clearly demarcated on all resulting plans and drawings, which describe the installation of utilities and all demolition and construction activities, and the TPZ should be fenced off.

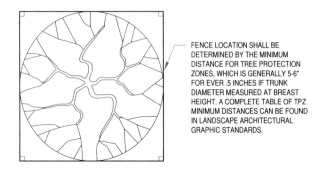

FENCE LOCATION SHALL BE DETERMINED BY THE MINIMUM DISTANCE FOR TREE PROTECTION ZONES, WHICH IS GENERALLY 5-6" FOR EVER .5 INCHES IF TRUNK DIAMETER MEASURED AT BREAST HEIGHT. A COMPLETE TABLE OF TPZ MINIMUM DISTANCES CAN BE FOUND IN LANDSCAPE ARCHITECTURAL GRAPHIC STANDARDS.

PLAN

Figure 3.4 Typical tree protection zone.

Acceptable Practices

Tree Protection Zone Specifications

Tree protection zones should meet the following specifications:

- Perimeter fencing—Minimum 4-ft-high orange plastic safety fence, wood barriers, wire snow fence or chain-link fence.
- Mulch—Two inches of composted mulch spread evenly over a geo-textile fabric throughout the entire zone.
- Maintain natural moisture levels.
- Do not alter the existing natural drainage.
- Signage—Affix to fencing as close to eye level as possible, containing the following directions: No vehicle movement; No storage of materials; No washing of equipment; Contact name and number for inquiries.
- Fertilizers—Healthy trees generally don't need to be fertilized, however, fertilizer is beneficial to compensate for root loss and to stimulate the growth of new feeder roots closer to the trunk. An efficient method of applying nutrients to large trees is to inject the soil with a water-based solution.

▶ Prior to establishing a tree protection zone, prune trees to be protected, focusing on removal of dead or broken branches. The purpose of this maintenance is primarily safety, but it also serves as a monitor for any new damage that may occur during construction.

Construction Activities within the Tree Protection Zone

If, during the course of construction, it does become necessary for activities to take place inside the tree protection zone, then a certified arborist should be consulted. The consulting certified arborist will recommend the most appropriate way to undertake such activities or suggest possible alternatives.

Vehicle and pedestrian movement can be particularly damaging to trees, causing soil compaction. A 6-in. layer of mulch over a geotextile fabric with an overlay of 3/4-in.-thick plywood sheets, along with 2 × wood planking loosely cabled around the tree trunk, is the recommended approach to reduce the effects of construction activity within the tree protection zone.

When trenching or excavation is to be undertaken, it is important that the roots be severed cleanly rather than be torn with a backhoe or other excavation equipment. The best way to achieve this is to expose the roots first and then cut them cleanly with a sharp saw or loppers. Roots with a diameter larger than 2 in. should be tunneled under, where practical.

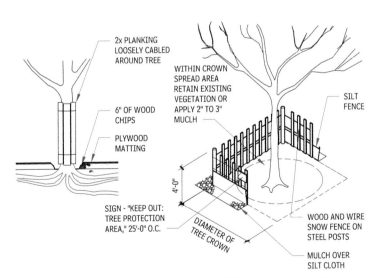

Figure 3.5 Tree trunk and root protection within the tree protection zone.
Source: Hopper, Landscape Architectural Graphic Standards. Copyright 2007, John Wiley & Sons, Inc.

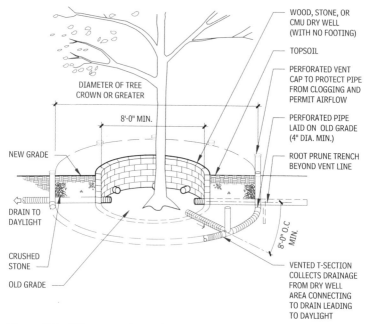

WOOD, STONE, OR
CMU DRY WELL
(WITH NO FOOTING)

TOPSOIL

PERFORATED VENT
CAP TO PROTECT PIPE
FROM CLOGGING AND
PERMIT AIRFLOW

PERFORATED PIPE
LAID ON OLD GRADE
(4" DIA. MIN.)

ROOT PRUNE TRENCH
BEYOND VENT LINE

DIAMETER OF TREE
CROWN OR GREATER

8'-0" MIN.

NEW GRADE

DRAIN TO
DAYLIGHT

CRUSHED
STONE

OLD GRADE

8'-0" O.C
MIN.

VENTED T-SECTION
COLLECTS DRAINAGE
FROM DRY WELL
AREA CONNECTING
TO DRAIN LEADING
TO DAYLIGHT

Figure 3.6 Filling around an existing mature tree utilizing a retaining wall to reduce the amount of fill within close proximity to the tree. Air vents and drainage pipe help mitigate some of the negative factors associated with the change in grade.
Source: Hopper, Landscape Architectural Graphic Standards. Copyright 2007, John Wiley & Sons, Inc.

Grade Changes within the Drip Line of Existing Trees

A change in grade either above or below the tree's natural level due to construction activity or design changes should be avoided. However, if absolutely necessary, proper procedures for filling or cutting around an existing tree should be employed to protect the tree.

Practices to Avoid

- Avoid construction activities within the drip lines of trees that result in soil compaction. If soil compaction remediation is required, a spoke-and-wheel trenching pattern utilizing an Air-Spade, a 6-in. by 6-in. trench, can be excavated radially, starting 5 ft from the base of a tree and extending to the edge of the critical root zone (CRZ). Each trench should be connected by a 6-in. by 6-in. trench that will

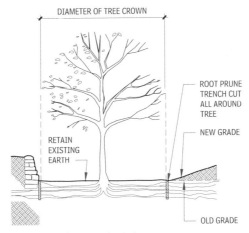

Figure 3.7   Raising grade around existing tree.
Source: Hopper, Landscape Architectural Graphic Standards. Copyright 2007, John Wiley & Sons, Inc.

demarcate the outer edge of the CRZ. The minimum amount of the CRZ trenched must be 40% of the total area of the CRZ. The trenches should then be filled with either compost or dehydrated manure.

- Avoid tearing roots with construction equipment. If roots are torn rather than cut cleanly, the resulting wound will have a much larger surface area, and will take longer to heal and be vulnerable to infection.

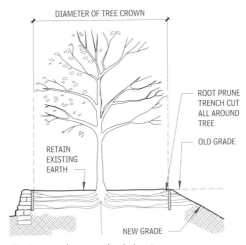

Figure 3.8   Cutting grade around existing tree
Source: Hopper, Landscape Architectural Graphic Standards. Copyright 2007, John Wiley & Sons, Inc.

- Avoid changing the existing drainage patterns around trees to be protected. Any increase or decrease in water can have devastating effects on tree health and stability. Changes in drainage patterns should not undermine roots or inundate trees with excessive water. If the natural runoff toward a tree has been cut off, or if a site is now being artificially drained after construction, then irrigation will be required to maintain tree health, particularly if substantial root loss has occurred.
- Construction contractors should never undertake any pruning during the course of construction, unless directed to do so.

References

ALSO IN THIS BOOK:

- Site Clearing
- Construction Layout

OTHER RESOURCES:

- Landscape Architectural Graphic Standards, First Edition, Hoboken, NJ: John Wiley & Sons, 2007.

Chapter 4

Temporary Controls

Temporary Erosion and
Sediment Controls

Temporary Storm Water Pollution Control

Temporary Erosion and Sediment Controls

Description

The control of erosion and subsequent transport of sediment from project sites is a critical part of the design and development process. Modification of land and land use can have severe impacts on-site, as well as upon adjacent lands and downstream areas. Most of the impacts can be mitigated by proper planning, implementation, and active maintenance of soil erosion and sediment control measures.

This has become a critical issue in recent years, and many local jurisdictions now require an erosion control plan as a part of the construction document package. The goal of erosion control measures is to protect areas outside of the project boundary, particularly bodies of water such as streams and lakes, from the harmful effects of increased silt load. Several methods can be used, including erosion control fencing, bales of straw placed in drainage channels, or "biobags," or filtration fabrics placed over the openings of catch basins or

Figure 4.1   Protective snow fencing with silt fence and hay bales to control erosion and prevent sediment from entering the river at the bottom of the embankment.

other drainage structures that are downhill from the site. Once construction is completed, these can be removed, but not until all work is completed.

Assessing Site Conditions

Construction Sequencing

Construction sequencing is a specified work schedule that coordinates the timing of land-disturbing activities and the installation of erosion and sediment control measures. The goal of a construction sequence schedule is to reduce on-site erosion and off-site sedimentation by performing land-disturbing activities and installing erosion and sediment control practices in accordance with a planned schedule.

Table 4.1 Scheduling Considerations for Construction Activities

Construction activity	Schedule consideration
Construction access, entrance to site, construction routes, areas designated for equipment parking	This is the first land-disturbing activity. As soon as construction begins, stabilize any bare areas with gravel and temporary vegetation.
Sediment traps and barriers, basin traps, sediment fences, outlet protection	After the construction site is accessed, install principal basins. Add more traps and barriers as needed during grading.
Runoff control diversions, perimeter dikes, water bars, outlet protection	Install key practices after installing principal sediment traps and before land grading. Install additional runoff control measures during grading.
Runoff conveyance system, stabilize stream banks, storm drains, channels, inlet and outlet protection, slope drains	If necessary, stabilize stream banks as soon as possible, and install a principal runoff conveyance system with runoff control measures. Install the remainder of the systems after grading.
Land clearing and grading, site preparation (cutting, filling, and grading, sediment traps, barriers, diversions, drains, surface roughening)	Implement major clearing and grading after installing principal sediment and key runoff-control measures, and install additional control measures as grading continues. Clear borrow and disposal areas as needed, and mark trees and buffer areas for preservation.
Surface stabilization, temporary and permanent seeding, mulching, sodding, riprap	Apply temporary or permanent stabilizing measures immediately to any disturbed areas where work has been either completed or delayed.

Continued

Table 4.1 *continued*

Construction activity	Schedule consideration
Building construction, buildings, utilities, paving	During construction, install any erosion and sedimentation control measures that are needed.
Landscaping and final stabilization, topsoiling, trees and shrubs, permanent seeding, mulching, sodding, riprap	This is the last construction phase. Stabilize all open areas, including borrow and spoil areas, and remove and stabilize all temporary control measures.

US EPA

Construction site phasing involves disturbing only part of a site at a time to prevent erosion from dormant parts. Grading activities and construction are completed and soils are effectively stabilized on one part of the site before grading and construction commence at another part.

Acceptable Practices

A wide variety of vegetative and structural measures may be used to limit erosion and prevent the transport of sediment off a disturbed site. The following measures are commonly referred to as soil erosion and sediment control measures:

- Buffer zone. A vegetated strip surrounding disturbed areas or along water body margins that filters solids and sediment from sheet flow used as a buffer on construction sites. Sometimes used with a level spreader to distribute runoff evenly.
- Level spreader. Converts concentrated runoff to sheet flow and disperses it uniformly across a slope without causing erosion. This structure is particularly well-suited for returning natural sheet flows to exiting drainage that has been altered by development, especially for returning sheet flows to receiving ecosystems such as wetlands where dispersed flow may be important to maintain pre-existing hydrologic regimes. Particular care must be taken to construct the outlet lip completely level in a stable, undisturbed soil to avoid formation of an outlet channel and subsequent erosion.
- Streambank stabilization. Vegetative and structural practices to prevent or reduce bank erosion.
- Check dam. A temporary structure to control concentrated stormwater flows in channels, slowing velocity and catching sediment.

Figure 4.2   Streambank stabilization with rock and vegetation.
Photo by Russell Adsit, FASLA.

Figure 4.3   A vegetated swale, usually dry except in rainfall events, channels storm water runoff.
Photo by Russell Adsit, FASLA.

- Vegetated swale. Used to help infiltrate runoff and convey storm water. Vegetation should be established before water flows are introduced.
- Channel stabilization. The creation, improvement, or stabilization of channels for safe conveyance.

Figure 4.4 Grass-lined channel with offset wattles to control velocity and stabilize channel banks during heavy storm water runoff.
Photo by Russell Adsit, FASLA.

Figure 4.5 Temporary stream diversion channel lined with stone for stabilization.
Source: adfg.Alaska.gov.

- Stream diversion channel. A temporary channel to conduct flow around construction in a stream.
- Temporary slope drain. A flexible conduit, serving as a temporary outlet to conduct flows safely down slopes. It reduces soil erosion and creation of gullies until permanent drainage measures can be employed. The ends of the flexible pipe usually have flared metal collars attached and the pipe itself needs to be anchored along the slope. The outlet should empty to a location that is erosion resistant and should be checked regularly for blockages or conditions that would render it ineffective. For flatter slopes, a half-pipe or channel can be used.
- Grade stabilization structure. A temporary or permanent structure designed to accommodate vertical grade change in natural or man-made channels dropping water to a lower elevation without causing erosion or gullies.
- Chemical stabilization. In areas where other measures to stabilize exposed soils are not effective, the spraying of vinyl, asphalt or rubber sprayed onto the soil surface can effectively bind and stabilize. The obvious environmental concerns of using these chemical stabilizers must be weighed against their erosion control value.
- Rock filter dam. A temporary or permanent dam used in streams or drainage channels to filter sediment and slow flow velocity. It forms a pool from which water flows downstream through a riser pipe or through the gravel of the rock dam.
- Retaining wall. A structural method to reduce slope face exposure to erosive forces. The use of a soil retaining structure during the construction phase can reduce steep slopes during construction. If the structure is to be permanent, careful sequencing of the construction

Figure 4.6 Temporary slope drain.
Photo by Russell Adsit, FASLA.

can facilitate grading operations and keep workers safe, without hindering the construction activities. The effect of changes to the site's drainage pattern need to be considered.

- Storm drain outlet protection. Typically, a rock or concrete device to reduce storm water velocity, dissipate flow energy and prevent channel erosion at pipe outlets.
- Surface roughening. Creating horizontal grooves running across a slope can decrease runoff velocity and erosion, improve water infiltration and help establish vegetation. They can be created by using grooving disks, tillers or heavy tracked machinery.
- Temporary seeding. Planting rapid germinating and growing annual grasses or other vegetation can be an effective measure to stabilize a slope. Surface roughening, fertilizer and raking in of seed are helpful to germination and growth. Hydroseeding mixes seed with mulch and fertilizer in one application.

These measures, plus those described in the following construction details, provide a palette of possible solutions to specific site conditions. Numerous trade products have been introduced that can simplify the installation and/or maintenance of many soil erosion and sediment control measures. Application of some measures

Figure 4.7 A stone or riprap apron is the most common measure for temporary storm water outlet protection, used here in conjunction with a series of hay bales and slope drains.
Photo by Russell Adsit, FASLA.

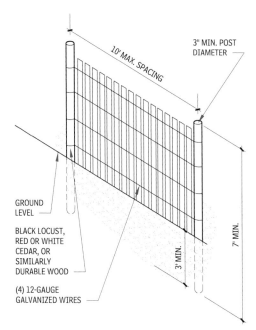

3" MIN. POST DIAMETER

10' MAX. SPACING

GROUND LEVEL

BLACK LOCUST, RED OR WHITE CEDAR, OR SIMILARLY DURABLE WOOD

(4) 12-GAUGE GALVANIZED WIRES

7' MIN.

3' MIN.

Figure 4.8a Sand fence detail.

varies by region; refer to local and state standards for specific requirements, limitations, or regional adaptations. Most states have a manual of soil erosion and sediment control standards specifically tailored to regional conditions.

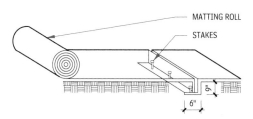

MATTING ROLL

STAKES

9"

6"

Figure 4.8b Erosion control mats.

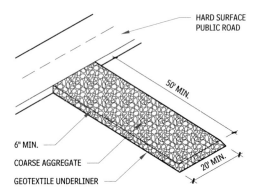

Figure 4.8c Construction exit.

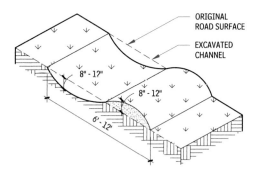

Figure 4.8d Diversion channel.

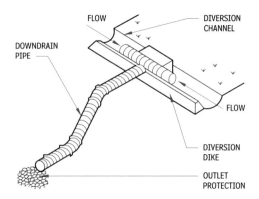

Figure 4.8e Temporary slope drain in conjunction with diversion channel.

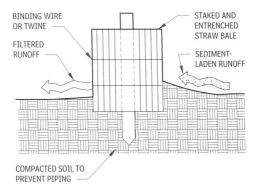

Figure 4.8f Hale bale sediment barrier.

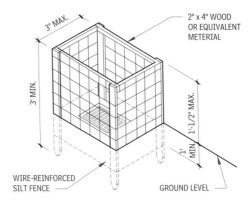

Figure 4.8g Fabric and frame sediment trap.

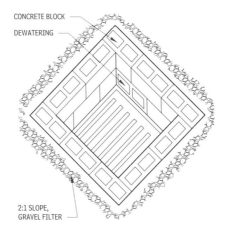

Figure 4.8h Block and gravel sediment trap.

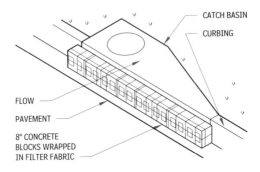

Figure 4.8i "Pigs in a blanket" sediment trap.

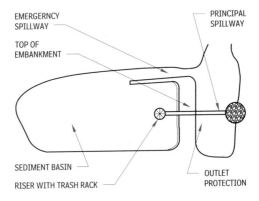

Figure 4.8j Sediment basin plan

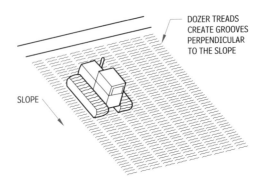

Figure 4.8k Track roughening.
Source: Hopper, Landscape Architectural Graphic Standards. Copyright 2007, John Wiley & Sons, Inc.

Temporary Storm Water Pollution Control

Description

Temporary storm water pollution control is required to prevent sources of pollution affecting the quality of storm water discharge from the site. The identification of potential sources of pollution which might affect storm water discharge quality and the measures that will be taken to address those concerns are very often outlined in a Storm Water Pollution Prevention Plan (SWPPP). The SWPPP should be part of the contract documents and monitored throughout construction to ensure compliance. A copy of the SWPPP should be kept on-site at all times.

Assessing Site Conditions

The following steps are part of the initial site condition assessment:

- Identify the location of all storm drainage structures, drainage swales and streams (or other water bodies) on or near the site.
- Identify all vegetation that is to be preserved before clearing at a height that will be visible to equipment operators.
- Identify potential sources of pollution which may be expected to affect the quality of storm water discharge from the site.
- Develop a set of measures that will be used to prevent sources of pollution from affecting the storm water discharge (the EPA has a description of best management practices that can be used as a reference).
- Check that practices and measures that will be taken are in compliance with Federal EPA as well as State and local requirements.
- Outline required filings, notifications, required permits and any other administrative tasks related to the temporary storm water pollution controls necessary during the construction.

Acceptable Practices

Temporary storm water pollution controls are often described as a series of Best Management Practices (BMPs) that are a list from which applicable choices for a specific project or set of conditions can be implemented. Some temporary storm water pollution controls BMPs that can be considered during construction are:

- Vegetation provides erosion control, storm water detention, biofiltration and post-construction aesthetic value. Existing vegetation outperforms new vegetation in every category and is valuable to preserve. Preservation and protection of existing vegetation usually includes some type of temporary fencing.

- Construction entrances should be stabilized with rock aggregate or other non-erodable material placed over a geotextile fabric. Where choices are available, locating the construction entrance at a high point where storm water runoff from the construction site will not be directed toward the entrance is most desirable. The construction entrance should not extend into the street, nor should it block or disrupt the flow of storm water in the gutter.

- Construction exits should be stabilized with coarse rock aggregate over a geotextile fabric. A steel grid (typically a series of 3 in. diameter or greater pipes or tubes, a minimum of 8 ft long and wide enough to accommodate the width of the anticipated construction vehicles) strong enough to support the heaviest construction vehicles anticipated should be firmly installed to agitate the tires in order to loosen and remove soil build-up (elevated 8 in. above the ground and spaced 4-$\frac{1}{2}$ in. apart or greater).

- A tire wash down area shall be provided at the construction exit so that on rainy days or when there is mud on the site, all vehicle tires can be washed with pressurized water to remove any mud or debris, in order to prevent material from leaving the site or being dropped on streets. The tire wash down area shall be sloped to divert any debris or soil back onto the site.

- Erosion control can be provided by using vegetated buffer strips (existing or newly planted vegetation). They slow storm water runoff, preventing soil erosion, filter sediment and allow storm water to percolate through the soil recharging ground water supplies. The width and slope of the vegetated buffer strips should be determined by the size and slope of the drainage area they need to accommodate.

- Erosion control of sheet flow on the down-slope side of a construction site can be provided by the use of hay bales placed with their ends perpendicular to the slope (contours) to trap sediment.

- Erosion control on slopes can be provided by the use of soil retention blankets anchored to the slope with wire staples 6 in. long and 1 in. wide. All rocks or other debris that would prevent the soil retention blankets from lying flat in direct contact with the soil need to be removed. The edges of the mat should be buried into a 6 in. wide by 6 in. deep trench, backfilled and tamped. Joints should be overlapped a minimum of 12 in. to provide a continuous blanket. Soil

Figure 4.9　A stone construction exit lined with filter fabric to agitate the vehicle in order to reduce the amount of soil being transported off-site. If mud needs to be removed from the tires, the tires should be washed with the waste water drained to an area where the sediment can be trapped.
Photo by Russell Adsit, FASLA.

retention blankets can be made from jute mat (jute yarn woven very loosely together); a wood fiber mat (constructed of wood fibers enclosed in nylon, cotton or other type of netting); or a synthetic matting creating a three-dimensional web to control erosion or facilitate vegetation establishment.

Figure 4.10　Three-dimensional web for erosion control.
Photo courtesy of Presto Geosystems.

▶ Soil retention blankets can help new vegetation by holding seeds, fertilizer and topsoil in place.

- Erosion control can be provided by the use of silt fence composed of a non-woven geotextile fabric (permeable to water but retaining sediment) supported by galvanized or painted metal posts (driven a minimum of 12 in. into the ground and spaced a maximum of 6 ft on center) on the down slope from the construction site. A wire backing or other temporary fencing should be used to help support the geotextile. Lengths of geotextile should be overlapped a minimum of 12 in. at stakes to provide a continuous barrier. A 6 in. deep and 6 in. wide trench should be dug on the side of the fence disturbed by construction and a 6 in. toe of the silt fence left at the bottom should be buried in the trench, backfilled and tamped firm. The ends of the silt fence should be turned up perpendicular to the slope (contours) to create a sediment trap. Accumulated silt should be removed and re-distributed on the site. If a chain-link fence is used along the same lines as the silt fence, it may be possible to attach the silt fence to the chain-link fence.

▶ Tilt the posts of the silt fence slightly, in an "uphill" direction for additional strength.

- On larger sites the excavation of a temporary detention structure may be a viable approach to containing storm water discharge and

Figure 4.11 A double silt fence with hay bales sandwiched between. The silt fence on the gravel construction entrance side is supported by chain-link mesh attached to galvanized posts.

controlling erosion. If a common low point can be identified, the area can be excavated to serve as temporary storm water detention area.

- A temporary sediment trap can be formed by creating an embankment or excavating to capture sediment and debris on drainage areas less than 3 acres. Sediment traps are often constructed with a pipe or stone outlet. They are usually created by excavating an area at the outlet of a channel, slope drain, swale, construction site entrance/exit or any storm water conveyance or discharge to capture any sediment or debris that it might be carrying.

- Rock check dams can be used to control erosion and sediment loss in areas of concentrated storm water flow. They slow velocity and catch sediment as the water runs through it. An effective measure used in drainage swales and ditches, when constructed in series, the top elevation of the downstream check dam should be set at the toe elevation of the adjacent upstream check dam and the top elevation of the last upstream check dam set to the invert elevation of the last stabilized portion of the drainage swale or ditch. The center of the check dam should be lower than the sides in order to channel water overflows away from the sides, preventing erosion.

- Rock berms of well graded rip-rap or open graded stone, secured with wire sheathing can be installed at the base of slopes to control erosion and trap sediment while allowing water to pass through.

- Stabilized earth berms are an effective perimeter control, keeping storm water runoff from leaving the site, as well as preventing storm water runoff from entering the site from the adjacent properties.

- Diversion dikes are constructed by forming a ridge of compacted soil, often accompanied by a ditch or swale with a vegetated lining, at the top or base of a sloping disturbed area. When on the up-slope side of a site, they help to prevent surface runoff from entering a disturbed construction site. When located on the down-slope side of a site, they divert sediment-laden runoff created onsite to sediment-trapping devices, preventing soil loss from the disturbed area.

- An interceptor swale channels storm water runoff to a stabilized outlet or sediment trap, in order to prevent off-site runoff from entering the construction site or prevent storm water from carrying sediment off the site.

- A thick layer of fibrous natural mulch (minimum 3 in.) can be used to control erosion and limit storm water runoff from the site. Mulch material can be straw, wood chips, shredded wood, post consumer paper content and yard trimming compost. Mulch can be used on slopes where establishing vegetation can be difficult or can help on slopes until seeded or planted areas can become established. When used on steeper slopes or in areas of concentrated runoff, the mulch should be held in place by netting anchored to the ground below.

Figure 4.12 Natural mulch material held in place to stabilize slope and control erosion.
Photo by Russell Adsit, FASLA.

- Hydromulch with seed can be used in place of regular seeding, wherever seeding is being considered as an erosion control measure. Hydromulch stabilizes the slope and applies seed and fertilizer all in one application.
- Storm drain inlet protection prevents soil and debris from entering into the structure. There are several protection measures: 1. Excavating around the inlet and letting water slowly pass through a filtering device; 2. Placing a fabric barrier around the inlet; 3. Forming a gravel barrier around the inlet.

An initial inspection and review of all measures taken to control erosion and storm water pollution should be conducted prior to the start of any site-disturbing construction activities. After initial implementation of the temporary storm water pollution protection measures, unusual or unforeseen conditions may still need to be addressed and additional measures may need to be taken.

The contractor should be responsible for maintaining all installations, equipment and services required for the temporary storm water pollution controls to remain effective until completion of construction. Any damage to storm water controls should be repaired immediately. Modifications or additional measures should be made to address changing site conditions or circumstances during the course of

Figure 4.13   Storm drain inlet protection during construction.
Photo by Russell Adsit, FASLA.

construction. All temporary storm water pollution control measures shall be removed after the completion of construction and the contractor should provide any necessary restoration to return those areas to their previous condition (or improved).

Figure 4.14   Storm drain inlet protection along street curb.
Photo by Russell Adsit, FASLA.

Practices to Avoid

Do not allow concrete truck wash-out water to be discharged off-site or into storm sewers. It can contaminate groundwater and area waterways, increase pH and clog storm drain pipes. Provide a concrete truck wash-out area to contain the discharge.

No construction dewatering should be discharged into sewers, storm drains or water bodies.

Do not allow sediment to accumulate in storm water pollution control measures. Inspect them regularly and remove sediment when necessary.

References

ALSO IN THIS BOOK:

- Construction Layout
- Site Clearing

OTHER RESOURCES:

- Dillaha, T.A., J.H. Sherrard, and D. Lee, 1989. Long-Term Effectiveness of Vegetative Filter Strips. *Water Environment and Technology*, 1:418–421.
- Landscape Architectural Graphic Standards, First Edition, Hoboken, NJ: John Wiley & Sons, 2007.

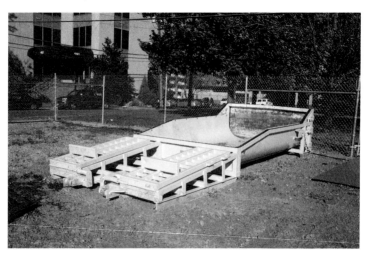

Figure 4.15 Manufactured concrete truck wash-out container.
Photo by Russell Adsit, FASLA.

- Smolen, M.D., D.W. Miller, L.C. Wyatt, J. Lichthardt, A.L. Lanier, W.W. Woodhouse, and S.W. Broome, 1988. *Erosion and Sediment Control Planning and Design Manual*. North Carolina Sedimentation Control Commission, NC Dept. of Natural Resources and Community Development, Raleigh, NC.

- USEPA, 1992. Storm Water Management for Industrial Activities: Developing Pollution Prevention Plans and Best Management Practices. EPA 832-R-92-006. U.S. Environmental Protection Agency, Office of Water, Washington, DC.

- USEPA, 1993. *Guidance Specifying Management Measures for Sources of Nonpoint Pollution In Coastal Waters*. EPA-840-B-92-002, January 1993. U.S. Environmental Protection Agency, Office of Water, Washington, DC.

- USEPA (U.S. Environmental Protection Agency). 1992. *Storm Water Management for Construction Activities: Developing Pollution Prevention Plans and Best Management Practices*. EPA 832-R-92-005. U.S. Environmental Protection Agency, Office of Water, Washington, DC

- SEE ALSO: TEMPORARY ENVIRONMENTAL CONTROLS AND TEMPORARY EROSION AND SEDIMENT CONTROLS

- SEE ALSO: TEMPORARY ENVIRONMENTAL CONTROLS AND TEMPORARY STORM WATER POLLUTION CONTROLS

PART III

DEMOLITION

Chapter 5
Demolition

Site Removals

Description

Most site improvement contracts involve the removal of site elements and pavements. Depending on what is to be removed and access in and out, the appropriate removal strategy and equipment will need to be used. Separating removed materials that can be recycled or re-used from general waste can lessen the amount of material that will be sent to a landfill. Identifying facilities that accept mixed waste to be separated and recycled can reduce the amount of material sent to a landfill. This approach to demolition and removal is not only environmentally sensitive but can reduce the cost of this initial phase of construction to the contractor.

▶ Removal and disposing of hazardous materials and safe procedures for removing them should be adhered to at all times.

Assessing Site Conditions

The initial site assessment should identify site elements that are to remain, document their condition, clearly mark them and specify the type of protection required during the construction phase. The contractor should exercise care not to damage these elements and should be held responsible for any damage to them during construction.

Some municipalities require a certain percentage of the total waste tonnage be recycled or re-used. During the assessment of existing conditions, an estimate should be made to calculate the total waste tonnage and a plan developed as to how the required percentage of material to be recycled or re-used will be met and how this will be documented.

Before any excavation takes place, local utilities should be contacted to determine where existing utility lines are located. These lines should be clearly marked. Any excavations or removals in close proximity to an existing utility should be done by hand. Any planned disruption of service should be coordinated with the utility company and notifications sent to those that will be affected. Any damage to existing utilities should be repaired at the contractor's expense.

▶ Some municipalities provide a "one call center" that can provide the contractor with the location of utilities and have them identified and marked.

Acceptable Practices

General Removals

The following general removal practices should be followed:

- Prior to construction commencement, a detailed plan for the demolition, abatement, removal and separation of general waste, recyclable or re-usable materials should be developed.
- All necessary tools and equipment for removal and demolition should be on-site and inspected for adequacy and appropriateness for the anticipated removal operations. In order to minimize disruption of the removal process, this should include replacements for components that can break or dull from usage (saw blades, drill bits, etc).
- Large areas of asphalt pavement are generally removed by a backhoe or excavator. For smaller projects or in areas where there may be utility lines or tree roots, portable jackhammers are generally used. The jackhammer operator will usually lightly score a series of lines or holes before driving the jackhammer tool deeper, to break up the pieces to a size that can be handled more easily.
- Large areas of concrete pavement are generally removed by a backhoe or excavator. It is always a cleaner joint when the concrete pavement can be removed to the nearest contraction or expansion joint.
- Removing large areas of pavers can be made easier by the removal of the edge restraint and removing the pavers starting at the edge and moving inward. If only a small section of pavers is to be removed within the field of pavers, one of the pavers may need to be broken in order to provide enough space to lift out the adjacent pavers.
- Footings and other supporting structures that extend to the frost line generally need to be removed by a backhoe or excavator that can dig around and break up the concrete or masonry into smaller pieces.
- Metal elements that require removal may need to be cut. Painted metal may contain lead and appropriate measures should be taken during the removal process.

▶ Site elements should be removed by pulling away from existing structures in order to prevent damage.

▶ The smaller pieces of asphalt or concrete can be broken into, the less void space created in the truck transporting the material. Although it may take a little extra work with the backhoe or jackhammer, it will require less truckloads and reduce removal costs.

Figure 5.1 Excavator with pointed tool to initially break up existing asphalt pavement to be removed. Area for removal has been sawcut along perimeter of where existing pavement is to remain.

Figure 5.2 Same machine with bucket to break up the asphalt into smaller pieces and load the removed pavement onto a truck for recycling.

Hand Excavation

In some areas where utilities are located, tree roots may exist or near site elements that are identified to remain, hand excavation and removal may be specified. Hand tools, hand-held power tools and/or air spades can be used to remove materials without damaging adjacent structures or plant roots.

Milling and Grinding

As an alternative to complete pavement removal, milling or grinding can be considered to remove surface imperfections if the pavement is otherwise structurally stable. The top course of asphalt pavement can be removed by milling, concrete pavement can have its surface removed by grinding.

- The milling of asphalt pavement is done by a machine that removes material to a specified depth uniformly throughout the milled area. The milling operation will result in the surface having a "macrotexture" of the specified depth (grooves). The milled asphalt pavement is a widely recycled material and should not be disposed of as general waste. After milling, any cracks or defects in the remaining layer of pavement can be addressed, the surface cleaned of any loose material, a tack coat applied, and an overlay of new asphalt pavement

Figure 5.3 Use of jackhammer, pick and sledge to carefully remove pavement around existing drain and pipe that was very close to the surface.

installed. Milling equipment is available in a number of different sizes to be matched to the size of the project.

- Concrete pavement surface irregularities can be removed by grinding with diamond blades. Grinding can remove surface roughness and uneven pavements at cracks or joints. It is a process that is generally used on roads to provide a smoother ride and noise reduction. It can also provide a "macrotexture" that improves drainage of water between the tire treads reducing skidding and hydroplaning. The diamond grinding heads and machines are not suited for smaller projects.

Selective Demolition and Removals

Selective demolition and removal techniques should be used wherever existing site elements are specified to remain and be protected or where existing elements need to be removed, stored, and re-installed as part of the proposed construction.

- Existing elements that will be stored and re-installed should be numbered to record their location and relationship to adjacent components. It is always better to re-install existing elements in the same configuration as they had been previously installed. This is particularly important with site elements like fence, railings or steps and can minimize additional cutting or grinding to get pieces previously not attached to each other to fit together.
- Where portions of pavement need to be removed adjacent to pavements that are to remain, the edge should be sawcut to provide a neat clean edge. It is best to set the saw blade to cut through the entire depth of the pavement. In concrete pavement, sawcutting is best done at an existing contraction or expansion joint and to sufficient depth to cut through any steel reinforcing or dowels.

Disposal of Removed Materials

The amount of removed material sent to landfills should be minimized. Diminishing space, increased costs and environmental concerns no longer make indiscriminate dumping of construction debris in a landfill an acceptable approach. Separating removed materials that can be recycled or re-used should be strongly encouraged, if not directly specified or required by local or state regulations. The value of recycled materials to the contractor can reduce the cost of demolition and removal in addition to being environmentally responsible.

If hazardous materials are encountered during demolition operations, all applicable regulations, laws, and ordinances concerning removal, handling, and protection against exposure or environmental pollution should be followed.

Figure 5.4 Sawcutting through asphalt pavement with a hand-held saw. For longer or deeper cuts, walk-behind or machine-mounted saws are available. There is always a slight overlap of cut lines in each corner that should be filled as part of the final construction.

Practices to Avoid

- Do not allow removal operations to be left to chance. Include detailed instructions for removals in the contract documents and ensure best practices by monitoring construction.
- Do not allow combined removed materials to be sent to a landfill because it is easier. Call for separation and recycling or re-use of materials to the maximum extent possible.

Utility Line Removal

Description

Existing utility line removal or re-routing is sometimes required during construction. Utilities to be removed may include gas, electric, communication, water or drainage lines. To protect the health, safety and welfare of the public this work should only be performed by qualified workers.

Assessing Site Conditions

The assessment of site conditions should identify:

- The type, location and status of any underground utilities (those to be removed and those that are to remain in service after construction);
- The location of any underground basements, storage tanks or vaults that may contain utility lines;
- The location of any above ground utility services and their status.

Some municipalities maintain a "one call center" where the location and status of underground utilities can be identified and marked on the site. Any digging on the site should not commence until the location of underground utilities have been determined with the utility companies. It is the contractor's responsibility to detect and protect utilities from damage during construction.

Acceptable Practices

The contractor should verify the location of utility lines provided by the utility companies or municipality by the use of exploratory excavations or subsurface exploratory devices. It is not unusual for utility lines to be installed in a slightly different location than may be shown on site utility plans and at a different depth than expected. Any excavation in close proximity to existing utilities should be done by hand and proceed with caution. Any inadvertent interruption

Figure 5.5 Utility lines flagged and marked prior to installation of temporary construction fence and before any excavation has taken place.

in service should be restored as quickly as possible at the contractor's expense.

Existing utilities that are to be abandoned (meaning taken out of service, disconnected and taken offline), are usually capped at both ends, with the utility line left in place. These lines may be uncovered during future construction or repair and requiring that their disposition be verified before construction can continue. This can be time consuming and unnecessarily disruptive. Therefore, utility lines that will be taken out of service should be removed completely whenever feasible.

▶ Any work involving utilities should only be performed by qualified personnel.

Practices to Avoid

- Avoid abandoning utilities in place. Some utilities if left in place, such as drainage or steam lines, will often be better supported than the adjacent area of new construction which can result in uneven settling, with the utility line maintaining the same elevation as the areas immediately adjacent settle. Other utilities can collapse, resulting in sinking. It is always best to remove any utilities that are being taken out of service.

- Avoid temporary interruptions in service without coordinating with the utility company and notifying those that will be affected by the interruption.

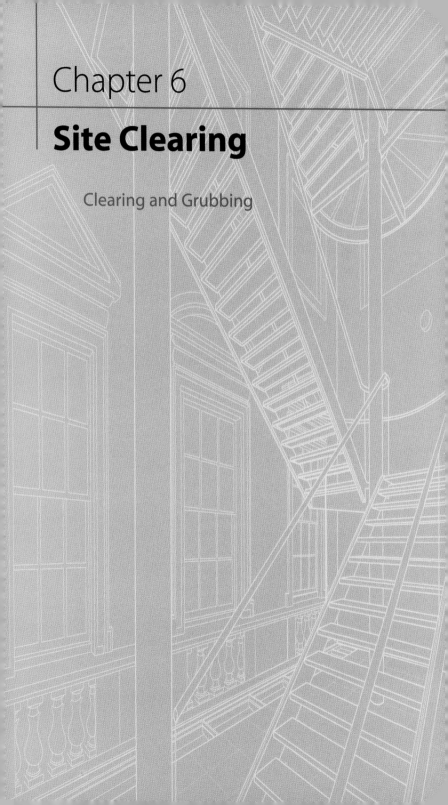

Chapter 6

Site Clearing

Clearing and Grubbing

Clearing and Grubbing

Description

Clearing and grubbing is one of the first phases of site construction. Clearing is a surface operation of removing unwanted materials such as trees (up to a specified size), vegetation, boulders and trash. Grubbing is the removal of unwanted subsurface materials such as sod, weeds, boulders, stumps, roots, buried logs or any other objectionable material. Clearing and grubbing is usually accomplished by the use of a bulldozer or grub hoe.

The area designated for clearing and grubbing should be clearly identified on the site plans. No clearing and grubbing activity should take place beyond this delineated area. All trees, shrubs and other vegetation to remain should be protected.

Assessing Site Conditions

A site inventory should be conducted to identify valuable existing vegetation to be preserved and protected during clearing and grubbing activities. Existing vegetation to be preserved should be protected with temporary fencing. Large trees to be preserved should be clearly marked with flags and their critical root zone protected with temporary fencing to prevent cutting of roots and compaction of the soil. All existing utility lines, both overhead and underground should be identified and the effects of clearing and grubbing might have on them evaluated (including falling limbs and ensuring worker safety).

A site inventory should include a list and location of invasive plants and weed infestations found on the site in order for effective control measures to be implemented.

The site assessment should include identifying areas where clearing and grubbing could cause damage to adjacent property or where access to adjacent property may be required. Typical potential damage includes:

- Cutting the roots of trees on the adjacent property.
- Having excess material distributed over the property line.
- Damaging septic systems.
- Utility damage.
- Causing erosion of the adjacent property's soil or allowing erosion and sediment to be directed toward the adjacent property.

If access is required to the adjacent property during construction activities, the written permission of the land owner should be secured prior to allowing any activity on the adjacent property.

▶ **If any damage occurs to private property, the contractor is responsible for the cost involved to return the site to its previous condition. A certified arborist should be consulted to provide recommendations for vegetation restoration or replacement.**

Acceptable Practices

General Clearing and Grubbing

The limits of the area designated on the site plan for clearing and grubbing should be clearly marked by stakes, flags or markings on trees. Trees to be preserved should be distinctively and clearly marked at approximately 6 ft above the ground in order that the marking will be visible to machine operators.

All vegetation not being preserved shall be completely cleared from the site to the depth specified in the contract documents (this may vary from 12 to 24 in. and may be dependent on the proposed contract work for this area). This includes all snags, logs, downed timber, brush, stumps, shrubs, roots, large rocks, boulders and rubbish. Any trees designated for removal should be taken down and their roots removed at this time. Usually trees up to a specified diameter or caliper are included in the general clearing and grubbing operation. Larger trees above the diameter or caliper specified are typically paid for as a separate item by their size. Mechanical stump chippers should be used to remove large stumps down to the depth below finished grade that is specified.

▶ **During clearing and grubbing it is advisable to include removal of any dead branches or trimming of low hanging branches on trees to remain that may interfere with the construction. All pruning should be done in accordance with acceptable nursery standards.**

Although a contractor may want to perform all clearing and grubbing at one time, it is desirable to coordinate clearing and grubbing with the rest of the construction sequence in order to leave vegetation in place as long as practically possible in order to minimize potential erosion. Vegetation on steep or unstable earth banks susceptible to erosion should be removed by hand. Wherever possible, understory and bank stabilizing vegetation should be left in place.

Large trees may have potential value to be milled into lumber or cut as firewood. Branches and small diameter trees can be chipped and made into mulch for use on the construction site (i.e., reduce soil compaction and dust control on temporary access roads) or other off-site purpose. The reuse of all removed material should be explored and encouraged.

All other removed material should be disposed of as specified in the contract documents and in accordance with all local, State and Federal regulations. Any holes or depressions resulting from the clearing and grubbing should be filled, compacted, and graded to blend with the adjacent grades unless the area is to be excavated further in a future construction phase.

▶ Use of wide track or large rubber tired equipment distributes the weight of the machine or vehicle over a wider area, resulting in less load per square inch on the ground. Use of this type of equipment will lessen the severity of soil compaction in these areas, particularly important if the area is proposed to receive new vegetation.

Any roots of existing vegetation to be preserved that are uncovered during clearing and grubbing, should be backfilled as soon as possible and the soil moistened to prevent the roots from dying.

Selective Clearing

Selective clearing can be specified to:

- Remove dead or diseased trees within areas of vegetation that are to remain.
- Increase the amount of sunlight into an area to facilitate growth and understory development.
- Improve sight distance.
- Increase security and safety.
- Open and/or frame desirable views.
- Prevent plant encroachment on to adjacent property.
- Create an environment that will provide long-term vegetation survival and vitality.

Where existing vegetation is designated to be preserved and will remain in place as part of the final design, selective clearing techniques should be utilized. Extra care is required so that the root systems of the existing vegetation are not damaged during clearing and grubbing as well as throughout the sequence of construction phases. This is particularly critical with trees, where the critical root zone extends out to the drip line of the tree and sometimes beyond.

The following selective clearing techniques and precautions should be employed:

- Avoid impacting trees with construction equipment as damaged bark can weaken a tree, leading to its ultimate demise.
- Clear and grub by hand under the drip lines of existing trees.

Figure 6.1 Clearing and grubbing with erosion and sediment control measures downslope.
Source: http://rentonwa.gov.

- Do not place or stockpile soil over the root zone.
- Do not expose roots of vegetation to remain.
- Do not mechanically disk or roto-till under existing tree canopies when preparing to seed.

Figure 6.2 Clearing and grubbing including tree removal.
Source: http://rentonwa.gov.

Practices to Avoid

- Avoid native vegetation removal and disturbance on streambanks unless absolutely necessary.
- Do not fasten ropes, cables or temporary fencing to trees.
- Do not clear or grub an area until work in that area is necessary.
- Do not clear and grub in any area where the existence of hazardous materials is suspected. Testing and evaluation should be performed before work is allowed to begin or continue.
- If evidence of artifacts that may be of archaeological, paleontological, historical or cultural value are encountered, clearing and grubbing should be stopped and the appropriate authorities notified.
- Avoid the accidental introduction of invasive plants during the clearing and grubbing operation by the cleaning of construction equipment prior to being used on the site and after leaving the site.
- Avoid having invasive plant species crowding out natives by re-vegetating as soon as possible after clearing and grubbing. Areas of disturbed soil can provide a favorable condition for invasive species to become established. Minimize the areas that need to be cleared and grubbed while still meeting the project's requirements.

Chapter 7

Construction Layout

Construction Layout

Construction Layout

Description

Measured drawing information provides the detailed location of various elements to be built on the site. The three basic methods for locating elements on a site are:

- Bearing angles and distances
- Coordinate system
- Dimensioning

Construction layout involves taking the information on the drawing and transferring that information to the site, to guide the construction phase.

Assessing Site Conditions

The layout plan must have fixed elements such as property lines, road centerlines and structures located exactly. Site elements that will remain after construction should be measured and the dimensions checked for accuracy to avoid a conflict during the construction phase. Site elements such as utility structures and existing trees can necessitate design changes (that can sometimes be difficult to make) during the construction phase.

Where a proposed design element needs to have a specific relationship to an existing site element (a walkway centered on a door or a bench centered between two existing trees), it should be dimensioned from that site element on the layout plan. All dimensions should be based on a site element or point that is to remain during the construction phase. The contractor must have an identifiable base point or point of beginning to use as a basis for laying out the proposed elements.

Acceptable Practices

Contractors use a variety of different methods to transfer layout plan information to the site. Some typical practices include:

- Stakes—that can show both horizontal layout location and vertical elevation;

Figure 7.1 The staking of proposed pavement perimeter with temporary tree protection.

- Flags—that can outline the horizontal layout;
- Strings—that can show the horizontal location and relative elevation or slope;
- Painted lines—using spray cans, the subgrade can be marked. This is particularly useful for curvilinear forms.

▶ Note that in order to install site elements that require formwork (like the curb example in Figure 7.4), the adjacent pavement must be removed in order to allow the contractor room to excavate, install and brace the forms. This additional area will need to be restored after the construction of the site element is complete.

Practices to Avoid

- Be sure all necessary dimensions to lay out the site elements are on the layout plan. The contractor should never need to measure distances from the plan in the field to determine a needed dimension.
- Avoid dimensioning site elements from a point inside the building or off the site, which sometimes is the case, particularly with large radii. These types of dimensions are difficult for the contractor to use to lay out site elements.

Figure 7.2 Example of a stake locating the perimeter of a proposed pavement with the elevation indicated by the ribbon and arrow.

Figure 7.3 Proposed path layout using flags.
Source: Photo by Mark K. Morrison, FASLA.

Figure 7.4 Proposed curb location and top of curb elevation indicated with string.

- Avoid dimensioning an existing structure or the distance between two fixed objects (such as a building wall and a retaining wall to remain, or an existing sidewalk), nor should any series of running dimensions add up to dimensioning these existing conditions. This can cause conflicts when laying out the site elements. (Leave one least important dimension open, a floating dimension, to avoid a conflict with the proposed design and existing conditions in the field).

▶ Avoid having a dimension based on a site element that is to be removed or a point in the proposed plan that is not yet built because of the logical sequence of construction. This will create a problem during the construction phase.

References

OTHER RESOURCES:

- Landscape Architectural Graphic Standards, First Edition, Hoboken, NJ: John Wiley & Sons, 2007.

PART IV

EARTHWORK

Chapter 8

Earthwork

Topsoil Stripping and Stockpiling

Topsoil Stripping and Stockpiling

Description

Topsoil is the top layer of undisturbed soil that contains organic material and nutrients that are essential to establishing and sustaining vegetative life. Existing topsoil should be preserved by stripping it from areas that are to be disturbed, compacted, filled or developed and stockpiling it for re-distribution later in the construction process. The re-use of existing topsoil is a practical and economical approach to successful establishment of new vegetation on the site.

Assessing Site Conditions

Prior to stripping the layer of topsoil, an inspection should be conducted to make sure it does not contain weeds or invasive vegetative species. All necessary erosion and sediment control measures should be in place prior to the stripping of topsoil.

Although the topsoil layer is generally removed to a depth of approximately 6 in., this depth can vary based on soil type and location. Core samples should be taken in several locations to determine the appropriate depth of topsoil to be stripped.

Acceptable Practices

After defining the areas where topsoil will be stripped, the top 6 in. (or the depth determined by core samples) should be scraped and removed. The removed topsoil should be stockpiled in areas located on the site plan. The area for stockpiling should not interfere with ongoing work on the site or disrupt drainage patterns or block drainage structures.

The slope of topsoil stockpiles should not exceed 2:1. Temporary measures should be used to contain sediment. Topsoil stockpiles can be covered to slow drying, prevent erosion, keep down dust and prevent contamination by wind-blown weed or invasive species seeds. Non-toxic soil binders can be applied to stockpiles for short-term stabilization. If topsoil stockpiles will not be re-distributed within a year, they should be stabilized by planting a quick-growing, erosion-preventing groundcover.

The stockpiling of topsoil for periods of a month or more will likely result in the loss of beneficial soil microorganisms which are an integral component of healthy soils. In order to minimize the loss of microorganisms, create many small stockpiles (4 to 6 ft high) rather than one large one and keep them moistened. When properly maintained, there is likely to be a greater concentration and less loss of microorganisms in the upper layer of the topsoil stockpile. In order to distribute the microorganisms throughout the topsoil, the top foot or so of the stockpile should be mixed with the balance of the soil, prior to re-distribution on the site. For topsoil stockpiled for a year or more, microorganism inoculates may need to be introduced into the soil mix prior to re-distribution on the site.

Practices to Avoid

- Topsoil is a valuable resource. Avoid the construction approach of cutting the topsoil layer away and using it in areas that require fill. This top organic layer removed first ends up at the bottom of the area to be filled, buried by the subsoil that is removed later and used to complete the filling operation. This puts valuable nutrients and organic material out of the reach of plant roots.

Figure 8.1   Stripped topsoil stockpiled in a low continuous pile along the edge of the site, waiting for rough grading to be completed and then re-distributed over the site.
Source: Photo by Mark K. Morrison, FASLA.

- Avoid stockpiling topsoil on steep slopes.
- Avoid leaving existing topsoil in areas designated for temporary staging or access. Compaction can destroy the topsoil structure, strip and stockpile topsoil from these areas as well as those being directly disturbed or built on as part of the construction.

References

ALSO IN THIS BOOK:

- Clearing and Grubbing
- Grading
- Spreading and Grading Topsoil
- Temporary Erosion and Sediment Controls
- Temporary Storm Water Pollution Control

OTHER RESOURCES:

- J. William Thompson and Kim Sorvig. Sustainable Landscape Construction, Washington, DC: Island Press, 2000.
- James Urban. Up By Roots, Champaign, IL: International Society of Arboriculture, 2008.

Chapter 9

Earth Moving

Grading

Spreading and Grading Topsoil

Grading

Description

Grading is the reshaping of the ground surface by moving earth on a site to desired finished elevations or subgrade elevations as shown on a proposed grading plan.

Grading can involve lowering the elevation in some areas (cutting) or raising the elevation in some areas (filling). Grading operations on a site can involve moving the existing earth already on the site to attain the desired elevations (balancing cut and fill). It may also require additional material be brought to the site or excess material removed from the site.

▶ Most grading plans strive to balance cut and fill. If site constraints prevent that approach, it is usually more desirable (and less costly) to remove material from a site rather than have to import additional material.

Assessing Site Conditions

During the preliminary design phase, the existing grades, slopes and drainage patterns of the site should be evaluated. As almost every site improvement involves some grading, understanding the existing conditions is a critical first step before considering grading changes. Thinking of grading as a strategy that should be integrated with other strategies to arrive at the final design rather than just a function that needs to be worked out later, maximizes the design impact of a creative grading plan as part of a comprehensive site improvement.

Existing site elements, trees and vegetation that could be negatively impacted upon by grading operations should be noted and addressed in the grading plan. There are several approaches to saving trees when the design requires that the grade around them change:

- Any changes in grade should be made as far away from the drip line as possible.
- If the grade around the tree needs to be raised significantly, a well can be created around the tree, ideally out to the drip line, to retain the existing soil and grade in the area of the feeder roots. A dry well

or perforated pipe system should be installed to provide drainage within the well.

- If the grade around the tree needs to be raised only a few inches, the existing root zone can be carefully scarified before adding a sandy loam mixed with organic matter. If the root zone area is compacted, compaction reduction techniques should be employed before adding any material over the root zone.

- If the grade around the tree needs to be raised a foot or more, a layer of large open graded stone and geotextile mat should be included in the profile, to provide a positive drainage layer and allow air to penetrate through to the original soil layer. A well will need to be constructed around the trunk, allowing room for growth, to keep the raised soil level away from the tree trunk itself.

- If the grade around the tree needs to be lowered, a tree wall should be constructed just outside the drip line to accommodate the change in grade. Drainage provisions should be made in the wall.

▶ **There are many variables involved when changing the grade around trees that are to be saved. Although general approaches provide a guide to techniques that can be used, the unique circumstances of each situation need to be studied in detail, in order to tailor the approach to the specific situation.**

Erosion and sediment control measures should be implemented prior to the grading operations. Vegetated buffer strips outside of the area to be graded as well as other areas should be incorporated into the plan to help provide temporary or permanent storm water control. Areas for stockpiling earth during the grading process should be identified and the stockpiles protected from erosion.

Prior to any grading operations being performed, potential damage to adjacent properties or installations should be evaluated. Where the potential for damage is high, a geotechnical engineer should be consulted to thoroughly evaluate the situation and propose mitigating measures to reduce the potential for damage.

Utility installation should be performed after rough grading operations have been completed and the surface drainage patterns are established. Storm sewers for site drainage are generally the first to be installed as they usually require the deepest and widest trench excavation. Depending on the project, the balance of utilities (sanitary, water, electric, gas, etc.) are installed immediately after, or at the same time, if there are no conflicts with location of the required trenches and utility routes.

Backfilling and compacting over installed utilities (or existing utilities where fill needs to be added) should be performed with lighter equipment compacting the layers in smaller lifts before heavier grading equipment is brought in to grade and compact the earth, in order not to crush or damage the utility.

Acceptable Practices

General

Based on the grading plan, the contractor (with the help of a surveyor if necessary) positions stakes on the site that represent a layout of the work that is to be done with the specified elevations required for each stake point. Often a ribbon or painted line on the stake indicates the required grade for the contractor to meet.

The grading plan should be studied to develop an efficient plan to cut and fill without having to haul earth long distances. Ideally, it is best if the soil can be scraped from high areas directly to low areas (basically cutting and filling in one operation). Grading should try to be sequenced in a way that does not require moving equipment over areas that have already been cut or filled.

Large areas can be graded using a scraper to cut areas to the required grades and move thin layers of soil to areas that require fill.

Figure 9.1 Stake with painted line and string indicating grade to be met.

Some scrapers are equipped with laser units to help set the equipment to grade more precisely. Graders, bulldozers and compactors are also used in the grading operation to complete grading done by the scraper and to get into areas that are not accessible to the scraper.

Areas of fill should be compacted in 6- to 12-in. lifts (layers) depending on the type of soil, equipment that is being used and desired level of compaction. Fill depths greater than 12 in. generally cannot be compacted effectively.

Rough Grading

Rough grading is the initial operation of shaping the earth on the site to within a few inches of the desired elevation. It involves moving, removing or importing the quantities of earth into the locations where the rough grading will take place. Rough grading will establish elevations that will parallel the elevations and slopes of the final grades. The rough grading operation includes any required compaction of areas that are filled. Proper compaction will require the addition of some water to provide the right moisture content that will allow the soil to be compacted to the required density.

Slopes that are created as part of the rough grading operation should be stabilized. This is particularly important with fill slopes that are difficult to compact without any restraint along the edge.

Fine Grading

After rough grading has been completed, fine grading establishes the elevations of the site at precisely the desired elevations to receive the proposed pavements or topsoil, which will bring the areas up to the finished grades shown on the grading plan. Fine grading is usually accomplished by using a grader and steel drum vibratory or rubber tire roller.

Grading Slopes

The maximum slope for lawn areas that will require mowing is 3:1 (three horizontal feet for one foot of vertical change in height). The maximum for other vegetated slopes is generally considered to be 2:1. These slopes will need to be stabilized until final grading is complete or vegetation is established. Slope roughening can provide easy, inexpensive and immediate erosion control after grading operations have been completed.

Slopes should be roughened using machine tracks or other attachments prior to seeding or planting in order to:

- Help vegetation get established from seed.
- Minimize erosion and trap sediment.
- Maximize storm water infiltration by slowing runoff velocity and increasing the surface area of the soil.

Some techniques to stabilize slopes after fine grading are:

- Stair step grading with the horizontal step sloped back toward the uphill slope. The ratio of vertical cut distance to horizontal distance should be less than 1:1 with vertical cuts not to exceed 2 ft in soft soils or 3 ft in rocky material. Each step catches material from above and provides a fairly level surface for vegetation to become established.
- Grooving the slope with a tiller, harrow or teeth of a front-end loader forming grooves perpendicular to the slope. Grooves should be at least 3 in. deep and no more than 15 in. apart with each series of grooves cut in the opposite direction of the preceding set of grooves to avoid buildup of loose material at one end.
- Tracking by running a tracked machine up and down the face of the slope, with the tracks leaving their horizontal impression perpendicular to the slope. Excessive compaction should be avoided by making as few passes as possible with the tracked equipment.

Finish Grading

Finish grading establishes the elevations that are indicated on the grading plans. For paved areas, this would include the finished elevations of proposed pavements after their installation. For landscaped areas, this would include the elevations shown on the grading plan after the spreading of new or stockpiled topsoil.

Practices to Avoid

- Do not place fill on saturated or frozen ground.
- Do not cut or fill so close to adjacent properties without providing protection against erosion, sedimentation, slippage or any other slope-related problem.

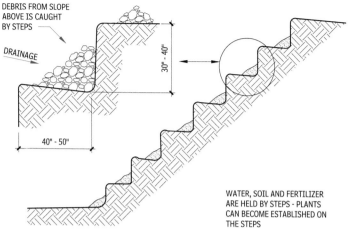

DEBRIS FROM SLOPE ABOVE IS CAUGHT BY STEPS

DRAINAGE

30" - 40"

40" - 50"

WATER, SOIL AND FERTILIZER ARE HELD BY STEPS - PLANTS CAN BECOME ESTABLISHED ON THE STEPS

STAIR STEPPING CUT SLOPES

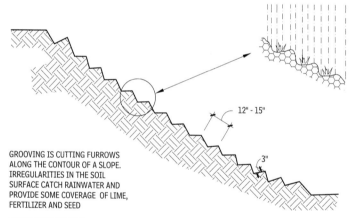

12" - 15"

3"

GROOVING IS CUTTING FURROWS ALONG THE CONTOUR OF A SLOPE. IRREGULARITIES IN THE SOIL SURFACE CATCH RAINWATER AND PROVIDE SOME COVERAGE OF LIME, FERTILIZER AND SEED

GROOVING SLOPES

Figure 9.2 Stair step grading and grooving slope diagrams.
Source: http://dcr.state.va.us_soil_and_water_documents_Chapter 3-3.

- Avoid placing fill adjacent to a water channel bank where it may cause bank failure with deposition of sediment downstream.
- Avoid grading adjacent to water bodies without leaving a vegetated buffer strip, berm or filter fabric fence to protect against erosion and sedimentation.
- Avoid excessive compaction in areas that will be vegetated. It inhibits germination and growth as well as increases runoff quantity and velocity.

EACH LIFT OF THE FILL IS COMPACTED, BUT THE OUTER FACE OF THE SLOPE IS ALLOWED TO REMAIN LOOSE SO THAT THE ROCKS, CLODS, ETC. REACH THE NATURAL ANGLE OF REPOSE.

FILL SLOPE TREATMENT

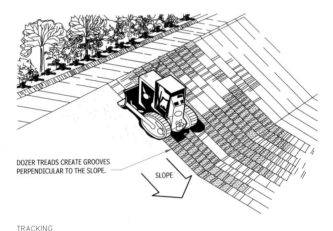

DOZER TREADS CREATE GROOVES PERPENDICULAR TO THE SLOPE.

SLOPE

TRACKING

Figure 9.3 Tracking creates impressions perpendicular to the slope.
Source: VA Chapter 3-3.29.

Figure 9.4 Tracking roughens surface perpendicular to the slope.
Source: Chattanooga BMP4-15.

Spreading and Grading Topsoil

Description

Topsoil is usually spread during finished grading to provide a suitable level of positive characteristics, nutrients and organic matter to encourage the growth of vegetation. It is the layer of soil where root development and biological activity occur. The coarser texture of topsoil increases its infiltration capacity and makes it less susceptible to erosion.

Topsoil to be spread can be from stockpiles of existing topsoil that has been stripped and stockpiled early in the construction phase or it can be imported from another site.

Assessing Site Conditions

Existing topsoil stockpiled for spreading during final site preparation should be used to provide a positive growing medium for vegetation. Before importing soil from another site, the restoration of existing soils on site should be considered. The addition of soil amendments can improve the quality of the existing soil characteristics to match the qualities of healthy local soils.

Existing or imported topsoil should be evaluated for quality, foreign matter, weed seeds, and the feasibility of distributing and grading topsoil on the site. In some cases, it may be more practical to enhance the quality of the soil or subsoil on site rather than transporting and spreading topsoil. If the existing soil or subsoil cannot be amended, or if the depth is not adequate to provide sufficient area for roots to develop or if the soil contains materials that may be toxic to vegetation, addition and spreading of topsoil may be the only alternative.

Because topsoil generally has a high level of infiltration, the soil beneath needs to be tested to determine if it is well draining. The different infiltration rates between the base soil and the topsoil overlay can create a situation where water will drain horizontally along the interface of the two different soil types. Low pockets created during the finished grading process can trap water beneath the surface. A percolation test should be performed to determine the rate of infiltration and need for any modification to the soil to improve its drainage characteristics to be compatible with the topsoil overlay.

▶ **Before spreading topsoil be sure that erosion and sediment control devices have been put into place.**

Acceptable Practices

- Prior to topsoil spreading be sure fine grading has established even and proper elevations as indicated on the plans, without low spots or other irregularities. Incorporate limestone into the existing soil if the pH is considered low for the proposed vegetation or is less than 6.0 for proposed turf areas or if the soil has a heavy clay content.
- The surface of the existing soil should be loosened and roughened to a depth of approximately 6 in. to create a bond between the existing soil and topsoil layers. This can be accomplished by running a disk over the area or using the teeth of a backhoe or loader to scarify the surface.
- It should be anticipated that some storm water will flow under the topsoil layer and along the surface of the subsoil, therefore, drainage may be required at low points.
- Topsoil should be spread uniformly over the area and compacted enough to bond the topsoil to the layer below and provide even storm water infiltration.
- Use low-impact equipment to minimize over-compaction and soil structure damage.
- On slopes that will not be mowed, the surface can be left rough to minimize erosion.
- Installation of topsoil on slopes carries the potential that it can slip down along interface with the subsoil. In order to minimize this possibility, consider:

  - Stepping the subgrade to provide a rougher surface.
  - Providing an intercepting swale at the top of the slope to minimize the storm water runoff down the face of the slope.
  - Install soil stabilizers, like a geoweb.

▶ **Surface matting is not effective in preventing topsoil from slipping down a steep slope.**

Practices to Avoid

- Do not spread topsoil while it is frozen or muddy or when the subgrade is wet or frozen.
- Do not apply topsoil to slopes steeper than 2:1 as it will likely slip down to the toe of the slope.
- Do not apply topsoil over a subsoil of a significantly different texture and infiltration rate.
- Avoid spreading topsoil on subsoils with high clay content, particularly on slopes.
- Avoid low spots in the grading of subsoils prior to topsoil spreading; they will hold water.
- Avoid having equipment repeatedly run over the area where topsoil has been previously placed to avoid compaction; loosen the soil if necessary.

References

ALSO IN THIS BOOK:

- Clearing and Grubbing
- Temporary Erosion and Sediment Controls
- Temporary Storm Water Pollution Control
- Temporary Tree Protection
- Topsoil Stripping and Stockpiling

OTHER RESOURCES:

- James Urban. Up By Roots, Champaign, IL: International Society of Arboriculture, 2008.
- Landscape Architectural Graphic Standards, First Edition, Hoboken, NJ: John Wiley & Sons, 2007.

PART V

EXTERIOR IMPROVEMENTS

Chapter 10

Surfaces and Paving

Asphaltic Concrete

Description

Asphaltic concrete is typically a combination of heated asphalt cement and heated aggregates mixed together in specific proportions and sizes ("hot mix" asphalt). The paving aggregate is dried and heated to approximately 300 degrees F and is thoroughly mixed with asphalt cement that is in a liquid state after being heated to 275 degrees F to coat all the aggregate particles entirely with the specified percentage of asphalt cement. The coated aggregate mix is delivered to the site hot and laid directly on a subgrade or base course of stone screenings. The mixture is compacted to a specific density and the pavement then hardens by cooling as the liquid asphalt turns solid, adhering to and binding the aggregate together.

▶ There are some types of asphaltic concrete that utilize emulsifiers or cut-back asphalt cement that allows pavements to be laid cold, that harden by evaporation. This is not as common or as preferred as "hot mix" asphaltic concrete.

The design mix of asphaltic concrete pavement varies using different sizes and percentages of different aggregates, laid in different thicknesses and using various percentages of asphalt cement. However, it is usually made up of a surface course that is laid over an aggregate base or on a binder course of asphaltic concrete that is composed of larger size aggregates for stability and strength. In all instances, a compacted subgrade is critical.

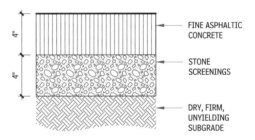

Figure 10.1 Light duty asphalt pavement.
Source: Hopper, Landscape Architectural Graphic Standards. Copyright 2007, John Wiley & Sons, Inc.

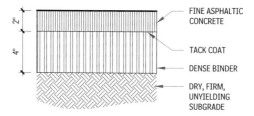

Figure 10.2 Heavy duty asphalt pavement (vehicular).
Source: Hopper, Landscape Architectural Graphic Standards. Copyright 2007, John Wiley & Sons, Inc.

Assessing Site Conditions

Types of Asphaltic Concrete Defects, Causes and Repair

One of the best sources for identification of asphalt pavement defects, their cause and possible solutions is the "Distress Identification Manual for the Long-Term Pavement Performance Program" published by the Federal Highway Administration (publication no. FHWA-RD-03-031)

Acceptable Practices

Subgrade Preparation

Asphaltic concrete pavement's role as a surface treatment is to transfer the load placed on it and distribute it over a larger area to the subgrade. Asphaltic concrete is considered a flexible pavement that, with some degree of resiliency, transfers loads to the subgrade over a smaller area than a more rigid pavement such as concrete. It is therefore highly dependent on the ability of the subgrade to support the load placed on it.

Asphaltic concrete pavements are often installed over a sub-base of compacted graded aggregate. This layer of aggregate adds stability and helps distribute the loads transmitted through the pavement over a larger area of the subgrade. This greater distribution of load allows the thickness of the asphaltic concrete pavement to be reduced.

Where freeze-thaw cycles are a consideration, the aggregate layer helps to keep any water away from the pavement and minimizes the effects of frost heave.

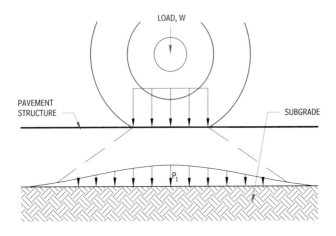

Figure 10.3 Spread of wheel-load through pavement structure.
Source: Hopper, Landscape Architectural Graphic Standards. Copyright 2007, John Wiley & Sons, Inc.

It is critical to properly prepare and compact the subgrade and/or the aggregate base course before the paving process:

▪ The subgrade should be free of soft or spongy material, organic matter or any materials that potentially could cause a weak spot or drainage problem.

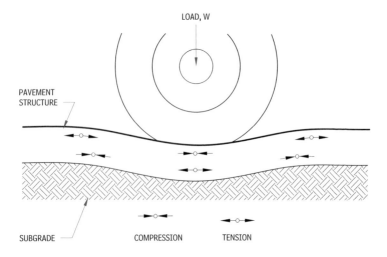

Figure 10.4 Pavement deflection results in tensile and compressive stresses in pavement structure.
Source: Hopper, Landscape Architectural Graphic Standards. Copyright 2007, John Wiley & Sons, Inc.

Figure 10.5 Aggregate sub-base being compacted with a roller. It is clear to see the difference in the surface texture between the areas that have already been compacted and the areas that still have not been gone over with the roller.

- A layer of aggregate as a base course can be used to help distribute the load over a greater area and to allow any water to drain through to the subgrade.
- The nature of asphaltic concrete pavement requires that the heavier the anticipated load the thicker the overall pavement needs to be in order to distribute the load over a larger area of the subgrade.

▶ If there is failure at the subgrade level, the asphalt pavement surface will follow the subgrade creating depressions or a rolling effect.

Asphaltic Concrete Pavement Reinforcement

Asphaltic concrete pavement has low tensile strength that often leads to surface defects. A geocomposite that integrally combines a nonwoven geotextile fabric with a geogrid can be used between the layers of asphaltic concrete pavement to add strength and stability to the asphaltic concrete pavement. The geocomposite combines the separation and filtering properties of the geotextile fabric with the strength of the geogrid. The addition of the geocomposite:

- Increases the tensile strength of the asphalt layer and absorbs shear forces.
- Distributes the load evenly over a larger area.
- Prevents formation and spreading of reflex cracks.
- Reduces deformations and rutting.

Aggregates

The size and proportion of each gradation of the aggregate specified in the asphaltic concrete design mix is critical to the strength, durability and skid resistance, and should be verified at time of delivery. Aggregates are classified by their size as it relates to the percentage of particles passing through a specific sieve size (a square screen) by weight. The different sized aggregates are combined in the desired proportions to meet the specified design mix. The specific mixes for different uses will vary by region and will often reference a standard set by the local Department of Transportation.

In general terms:

- Coarse aggregate is retained on a No. 8 sieve;
- Fine aggregates pass through a No. 8 sieve;
- Mineral filler passes through a No. 30 sieve.

The percentage of aggregate passing through the sieve size is given as a range (i.e., 65 to 90%). The maximum aggregate size is the smallest sieve that will allow 100% of the aggregate to pass through. The nominal aggregate size is the largest sieve that will retain any of the aggregate. The coarser aggregate gives the asphaltic concrete pavement strength and stability. The fine aggregate helps increase the density of the pavement. The mineral filler and smallest particles fill the voids between the larger aggregates making the pavement more dense and less pervious.

A dense graded asphaltic concrete pavement:

- Prevents water from being trapped in the voids, which is extremely detrimental during freeze/thaw cycles.
- Prevents water penetration to the subgrade, which can affect its load bearing capacity.

Although a coarse aggregate provides strength, stability and distribution of a load over a wider area, it is not suitable for a wearing surface because of its rough texture. Therefore, it is most often the case that the coarser aggregate mix is laid first as a binder course and a surface course of fine aggregate asphaltic concrete is overlaid on top. This combination benefits from the strength of the coarse binder and the smooth textured surface of the fine aggregate asphaltic concrete mix.

▶ After a thorough sweeping, a tack coat of asphalt cement should be sprayed between the courses of asphalt, just prior to laying the next paving course, to bind them together.

▶ Pervious asphalt is an exception containing an open graded aggregate mix that is a bit rougher texture. This is covered later in this section.

Pavement Thickness and Layers

The thickness of the asphaltic concrete pavement is directly related to its ability to:

- Support anticipated loads without exceeding the limits of the bond strength of the asphalt cement binding the aggregates together.
- Distribute anticipated loads over a large enough area as to not exceed the load bearing capacity of the subgrade.

The greater the anticipated load, the thicker the asphaltic concrete pavement.

Asphaltic concrete pavement can be laid as a "full depth pavement" or over an aggregate base course. A full depth asphaltic concrete pavement is laid directly on a compacted subgrade. Asphaltic concrete pavement can also be laid over an aggregate base course spread and compacted over a compacted subgrade.

A full depth asphaltic concrete pavement has the following characteristics:

- The ability to transfer compressive and tensile forces that can be generated by vehicular traffic over a larger area of the subgrade.
- One inch of a full depth asphaltic concrete layer is equal to approximately 3 in. of an aggregate base.
- It can be susceptible to freeze/thaw damage when used in areas of deep frost or where subgrade composition is susceptible to frost heave.

Asphaltic concrete laid over an aggregate base has the following characteristics:

- Transfers compressive but not tensile forces, and therefore needs to be thicker than a full depth pavement for vehicular usage.

- Minimizes the potential damage from freeze/thaw cycles as it keeps any water away from the asphalt layer and provides load distribution to the compacted subgrade.
- Can reduce the thickness of the asphalt layers, as 3 in. of an aggregate base is equal to 1 in. of asphaltic concrete.

▶ **An aggregate base course can be stabilized using asphalt cement, roughly doubling its load bearing capacity over an untreated aggregate base.**

The thickness of a layer of asphaltic concrete pavement that can be laid at one time is limited by the size of the roller that is necessary to achieve the specified density of the pavement after compaction. As some sites limit the size of the roller that can be used, the asphaltic concrete can be laid in lifts (separate layers that are compacted before another layer of asphaltic concrete is laid on top) that can range from 3/4 to 12 in. (depending on the size of the roller).

▶ **The thickness of a lift should be at least twice the maximum particle size of the aggregate.**

Between each lift, the surface must be cleaned thoroughly and the surface sprayed with a tack coat of asphalt cement to bind the layers together.

The Paving Process

The paving mixture is delivered to the site hot and is placed directly over compacted subgrade or on a compacted aggregate base course or on a base of concrete by a mechanical paving machine or raked into place by hand and is installed as follows:

- The mixture is placed to a depth which, after compaction, will be equal to the specified depth shown on the detail drawings.
- It is then compacted by use of a power-driven roller or other approved method to achieve the specified density and firmness.
- Proper compaction should result in a pavement that has approximately 3 to 5% air voids to increase durability relating to the stresses of expansion and contraction.
- As the mixture cools, the asphaltic concrete pavement hardens. This time can vary but is generally within 24 hours that the pavement has cooled and is ready for use.

▶ **The area of asphaltic concrete pavement must have a firm edge to contain the material, allow proper compaction and prevent the edges from crumbling.**

Typically, hot asphaltic concrete is dumped from a truck into the spreader box hopper. The truck moves forward and is ready to fill the hopper when it is empty. The spreader box hopper lays a uniform level of asphaltic concrete, which will be compacted to the pavement thickness specified. The freshly laid asphaltic concrete is compacted by several passes with the roller while it is still hot. Areas that are inaccessible to the spreader need to have asphaltic concrete shoveled in by hand and then leveled by hand raking. Areas inaccessible to the roller need to be compacted with a plate vibrator. After several passes with the roller, the compaction density is checked with a nuclear density gauge.

After the compaction of the surface course, the entire paved area is checked for depressions using a 10-foot wood or metal straight edge. Any depression greater than allowable in the specification, shall be corrected by removing the surface course of the affected areas, and replacing with new material to form a true and even surface.

▶ **The asphaltic concrete paving process by its nature can result in slight surface irregularities creating "bird baths" after a rainstorm. The rule of thumb that is often applied is to place a nickel at the deepest point in the bird bath. If Thomas Jefferson's head is above water, the deviation in the surface is acceptable. If his head is below**

Figure 10.6 Hot asphaltic concrete from the truck being dumped into the spreader box hopper. The truck moves forward ready to refill the hopper when it is emptied.

Figure 10.7 The spreader lays a uniform level of asphaltic concrete, which will be compacted to the pavement thickness specified. Note the small area around the curb radius that is inaccessible to the spreader.

water, the area of pavement should be removed and the depression corrected. The exceptions to this rule would be areas at the top or bottom of steps or ramps, door entries, or any area that might be part of a primary circulation route. These areas should always be free of any ponding water, particularly if an area is subject to freezing temperatures. A surface area with a large percentage of bird baths may also be considered not acceptable requiring removal and repaving to correct the condition.

Weather Conditions

The installation of asphaltic concrete pavement is sensitive to weather conditions.

- Asphaltic concrete pavement should never be installed under rainy conditions or when there is excessive moisture.
- Winds will increase the heat loss rate of the paving mixture and reduce the time the asphaltic concrete can be laid and compacted while still hot.
- Air and surface temperatures should be a minimum of 40 degrees F.

The asphaltic concrete pavement needs to be laid and compacted while still hot. Therefore, temperature is a limiting factor in how long the contractor has to lay and compact the pavement before it cools. A thicker layer of asphaltic concrete being laid retains its heat longer and can be successfully laid at a temperatures closer to 40 degrees F. Thinner layers or lifts of asphaltic concrete cool more quickly and therefore should be laid when temperatures are significantly higher than the minimum temperature of 40 degrees F. Ideally, temperatures of approximately 70 degrees F are best for asphaltic concrete installations.

In order for proper compaction to take place, the temperature of the hot mixture must be between 185 degrees F and 300 degrees F. It is between these temperatures that the asphalt cement is in a liquid form that facilitates the movement of the aggregate that creates the desired density upon compaction. Once the mixture cools below 185 degrees F, it begins to stiffen and the asphaltic cement hardens to bond the aggregate particles together before it can be spread and compacted. If the temperature of the mixture falls below 185 degrees F it is no longer suitable to be used as a paving material and should be rejected and removed from the site.

▶ **The temperature of the asphaltic concrete in the truck and in the spreader hopper should be recorded at regular intervals during the paving process.**

Maintenance

There are three basic types of asphalt pavement maintenance:

- **Preventative Maintenance** is work that is done to prevent deterioration of a pavement which reduces the need for substantial maintenance. Types of preventative maintenance are drainage maintenance and fog seals.
- **Routine Maintenance** is the day-to-day work that is necessary to preserve and keep a pavement as close to an as-constructed condition as possible such as crack sealing and pothole patching.
- **Major Maintenance** is work that is needed to restore a pavement to its as-constructed condition.

Crack Sealing is necessary to prevent the intrusion of water into the underlying pavement layers. All crack sealing materials require the following properties:

- Good bonding/adhesion;
- Flexibility and extendibility;
- Ease of application;
- Resistance to softening; resistance to tracking;
- Resistance to weathering;
- Compatibility with asphalt.

Surface treatments that improve the waterproofing properties or texture of a pavement surface are referred to as seal coats. Surface treatments can be applied in multiple layers. A fog seal refers to an application of asphalt emulsion that is diluted with water that coats surface particles and flows into surface cracks and voids. It can restore old pavement installations that have become dry, brittle and cracked with age, extending the time before more extensive maintenance or replacement would be required.

A high-grade asphalt emulsion sealer (sometimes called bituminous emulsified sealer) should be applied every two to five years (the first application should wait a minimum of six months after the installation of the pavement), depending on climate, load and volume of traffic. Emulsion sealers consist of asphalt cement treated to mix with water. Once applied, the water evaporates, the material hardens, and the surface is waterproof.

Another restoration method involves the use of a slurry mixture of emulsified asphalt cement and a thin layer of fine aggregate. It performs the same function as a fog seal with additional structural benefits, improved traction on slopes and improvement of skid resistance. It can be applied with a slurry seal machine to ensure the even distribution of the treatment over an area.

Asphaltic Concrete Pavement Rehabilitation

Asphaltic concrete pavement rehabilitation is required when repeated maintenance is required or if the problem is more extensive than maintenance can address. Pavement rehabilitation can include:

- The addition of a thin (typically ¾ to 2 in.) layer of asphaltic concrete over the existing pavement after all cracks and other deficiencies have been addressed. For extra protection against cracks making their way through to the new surface, the overlay can be combined with the use of a geotextile fabric that is placed over the existing pavement after a tack coat has been applied, and the re-surfacing course of asphalt placed over the geotextile.
- Milling of the existing asphalt surface and adding a layer (1-½ to 2 in.) of asphaltic concrete pavement over the remaining asphalt base, after all cracks and other deficiencies have been addressed.
- Removing complete sections or partial sections of pavement by sawcutting and replacing those sections with full depth asphaltic concrete pavement.

For pavements that exhibit more extensive structural problems, total removal and replacement may be the only approach. This is particularly the case where the visible problems indicate that the cause may be related to issues with the subgrade.

Patching

There are two basic types of asphalt pavement patches:

- **Deep or Full Depth Patches** are at least 4 in. deep and are used for making permanent repairs to the pavement. The material to be repaired needs to be removed to a depth necessary to reach firm support. The excavation should also extend at least one foot into the good pavement surrounding the area to be patched.
- **Surface Patches** do not require the removal of existing pavement. A surface or "skin" patch is all that is required to repair small hairline cracks, minor surface distortion or raveling which typically only a layer of hot-mix asphalt or a chip seal will cover.

Resurfacing Overlays

Prior to resurfacing the existing pavement should have all weak areas replaced, all cracks sealed and any depressions filled with leveling wedges of asphaltic concrete. After proper preparation the area should be thoroughly swept to remove any debris that might interfere with the new asphaltic concrete overlay bonding to the existing.

After the surface has been thoroughly prepared and cleaned, a tack coat of liquid asphalt cement should be sprayed over the entire area and the resurfacing mixture should be laid hot over the surface and compacted. During compaction, the tack coat binds the existing pavement to the resurfacing overlay. The edges of a resurfaced area can be tapered to meet the grade of adjacent pavements flush and can also be "keyed in" at the edges for extra stability.

However, because the area after resurfacing is approximately an inch higher than the previous grade, care needs to be taken that the drainage pattern of the resurfaced and surrounding areas are not adversely impacted. It is easy for the newly resurfaced area to become a dam when the raised grade disrupts the flow of stormwater from an adjacent area to the drainage structure that is designed to accommodate the runoff.

Milling

As part of an asphalt pavement resurfacing effort, it is possible to mill the top surface of the existing asphaltic concrete and install a new wearing course on top of the remaining pavement. Milling allows the

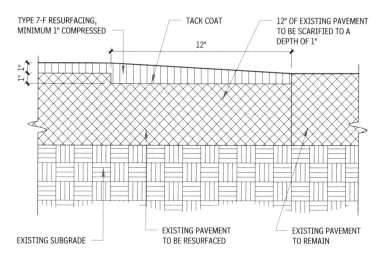

Figure 10.8 Asphalt pavement resurfacing.

restored finished grade to match the pre-restored elevations, while a resurfacing course increases the elevation which can disrupt the drainage pattern of the adjacent surfaces.

Removed or milled asphaltic concrete pavements can be recycled. The millings can be re-used to create new asphaltic concrete mixes that result in a savings on energy costs, reduces the construction materials that would need to be sent to a landfill and saves on the component materials that make up asphaltic concrete, particularly those that are petroleum based.

- The milling machine removes the existing pavement to the desired depth.

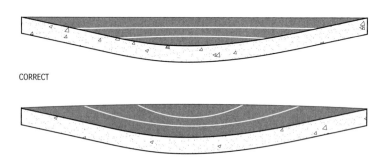

Figure 10.9 Multi-layer leveling wedges.

- As it goes along the material is put into a dump truck that runs behind the milling machine via a chute.
- The removed asphaltic concrete can be recycled at the plant and after processing used again for pavement, commonly referred to as recycled asphalt pavement or RAP.
- A brooming machine cleans the pavement (hand broomed on smaller projects),
- A tack coat is sprayed on the surface, and
- The asphaltic concrete is laid and compacted.

Quantity Calculations

Often there is a need to calculate the amount of asphalt that is being laid. This can be difficult as site plans can calculate the square feet or yards to be installed, and the asphalt plants generally deliver the asphaltic concrete material measured in tons. Aggregate is generally measured in cubic yards. There are some generally easy steps that can help convert and compare these different units.

- The first step is to calculate the volume of asphalt or aggregate required in cubic feet, taking the necessary dimensions from the site plan. This is done by calculating the square footage and multiplying by the specified depth of pavement or aggregate. Remember to keep all the units the same, so when the depth is multiplied it should be in the form of a decimal of a foot (i.e., a 6-in. depth would be represented by .5 ft, a 4-in. depth by .33 ft, etc.). The result will be a volume measured in cubic feet.
- For an aggregate base, the resulting cubic feet needs to be converted to cubic yards by dividing by 27. There are 27 cubic ft in a cubic yard.
- To convert the cubic feet of asphalt pavement needed to tons, it is necessary to know the in-place density (pounds per cubic foot of material) of the design mix specified, as the weight does vary between mixes. Once this is known, multiply the volume in cubic feet times the in-place density, which will give the weight of the asphalt pavement required in pounds. Take the resulting number of pounds and divide by 2,000 (there are 2,000 lbs in one ton) and the result is the amount of asphalt in tons.

▶ When calculating the area of a curvilinear path or road, use the centerline as the length times the width.

Porous Asphaltic Concrete Pavements

Porous or pervious asphaltic concrete pavements are composed of similar materials and installed in a similar manner as regular asphaltic concrete pavements with some small but significant differences:

- The aggregate base course provided must be thicker. As the water passes through the porous surface it must have someplace to go. The aggregate base provides a place for the water to go and acts as a reservoir, storing the water below the surface until it can infiltrate into the subgrade. The aggregate base can vary anywhere from 18 in. or more depending on the anticipated storm design and the rate of infiltration of the subgrade. This is usually calculated by the landscape architect or engineer and figured into the specified depth for each project on a case by case basis, so that the level of water in the aggregate base does not rise to the level of the pavement.
- The asphaltic concrete design mix is made up of primarily the same size aggregates, commonly referred to as gap-graded or open-graded. Without fine aggregates or filler, voids are created between the aggregates that allow water to pass through to the aggregate base.
- Once laid, the asphaltic concrete mix is compacted just enough to bind the aggregate particles together. Too much compaction or compaction with too heavy a roller will result in a denser pavement, lesser percentage of voids and reduce the infiltration rate of the pavement.

While the porous asphaltic concrete mix uses conventional materials, the additional depth of the aggregate base can be expected to cost more in excavation and material, but this is often offset by the reduced cost of providing other manmade, traditional storm drainage systems, which often requires the purchase of additional land or dedicating existing land to storm water purposes.

Due to the coarser aggregate, the surface of porous asphaltic concrete pavement is a bit coarser than regular asphaltic concrete pavement. However, it still meets the requirements of the American Disabilities Act Accessibility Guidelines for an accessible route.

Porous asphaltic concrete pavement does benefit from an annual vacuuming to lift fine particles that have infiltrated into the surface. Porous pavements that have been installed for over 20 years have exhibited little cracking, pothole damage or reduction in their infiltration rates.

Practices to Avoid

- An asphaltic concrete mix must be laid hot, above 185 degrees F. Therefore, a partial load from another site should never be accepted, as its temperature and time away from the plant cannot be verified.

- Asphaltic concrete pavement should not be laid unless the surface and air temperature is above 40 degrees F. Cooling time of the asphaltic concrete mix should be calculated to determine how long the contractor has to lay and compact the pavement before the mix cools to below 185 degrees F.
- Asphaltic concrete pavement should never be laid in the rain or when rain is anticipated.
- Overlay treatments should not be used if it will disrupt the drainage pattern of the area in which they are installed.
- Surface treatments should not be considered a permanent solution to more serious problems that require more extensive repairs or pavement replacement.
- Porous asphaltic pavements should not be power washed, as it drives the fine particles further into the pavement, filling the voids and reducing infiltration rates.
- Porous asphaltic concrete pavements should not be sealed; this will totally negate its infiltration characteristics, rendering it useless as a storm water management tool.

Concrete

Description

Concrete is a mixture of Portland cement, aggregates of various gradations, and water. The water mixes with the cement to form a paste that hardens by a chemical process (called *hydration*) that in turns binds the aggregate into a monolithic mass. The combinations of these ingredients in their various forms and proportions determine the strength, workability, and other characteristics of the concrete. Supplementary cementitious materials and chemical admixtures may also be included in the paste.

The quality of the concrete depends upon the quality of the paste and aggregate, and the bond between the two. In properly made concrete, each and every particle of aggregate is completely coated with paste and all of the spaces between aggregate particles are completely filled with paste.

Aggregates are generally divided into two groups: fine and coarse.

- Fine aggregates consist of natural or manufactured sand with particle sizes ranging up to 9.5 mm ($^3/_8$ in.).
- Coarse aggregates are particles retained on the 1.18 mm (No. 16) sieve and ranging up to 150 mm (6 in.) in size. The maximum size of coarse aggregate is typically 19 mm or 25 mm ($^3/_4$ in. or 1 in.).
- Intermediate sized aggregate, around 9.5 mm ($^3/_8$ in.), can be added to improve the overall aggregate gradation.

The paste is composed of:

- Cementitious materials;
- Water;
- Entrapped air or purposely entrained air.

The paste constitutes about 25% to 40% of the total volume of concrete. The absolute volume of cement is usually between 7% and 15% and the water between 14% and 21%. Air content in air-entrained concrete ranges from about 4% to 8% of the volume.

The introduction of air into the concrete mix has positive effects on the characteristics of concrete during installation and after it has hardened. After concrete has hardened, air entrainment improves resistance to freeze-thaw cycles by providing microscopic voids for the expansion of water as it freezes, relieving internal pressure that can cause cracking. The benefits of air-entrainment during concrete installation include:

- Increases slump allowing a decrease in the amount of water in the concrete mix resulting in:
  - Higher strength without sacrificing workability;
  - Less drying shrinkage;
  - Less bleed water that can cause the adverse effect of a higher water/cement ratio on top of slabs.
- High degree of workability.
- A more cohesive concrete mix, with less segregation of aggregate.

In order for concrete to fully benefit, these microscopic air bubbles must have the proper size, distribution and volume. ASTM C 260 specifies requirements for air-entraining admixtures.

In order to maintain a constant percentage of air during installation:

- Concrete should be ready to be poured as soon as possible after the mixer truck arrives at the site, as prolonged mixing can reduce the percentage of air entrainment.
- Being more cohesive and workable, excessive internal vibration of the concrete is not only unnecessary but should be avoided, as it can reduce the initial air content of the concrete.

For any particular set of materials and conditions of curing, the quality of hardened concrete is strongly influenced by the amount of water used in relation to the amount of cement. Unnecessarily high water contents dilute the cement paste. Following are some advantages of reducing water content:

- Increased compressive and flexural strength.
- Lower permeability, thus lower absorption and increased water tightness.
- Increased resistance to weathering.
- Better bond between concrete and reinforcement.
- Reduced drying shrinkage and cracking.
- Less volume change from wetting and drying.

The less water used, the better the quality of the concrete, provided the mixture can be consolidated properly. Smaller amounts of mixing water result in stiffer mixtures, but with vibration, stiffer mixtures can be easily placed. Thus, consolidation by vibration permits improvement in the quality of concrete.

Assessing Existing Condition

Subgrade Preparation

Cracks, slab settlement, and structural failure can often be traced to an inadequately prepared and poorly compacted subgrade. The subgrade on which a slab on ground is to be placed should be well drained, of uniform bearing capacity, level or properly sloped, and free of sod, organic matter, and frost. The three major causes of non-uniform support are:

- The presence of soft unstable saturated soils or hard rocky soils.
- Backfilling without adequate compaction.
- Expansive soils.

Uniform support cannot be achieved by merely dumping granular material on a soft area. To prevent bridging and settlement cracking, soft or saturated soil areas and hard spots (rocks) should be dug out and filled with soil similar to the surrounding subgrade or if a similar soil is not available, with granular material such as sand, gravel, or crushed stone. All fill materials must be compacted to provide the same uniform support as the rest of the subgrade. During subgrade preparation, it should be remembered that undisturbed soil is generally superior to compacted material for supporting concrete slabs.

▶ Proof rolling the subgrade by running a piece of heavy construction equipment over an area is commonly used to identify areas of unstable soils that need to be addressed.

▶ The subgrade should be moistened with water in advance of placing concrete, without creating puddles or wet, soft, muddy spots. Large areas can be watered down with a water truck equipped with spray nozzles. This will prevent the dry subgrade from wicking up the water away from the freshly laid concrete.

Sub-base

A sub-base is frequently placed on the subgrade:

- As a leveling course to address minor surface irregularities;
- To improve uniformity of support;
- To bring the site up to the required elevation;
- As a capillary break between the slab and the subgrade.

A sub-base of a 4-in. thick layer of granular material such as sand, gravel, crushed stone, recycled concrete or slag, should be compacted to near maximum density. If a thicker sub-base is specified,

Figure 10.10   Large area being proof rolled by running heavy tracked equipment back and forth over the same area repeatedly.

the material should be compacted in layers (lifts) of approximately 4 in. in depth unless tests determine compaction of thicker a lift is possible.

Subgrades and sub-bases can be compacted with:

- Rollers (walk behind or ride-on);
- Vibratory rollers;
- Vibratory plates;
- Rammers;
- Hand tampers.

Ideally, the compaction equipment used should be matched with the soil type. Cohesive soils (containing a large percentage of clay) are best compacted with a rammer or pad-foot vibratory roller (for larger areas), that are high impact and force the air out of the soil. Granular soils require a vibratory action to move and compact the soil particles, making vibratory plates the better compaction equipment method.

▶ A sub-base should be considered in areas that contain expansive soils. This is a common condition in some parts of the country, particularly in some western states.

Acceptable Practices

Forms

Cast-in-place concrete requires formwork to define its shape as it cures. Plywood and milled lumber are the most common form materials. However, their use depletes resources and their disposal contributes to construction waste. Reuse of formwork can save resources and reduce material sent to landfills. Steel, aluminum or plastic forms can be reused many times. Wood forms can be reused if form release agents that don't damage the wood are used such as low- and zero-VOC water-based, soy-derived or those made from other biologically derived oils that also reduce health risks to construction staff.

Edge forms and intermediate screeds should be set accurately and firmly to the specified elevation and contour for the finished surface. Slab edge forms are usually metal or wood braced firmly with wood or steel stakes to keep them in horizontal and vertical alignment. The forms should be straight and free from warping and have sufficient strength to resist concrete pressure without bulging. They should also be strong enough to support any mechanical placing and finishing equipment used.

▶ Earth forms can minimize use of resources and save cost of formwork materials. Footing width should be increased by 1 in. for each earth form side. Concrete that will show above grade should be formed with formwork.

Concrete Slump

Slump is a measure of concrete's consistency, texture and uniformity. Performing a slump test on the concrete that is delivered to the project site is the only way to ensure that the concrete mix specified is the concrete mix that is being delivered. The slump test is based on American Society for Testing and Materials C 143-74 "Standard Test Method for Slump of Portland Cement Concrete" and ASTM 172-71 "Standard Method Sampling Fresh Concrete."

Samples taken for the test must be representative of the entire batch. This is accomplished by taking the samples at two or more regularly spaced intervals during discharge of the middle portion of the batch. These samples are then combined into one sample for testing purposes. The first and last portions of the composite sample should be taken as quickly as possible, and never more than 15 minutes apart.

A slump test is performed with a galvanized steel cone, 12 in. high that has a base opening of 8 in. in diameter and a top opening of 4 in. in diameter. The top and bottom openings are perpendicular to the vertical axis of the cone. There are handles on the sides to hold down the cone while filling and facilitate raising it up. The tamping rod is a straight ⁵⁄₈ in. diameter steel rod, 24 in. long, with one end rounded to a diameter of ⁵⁄₈ of an in.

Although the equipment may seem quite simple, the test must be performed with specific criteria as outlined:

- Dampen the slump cone and place it on a flat, moist, nonabsorbent, rigid surface.
- Stand on the two foot pieces of cone to hold it firmly in place while filling the cone with the concrete sample.
- Fill the cone mold ⅓ by volume (2-⁵⁄₈-in. high) with the concrete sample, rotating the scoop around the top edge of the cone as the concrete slides from it to ensure the concrete is evenly distributed within the mold.
- Rod it with 25 strokes using the rounded end of the tamping rod. Distribute rodding strokes evenly over entire cross section of the concrete by using approximately half the strokes near the perimeter (outer edge) and then progressing spirally toward the center.
- Fill the cone ⅔ full by volume (half the height) and again rod 25 times with rod just penetrating into, but not through, the first layer. Distribute strokes evenly.
- Fill the cone to overflowing and again rod 25 times with the rod just penetrating into, but not through, the second layer, distributing the strokes evenly. If during rodding the level of concrete should fall below the top of the cone, add additional concrete to keep the level above the top of the cone.
- Strike off excess concrete from top of cone with the steel rod so the concrete is level with the top of the cone. Clean any overflow away from the base of the cone.
- Immediately after leveling the concrete to the top of the cone, remove the cone by carefully and steadily lifting straight up with no lateral or torsional motion being imparted to the concrete. The entire operation from the start of the filling through removal of the mold shall be carried out without interruption and should not exceed an elapsed time of 2-¹⁄₂ minutes.
- Invert the cone and place it next to the concrete sample, placing the steel rod horizontally across the inverted cone so the rod extends over the slumped concrete.
- Measure the distance from bottom of the steel rod to the original center of the top of the specimen. This measurement is the slump of the concrete.
- If a decided falling away or shearing off of concrete from one side or portion of the mass occurs, disregard the test and make a new test on another portion of the sample.

Figure 10.11a   Slump cone is filled and rodded to consolidate concrete.
Source: Photo courtesy of the Portland Cement Association.

If the slump is too small or too great, a decision will need to be made as to either accept or reject the concrete or consider modifying the slump.

Adjusting Slump in the Field

There are a number of variables that will result in the need to adjust slump at the concrete delivery site, including the supplier holding back on batch water to ensure a safe water-cement ratio in anticipation of

Figure 10.11b   After filling and rodding the slump cone concrete is leveled off.
Source: Photo courtesy of the Portland Cement Association.

Figure 10.11c Slump cone is lifted off vertically.
Source: Photo courtesy of the Portland Cement Association.

additions of water at the site. Rather than guess at the slump of the delivered concrete, most contractors will use two tests, one to determine the initial slump of the concrete and the other for compliance with the specifications. The first slump test is performed on a wheelbarrow of concrete taken from the first part of the truck. This first sample typically has a higher slump than the rest of the batch,

Figure 10.11d Slump cone is inverted and a ruler is used to measure the difference in height (slump) between the top of the cone and the top of the concrete. In this example, the slump is about 4 in.
Source: Photo courtesy of the Portland Cement Association.

therefore, any decisions to adjust the slump at this initial stage are made very carefully.

If it is determined that the concrete has a slump below the specified slump and it is unsuitable for placement at that slump, water may be added in accordance with ASTM C 94, to achieve the desired slump, providing the specified water-cement ratio is not exceeded. After any plasticizing or high-range water-reducing admixtures are introduced to the concrete, water should not be added. The slump and air content of air-entrained concrete should be measured after slump adjustments are made to verify compliance with the specifications.

When using water to increase slump, it must be added to the entire batch; water should not be added to the middle or end of a batch to increase workability. Make sure on-site water is added correctly. Introduce water into the batch at the head section of the drum or by dual injection into the head and discharge section of the drum. Don't use a hose to spray additional water into the mix. Check that the ready mix truck has a Truck Mixer Manufacturer's Bureau rating plate attached to the body indicating its conformance to truck mixer and agitator standards. These standards require the truck to have a mixer water system with a working, visible sight gauge and an automatic measuring device accurate to 1% of the total capacity of the water tank. ASTM C 94 requires an additional 30 revolutions at mixing speed when water is added to the truck and prohibits water being added to the truck when the combined revolutions from a long haul or waiting time exceed 270.

Concrete properties change when water is added to the mix. Adding just 1 gallon of water per cubic yard can:

- Increase slump 1 in.
- Decrease compressive strength 150 to 200 psi.
- Waste about 1/4 bag of cement.
- Increase shrinkage by 10%.

However, water isn't the only way to adjust slump. A water reducer or superplasticizer can be added at the site to increase slump. Using admixtures have the advantage of maintaining the water-cement ratio, at the same time providing a workable slump. If the concrete is already at the maximum water-cement ratio, an admixture may be the only acceptable method of increasing slump. These admixtures come in pre-measured bags to be used for each cubic yard of concrete, which will predictably raise the slump to meet the specification.

Sometimes, slump needs to be decreased. Although ready mix drivers typically carry a couple of extra sacks of cement to dry up the mix the additional revolutions to mix the cement into the batch is time consuming and is not always effective at reaching the desired slump. A more effective method for reducing slump is to add powdered silica fume. Prepackaged powdered silica will dry up a mix, but will also darken the concrete.

Water/Cement Ratios

Low water/cement ratios increase:

- Durability
- Strength
- Desired characteristics of concrete

As an example, a .45 water/cement ratio can reach a compressive strength of 4500 psi, while a .50 water/cement ratio will likely reach a compressive strength of 4000 psi. A concrete mix with a greater than .50 water/cement ratio increases permeability significantly, that can have a negative effect on durability, particularly in areas that are exposed to freeze/thaw conditions.

The water/cement ratio is calculated by dividing the water in one cubic yard of concrete mix (in pounds) by the cement in the concrete mix (in pounds). Therefore, a .50 water/cement ratio mix would contain half the amount of water, as cement (in pounds).

▶ If a mix identifies the amount of water in gallons, convert this amount to pounds by multiplying the number of gallons by 8.33 pounds to determine the total number of pounds of water, and then divide by the number of pounds of cement, to determine the water/cement ratio.

Placing and Spreading

The freshly poured concrete should be placed as close as possible to its final position, should slightly overfill the forms and be roughly leveled with square-ended shovels or concrete rakes and then screeded with a straight edge. Short handled, square-ended shovels are recommended for spreading concrete. A come-along (a tool that looks like a hoe and has a long straight edged blade) can also be used.

Excessive handling or movement of the poured concrete over long distances can cause segregation of the coarse and fine aggregates, negatively affecting strength and durability. Large voids trapped in the concrete during placing should be removed by consolidation.

▶ Do not use a round edge shovel for spreading concrete since it does not spread the concrete evenly.

Protect Your Head and Eyes

It is recommended that a hard hat or safety hat be worn when working any construction job, large or small. Proper eye protection is essential when working with cement or concrete. Eyes are particularly vulnerable to blowing dust, splattering concrete, and other foreign objects. On some jobs it may be advisable to wear full-cover goggles or safety glasses with side shields.

Consolidating Concrete

Consolidation is the process of compacting fresh concrete; to mold it within the forms and around embedded items and reinforcement; and to eliminate stone pockets, honeycomb, and entrapped air. It should not remove significant amounts of intentionally entrained air in air-entrained concrete.

Consolidation is accomplished by hand or by mechanical methods. The method chosen depends on the consistency of the mixture and the placing conditions, such as complexity of the formwork and amount and spacing of reinforcement. Generally, mechanical methods using either internal or external vibration are the preferred methods of consolidation.

Vibration

Vibration, either internal or external, is the most widely used method for consolidating concrete. When concrete is vibrated, the internal friction between the aggregate particles is temporarily destroyed and the concrete behaves like a liquid; it settles in the forms under the action of gravity and the large entrapped air voids rise more easily to the surface. Internal friction is reestablished as soon as vibration stops.

Vibrators, whether internal or external, are usually characterized by:

- Frequency of vibration, expressed as the number of vibrations per second (Hertz), or vibrations per minute (vpm);
- The amplitude of vibration, which is the deviation in millimeters (inches) from the point of rest.

▶ When vibration is used to consolidate concrete, a standby vibrator should be on hand at all times in the event of a mechanical breakdown.

Internal Vibration

Internal or immersion-type vibrators, often called spud or poker vibrators, are commonly used to consolidate concrete in walls, columns, beams, and slabs. Flexible-shaft vibrators consist of a vibrating head connected to a driving motor by a flexible shaft. Inside the head, an unbalanced weight connected to the shaft rotates at high speed, causing the head to revolve in a circular orbit. The motor can be powered by electricity, gasoline, or air.

Proper use of internal vibrators is important for best results. Vibrators should not be used to move concrete horizontally since this causes segregation. Whenever possible, the vibrator should be lowered vertically into the concrete at regularly spaced intervals and allowed to descend by gravity. It should penetrate to the bottom of the layer being placed and at least 150 mm (6 in.) into any previously placed layer. The height of each layer or lift should be about the length of the vibrator head or generally a maximum of 500 mm (20 in.) in regular formwork.

In thin slabs, the vibrator should be inserted at an angle or horizontally in order to keep the vibrator head completely immersed. However, the vibrator should not be dragged around randomly in the slab. For slabs on grade, the vibrator should not make contact with the subgrade. The distance between insertions should be about 1 ½ times the radius of action so that the area visibly affected by the vibrator overlaps the adjacent previously vibrated area by a few centimeters (inches).

External Vibration

External vibrators can be form vibrators, vibrating tables, or surface vibrators such as vibratory screeds, plate vibrators, vibratory roller screeds, or vibratory hand floats or trowels. Form vibrators, designed to

Figure 10.12 Internal vibrators consolidating concrete as the concrete is pumped in behind.
Source: Photo courtesy of the Portland Cement Association.

be securely attached to the outside of the forms, can be especially useful:

- For consolidating concrete in members that are very thin or congested with reinforcement;
- To supplement internal vibration;
- Stiff mixes where internal vibrators cannot be used.

Curing Concrete

Curing is the maintenance of a satisfactory moisture content and temperature in concrete for a period of time immediately following placing and finishing so that the desired properties may develop properly. Curing has a strong influence on the properties of hardened concrete. Proper curing will increase:

- Durability
- Strength

Figure 10.13a   External vibrator being applied to the sides of the form to supplement the internal vibrator directly in the concrete.
Source: Photo courtesy of the Portland Cement Association.

Figure 10.13b   A screed box with a vibrator attached.
Source: Photo courtesy of the Portland Cement Association.

- Watertightness
- Abrasion resistance
- Volume stability
- Resistance to freezing and thawing and deicers

When Portland cement is mixed with water, a chemical reaction called hydration takes place. The extent to which this reaction is completed influences the strength and durability of the concrete. Freshly mixed concrete normally contains more water than is

Figure 10.13c   A truss vibrating screed levels and consolidates at the same time.
Source: Photo courtesy of the Portland Cement Association.

required for hydration of the cement; however, excessive loss of water by evaporation can delay or prevent adequate hydration.

Exposed slab surfaces are especially sensitive to curing as strength development and freeze-thaw resistance of the top surface of a slab can be reduced significantly when curing is defective. The most effective method for curing concrete depends on the materials used, method of construction, and the intended use of the hardened concrete.

Forms provide satisfactory protection against loss of moisture if the top exposed concrete surfaces are kept wet. Wood forms left in place should be kept moist by sprinkling, especially during hot, dry weather. For most jobs, curing generally involves applying curing compounds, or covering the freshly placed and finished concrete with impermeable sheets or wet burlap.

During the curing period, the correct temperature must be maintained in order for the concrete to harden properly. Hydration slows when the temperature goes below 50 degrees F and completely stops at temperatures below 40 degrees F. At temperatures greater than 85 degrees F, the chemical reaction occurs too quickly and temperature differences within the concrete can lead to internal stresses that result in cracks.

The acceptable methods for proper concrete curing are (right after finishing):

- Covering the concrete with impermeable plastic sheeting.
- Covering the concrete with burlap that is kept wet for the entire curing period.
- Applying a liquid curing compound over the freshly finished concrete that establishes a membrane that prevents moisture from leaving the concrete (the most common method).

▶ Many liquid curing compounds are tinted making it easy to observe whether the entire surface of concrete has been thoroughly covered. The tint fades and disappears completely after the completion of the initial month of the curing period.

Rain Protection

Protective coverings such as polyethylene sheets or tarpaulins should be available and on-site at all times. When rain occurs, all batching and placing operations should stop and the fresh concrete should be covered to the extent that the rain does not indent the surface of the concrete or wash away the cement paste. When rain ceases, the covering should be removed and remedial measures taken such as surface retexturing or reworking in-place plastic concrete, before concrete placing resumes.

Concrete Strength

Generally a concrete mix is required to provide a specified compressive strength measured in pounds per square inch (psi). A common testing method to determine compressive strength is a cylinder test. The cylinder test involves taking a pre-molded concrete sample that has been properly cured, subjecting it to a test load, measuring the maximum load reached at the point that the concrete sample fails and calculating the compressive strength measure in pounds per square inch. Test results are only accurate when the concrete cylinders have been prepared, handled and cured properly.

The cylinder itself can be either 12 in. high by 6 in. in diameter or 8 in. high by 4 in. in diameter, typically made from steel, cast iron or a hard plastic material. The tamping rod to consolidate the concrete in the cylinder mold should be ⅝ in. diameter for the 6 in. diameter cylinder and ⅜ in. diameter for the 4-in. diameter cylinder, both with a hemispherically shaped tip.

▶ **Although the smaller diameter cylinders are easier to handle, the diameter of the cylinder should be at least 3 times the nominal maximum size of the coarse aggregate used in the concrete.**

A cylinder test procedure outline is as follows:

- A representative sample of concrete should be taken from the middle of the load (in accordance with ASTM C 172) by diverting the chute into a wheelbarrow with two portions of concrete taken within 15 minutes of each other. The sample should be a minimum of 1 cubic foot.
- After treating the molds with a release agent, the cylinders should be placed on a level surface and filled by distributing the concrete along the inside of the mold with the scoop.
- For concrete with a slump of 1 in. or less, the concrete should be consolidated by vibration. For concrete with a slump of 1 in. or more, the concrete sample can be consolidated by vibration or rodding. For vibration (one insertion for a 4-in. diameter cylinder, two insertions for a 6-in. diameter cylinder) the cylinder should be filled in two equal layers. For rodding, a 6-in. diameter cylinder should be filled in three equal layers and for 4-in. diameter cylinders two equal layers. Each layer should be rodded 25 times evenly distributed throughout the layer. Tap the sides of the cylinder with a mallet after

Figure 10.14 The concrete is rodded in the cylinder by layers to consolidate the concrete.
Source: Photo courtesy of the Portland Cement Association.

each layer of concrete is consolidated, to close any voids created by the vibrator or tamping rod.

- Strike off the top of the cylinder to level the concrete with the top of the cylinder and cover with a plastic lid or bag to prevent water evaporation. During the initial curing period (approximately 24 hours), the cylinders should be kept between 60 to 80 degrees F.

Figure 10.15 The top of the cylinders are leveled off.
Source: Photo courtesy of the Portland Cement Association.

Figure 10.16   The plastic cylinders filled with concrete are allowed to cure at 70 degrees F for 28 days in a controlled environment curing box.
Source: Photo courtesy of the Portland Cement Association.

Then each cylinder is loaded axially in a laboratory, the cylinder is stood up in a loading machine and an arm of the machine pushes down on the top of the cylinder until the cylinder breaks. The maximum amount of force the machine used on the cylinder is important, it tests the maximum strength of the concrete. The compressive strength of the concrete is calculated using the load at which the cylinder failed divided by the cross-sectional area of the cylinder.

Air-Entrainment Testing

There are three ways to measure the air content of fresh concrete upon delivery at the site:

- The pressure method—pressure is applied to the concrete sample compressing the entrained air in the pores. This test relies on the relationship between pressure and volume (Boyles Law) to determine the air content of a concrete mixture.

Figure 10.17 A field test for air entrainment.

- The volumetric method—air is removed from a known volume of concrete by agitation in an excess of water. This test is typically used for lightweight and porous aggregate concrete mixtures. Care must be taken to assure that the sample has been agitated sufficiently to remove all of the air from the sample.
- The free air method—a concrete sample is placed in a vial and alcohol is added to free the air. The change in level of the alcohol in the vial stem indicates the air content. The test takes about 3 minutes to perform and is therefore ideal for field use at either a pour site or batch plant.

Practices to Avoid

Hot Weather Conditions

Working with concrete in hot weather conditions should be avoided whenever possible. Hot weather conditions adversely influence concrete quality primarily by accelerating the rate of moisture loss and rate of cement hydration that occur at higher temperatures.

Detrimental hot weather conditions include:

- High ambient temperature;
- High concrete temperature;
- Low relative humidity;
- High wind speed;
- Solar radiation.

Hot weather conditions can create difficulties in fresh concrete, such as:

- Increased water demand;
- Accelerated slump loss leading to the addition of water on the jobsite;
- Increased rate of setting resulting in placing and finishing difficulties;
- Increased tendency for plastic cracking;
- Critical need for prompt early curing;
- Difficulties in controlling entrained air;
- Increased concrete temperature resulting in long-term strength loss;
- Increased potential for thermal cracking.

Adding water to the concrete at the jobsite can adversely affect properties and serviceability of the hardened concrete, resulting in:

- Decreased strength from higher water to cement ratio;
- Decreased durability due to cracking;
- Increased permeability;
- Non-uniform surface appearance;
- Increased tendency for drying shrinkage;
- Reduced abrasion resistance from tendency to sprinkle water during finishing.

As concrete temperature increases there is a loss in slump that is often unadvisedly compensated for by adding water to the concrete at the jobsite. At higher temperatures a greater amount of water is required to hold slump constant than is needed at lower temperatures. Adding water without adding cement results in a higher water-cement ratio, thereby lowering the strength at all ages and adversely affecting other desirable properties of the hardened concrete.

Cold Weather Conditions

Working with concrete in cold weather without special precautions should be avoided. Cold weather is defined by ACI Committee 306 as a period when for more than 3 successive days the average daily air temperature drops below 5°C (40°F) and stays below 10°C (50°F) for more than one-half of any 24-hour period. Under these circumstances, all materials and equipment needed for adequate protection and curing must be on hand and ready for use before concrete placement is started. Normal concreting practices can be resumed once the ambient temperature is above 10° C (50°F) for more than half a day

During cold weather, the concrete mixture and its temperature should be adapted to the construction procedure and ambient weather conditions. Preparations should be made to protect the concrete; enclosures, windbreaks, portable heaters, insulated forms and blankets should be ready to maintain the concrete temperature. Forms, reinforcing steel, and embedded fixtures must be clear of snow and ice at the time concrete is placed. Thermometers and proper storage facilities for test cylinders should be available to verify that precautions are adequate.

▶ **The concrete's temperature will tell whether the covering is adequate. The heat liberated during hydration will offset to a considerable degree the loss of heat during placing, finishing, and early curing operations. As the heat of hydration slows down, the need to cover the concrete becomes more important.**

Concrete gains very little strength at low temperatures. Freshly mixed concrete must be protected against the disruptive effects of freezing until the degree of saturation of the concrete has been sufficiently reduced by the process of hydration. The time at which this reduction is accomplished corresponds roughly to the time required for the concrete to attain a compressive strength of 3.5 MPa (500 psi). At normal temperatures and water-cement ratios less than 0.60, this occurs within the first 24 hours after placement. Significant ultimate strength reductions, up to about 50%, can occur if concrete is frozen within a few hours after placement or before it attains a compressive strength of 3.5 MPa (500 psi). Concrete to be exposed to deicers should attain a strength of 28 MPa (4,000 psi) prior to repeated cycles of freezing and thawing.

▶ **Concrete that has been frozen just once at an early age can be restored to nearly normal strength by providing favorable subsequent curing conditions. Such concrete, however, will not be as resistant to weathering or as watertight as concrete that had not been frozen. The critical period after which concrete is not seriously damaged by one or two freezing cycles is dependent upon the concrete ingredients and conditions of mixing, placing, curing, and subsequent drying. For example, air-entrained concrete is less susceptible to damage by early freezing than non-air-entrained concrete.**

Concrete Pavement

Description

Concrete pavement is a versatile, durable, and cost-effective site design element. The various textures, finishes, patterns, and colors available provide important design opportunities to strengthen an overall site plan that should not be lost.

Assessing Site Conditions

Evaluating Existing Concrete Pavement

When evaluating the condition of existing concrete pavement that is exhibiting problems, a determination as to whether the concrete pavement needs to be replaced or repaired may need to be made. Understanding the possible reasons for the problem with the existing pavement and how to rectify those conditions is an important part of the evaluation process.

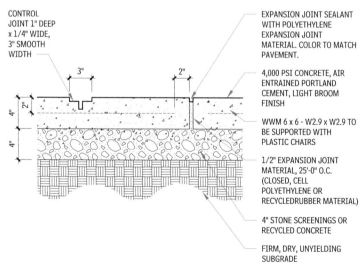

CONTROL JOINT 1" DEEP x 1/4" WIDE, 3" SMOOTH WIDTH

EXPANSION JOINT SEALANT WITH POLYETHYLENE EXPANSION JOINT MATERIAL. COLOR TO MATCH PAVEMENT.

4,000 PSI CONCRETE, AIR ENTRAINED PORTLAND CEMENT, LIGHT BROOM FINISH

WWM 6 x 6 - W2.9 x W2.9 TO BE SUPPORTED WITH PLASTIC CHAIRS

1/2" EXPANSION JOINT MATERIAL, 25'-0" O.C. (CLOSED, CELL POLYETHYLENE OR RECYCLEDRUBBER MATERIAL)

4" STONE SCREENINGS OR RECYCLED CONCRETE

FIRM, DRY, UNYIELDING SUBGRADE

Figure 10.18   4-in. Reinforced Concrete Pavement.
Source: Hopper, Landscape Architectural Graphic Standards. Copyright 2007, John Wiley & Sons, Inc.

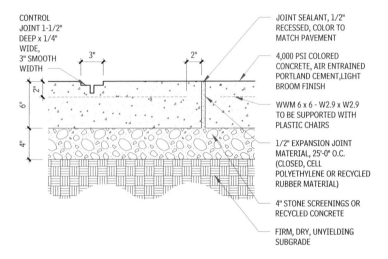

CONTROL JOINT 1-1/2" DEEP x 1/4" WIDE, 3" SMOOTH WIDTH

3"

2"

6"

2"

4"

JOINT SEALANT, 1/2" RECESSED, COLOR TO MATCH PAVEMENT

4,000 PSI COLORED CONCRETE, AIR ENTRAINED PORTLAND CEMENT, LIGHT BROOM FINISH

WWM 6 x 6 - W2.9 x W2.9 TO BE SUPPORTED WITH PLASTIC CHAIRS

1/2" EXPANSION JOINT MATERIAL, 25'-0" O.C. (CLOSED, CELL POLYETHYLENE OR RECYCLED RUBBER MATERIAL)

4" STONE SCREENINGS OR RECYCLED CONCRETE

FIRM, DRY, UNYIELDING SUBGRADE

Figure 10.19   6-in. Reinforced Colored Concrete Pavement.
Source: Hopper, Landscape Architectural Graphic Standards. Copyright 2007, John Wiley & Sons, Inc.

Three existing concrete conditions and their possible underlying causes of failure that would require replacement are:

- Deep cracks that go all the way through the pavement, often accompanied by differential settling of the pavement between the cracks: This can be caused by heavier loads than the pavement was designed to handle, a problem with the subgrade preparation, or both. To address this condition the existing pavement needs to be removed; any unsuitable material in the subgrade replaced; the subgrade and sub-base properly compacted; the pavement design modified if necessary; and then the installation of new concrete pavement.
- Sunken concrete pavement: Often occurring at expansion or control joints, this type of sinking is usually the result of improper subgrade preparation that leaves the concrete pavement unsupported and susceptible to sinking from heavy loads placed upon it or simply the weight of the concrete itself. To address this condition the existing pavement needs to be removed; any unsuitable material in the subgrade replaced; the subgrade and sub-base properly compacted; and then the installation of new concrete pavement.
- Frost heave: Concrete pavements in areas that are susceptible to freeze/thaw cycles can be pushed upwards as the moisture contained in the soil below freezes and expands. Often the pavements do not settle back evenly after the frozen soil thaws. To address this condition the existing pavement needs to be removed; any unsuitable

material in the subgrade removed (with particular attention paid to soils that absorb and retain moisture) and replaced with well drained and compactable material; the subgrade and sub-base properly compacted; and then the installation of new concrete pavement.

Acceptable Practices

Subgrade Preparation

Uniformity, in both soil composition and compaction, is the key to a good subgrade—one that will provide adequate support, ensure an even slab thickness, and prevent slab settlement and structural cracking. Soft spots should be removed and replaced with good material, such as gravel or crushed rock. Compaction is particularly important along the pavement edges and expansion joints where subgrade support is critical to prevent cracking or sinking. The subgrade should be graded parallel to the proposed finished grade.

Utility trenches or other excavations that extend deeper than the prepared subgrade must be brought back up to the required subgrade elevation by backfilling and compacting in 6-in. thick layers (lifts). If these areas are not compacted properly, this soil will settle while the adjacent undisturbed subgrade does not, resulting in a void under this section of concrete, leaving it susceptible to cracking.

Expansive clay soils can be a problem for a subgrade as they swell when they get wet and shrink when they get dry. One way to address this situation would be to ensure that the soil is compacted well when dry, and then not allow the soil to become wet and expand. Another approach would be to replace the top layer of expansive soil with 2 to 8 in. of crushed stone (the depth a factor of the degree of expansiveness; consulting with a soil engineer may be necessary). Despite the best compaction, as the clay soils dry and shrink, the pavement may sink slightly. To minimize any related problems, these slabs should be isolated from other construction with sleeves or expansion joints.

In some cases where soil resists good compaction or heavy loads are anticipated, soil stabilization may be specified in order to improve the characteristics of the soil. Soil stabilization is the process of blending and mixing materials with a soil to improve certain properties of the soil. The process may include the blending of soils to achieve a desired gradation or the mixing of commercially available additives that may alter the gradation, texture or plasticity, or act as a binder for cementation of the soil.

This may be accomplished by:

- Mechanical stabilization: Mechanical stabilization is accomplished by mixing or blending soils of two or more gradations to obtain a material meeting the required specification. The soil blending may take place at the construction site, a central plant, or a borrow area. The blended material is then spread and compacted to required densities by conventional means.
- Additive stabilization: Additive stabilization is achieved by the addition of specified percentages of Portland cement, lime, fly ash, calcium chloride, bitumen, or combinations of these materials to the soil. The selection of type and determination of the percentage of additive to be used is dependent upon the soil classification and the degree of improvement in soil quality desired. Generally, smaller amounts of additives are required when it is simply desired to modify soil properties such as gradation, workability, and plasticity. When it is desired to improve the strength and durability significantly, larger quantities of additive are used. After the additive has been mixed with the soil, spreading and compaction are achieved by conventional means.

Another common approach is the use of woven geotextiles or a geogrid for stabilization and separation of the aggregate from the subgrade. Their high tensile strengths stabilize the subgrade and prevent the aggregate and subgrade from intermixing. This can reduce the thickness of the aggregate layer and increase the longevity of the pavement. The geotextile fabric should be rolled out smoothly over the compacted subgrade with an overlap at seams of 2 to 3 ft. The specified depth of aggregate can then be back dumped onto the fabric, being careful not to drive equipment directly on the fabric. The aggregate can then be spread and compacted using conventional techniques.

Soil compaction is about squeezing out as much air and moisture as possible to push the solid soil particles together making the soil more dense and increasing its bearing capacity. A Proctor test is used to determine the relationship between soil density and moisture and calculates a reasonable soil density that can be achieved. To achieve the highest levels of compaction the moisture level in the soil should be between 10 to 20%.

To get an approximation of the soil-bearing capacity in the field, a hand penetrometer can be used. It is a spring loaded probe that measures the pressure the soil can resist. This can give quick and valuable information in the field about the critical factor of bearing capacity.

To check moisture content and related bearing capacity in the field, when a Proctor test is not being done, some useful rule-of-thumb techniques are:

- To check for moisture, squeeze a ball of soil in your hand. If it won't hold a shape, it's too dry; if it molds easily and then breaks into several pieces when dropped, the moisture content is within the desired range; if it leaves moisture in your hand and doesn't break when dropped, it's too wet.
- A clay soil that you can push your thumb into a few inches with moderate effort will yield a bearing strength of between 1,000 to 2,500 psf.
- Loose sand that you can barely push a #4 rebar into by hand will yield a bearing capacity of between 1,000 to 3,000 psf.
- Sand that you can drive a #4 rebar into about a foot with a 5 pound hammer will yield a bearing capacity of over 2,000 psf.

See Subgrade Preparation under the Concrete section of this Field Guide for more information.

Sub-base

A sub-base is frequently placed on the subgrade as a leveling course to:

- Equalize minor surface irregularities;
- Enhance uniformity of support;
- Bring the site to the desired grade;
- Serve as a capillary break between the slab and the subgrade.

The specified depth of aggregate for the sub-base should be evenly distributed over the subgrade and compacted. The contractor should place and compact to near maximum density a 4-in. thick layer of granular material such as sand, gravel, crushed stone, or slag. If a thicker sub-base is needed for achieving the desired grade, the material should be compacted in layers between 4 to 6 in. thick unless tests determine compaction of a thicker lift is possible. The thicker the sub-base the greater the load the slab will be able to support.

▶ If the specifications allow, recycled crushed concrete is an excellent source for sub-base material.

A base course of smaller aggregate being placed on top of the coarser aggregate sub-base is a common practice that:

- Makes fine grading to meet the desired sub-base elevations easier.
- Provides a flat base which results in a uniform slab thickness.
- Provides a flat base that allows the concrete slab to slide as it shrinks and expands, reducing the risk of cracking.

See Sub-base under the Concrete section of this Field Guide for more information.

Formwork

The area that is to be paved with concrete requires forms to be erected that will contain the concrete when it is placed. Edge forms and intermediate screeds should be set accurately and firmly to the specified elevation and contour for the finished surface. Slab edge forms are usually metal or wood braced firmly with wood or steel stakes to keep them in horizontal and vertical alignment. The forms should be straight and free from warping and have sufficient strength to resist concrete pressure without bulging. They should also be strong enough to support any mechanical placing and finishing equipment used.

Reuse of formwork can save resources and reduce material sent to landfills. Steel or plastic forms can be reused many times. Wood forms can be reused if treated with form release agents that don't damage the wood such as low- and zero-VOC water-based, soy-derived or those made from other biologically derived oils, to prevent the concrete from bonding with the form, which would result in the concrete pulling away from the pavement when the forms are stripped.

The most common choices of materials for curved forms are thin pieces of wood or plywood or flexible metal. Formwork should be

Figure 10.20   Wood forms for pavement are held in place by metal stakes. The boards between the edge forms indicate where the expansion joint will be placed.
Source: Photo courtesy of the Portland Cement Association.

Figure 10.21   Spraying the inside of the forms with a release agent prevents the concrete surface from being damaged when the forms are stripped. Diesel fuel, sometimes used in the past, should never be used as a form release agent. *Source:* Photo courtesy of the Portland Cement Association.

secured in place, particularly for curves formed from thinner wood, where the bracing needs to be spaced close enough together to prevent shifting of the form during the pouring of concrete to ensure a smooth and flowing curve.

It is best to always have the top of the forms set flush with the proposed finished grade of the pavement.

Reinforcement

Reinforcement is used in concrete pavements to increase the tensile strength of concrete pavement. Typical reinforcement of concrete pavements includes:

- Welded steel wire mesh fabric;
- Steel reinforcing bars;
- Various fibers that are integrally mixed with the concrete.

The most common reinforcement for concrete pavement is the use of wire mesh. It is manufactured of steel wire of various sizes that is welded together to form square grids of either 4 in. or 6 in.

Welded wire mesh is specified using four numbers that relate to the size of the grid and the cross-sectional area of the wire. An example of a typically specified welded wire mesh for reinforcing concrete pavement is 6 x 6 – W2.9 x W2.9. The first number refers to the spacing of the longitudinal wire in inches (6″). The second number refers to the spacing of the transverse wires in inches (6″). The third number refers to the cross-sectional area of the longitudinal wires in hundredths of an inch (.029″). The fourth number refers to the cross-sectional area of the transverse wires in hundredths of an inch (.029″). The letter "W" refers to plain wire, the letter "D" would designate a deformed wire. If the wire is specified in metric measurement, the "W" or "D" prefix is preceded by an "M" (MW or MD).

▶ **The welded wire mesh can be specified with a galvanized coating or epoxy coating, where additional corrosion resistance is required. The galvanized coating is applied to the individual wires before welding. The epoxy coating is done after the wire has been welded to form the mesh fabric.**

For the welded wire mesh to be effective, the reinforcing needs to be securely anchored in place prior to the pouring of the concrete. To provide this support, different types of chairs and rails can be used that have been specially designed to clip to the mesh and keep the reinforcing at the correct depth throughout the placement of the concrete.

▶ **Welded wire mesh reinforcement comes in large rolls or sheets. The rolls can be difficult to anchor at the proper depth within the concrete pavement because it is difficult to get it to lay flat. The sheets lay flat and are easier to support at the correct depth within the concrete.**

Steel reinforcing bars are sometimes used to reinforce concrete pavement. Typically, the bars used are called "deformed" because they are not smooth but are manufactured with a ribbed pattern. The ribbed pattern increases the surface area of the bar that comes in contact with the concrete. It does so in a pattern that allows the concrete to get a firm grip on the steel and prevents slippage.

Steel reinforcing bars are specified by a number, that when multiplied by $1/8$ in., represents the bar's nominal diameter in inches. The reinforcing bars must be secured in place by special chairs and clips. These secure the bars in place and at the proper depth during the placement of the concrete.

Glass or plastic fiber products can be integrally mixed with the concrete to provide additional reinforcement, which can help to relieve internal stress and minimize cracking. The addition of fiber reinforcing helps develop early tensile strength along the surface of the concrete to resist the tensile forces that cause plastic shrinkage cracking.

See the Steel Reinforcement section of this Field Guide for more information.

Placing the Concrete

Generally, concrete should be placed within an hour after cement has been added to the mix. If more time than an hour elapses, the concrete mix could dry and stiffen, affecting its strength and workability. The delivery of concrete needs to be coordinated with the construction crew's ability to screed, consolidate and bullfloat the concrete already delivered before the next delivery is made. Thoroughly mixed concrete is placed within the formwork, starting at one end and working evenly toward the other, with each batch being placed against the previous placed concrete. The concrete should be deposited evenly across the area that is being paved. The concrete should not be deposited in piles that need to be mixed together and spread between the formwork.

Short-handled, square-ended shovels, concrete rakes or a come-along (a hoe-like tool) are recommended for spreading the concrete evenly. The concrete should be placed as close as possible to its final position as moving the concrete over excessive distances can separate the coarse aggregates from the fine aggregates as well as separate them both from the cement paste that ultimately binds them together.

The concrete should be consolidated in the forms by using handtools or by the use of internal vibrators. Consolidation compacts fresh concrete to mold it within the forms and around embedded items and reinforcement and to eliminate stone pockets, honeycomb, and entrapped air. It should not remove significant amounts of intentionally entrained air.

▶ With the concrete spread and consolidated, it is then leveled by screeding with a board or other straight edge to remove excess concrete and bring the top surface of the slab to its proper grade. It should be moved across the concrete with a sawing motion while advancing forward a short distance with each movement. There should be a surplus of concrete against the front face of the straightedge to fill in low areas as the straightedge passes over the slab.

Figure 10.22   The concrete truck pulls up as close as possible and the chute is moved back and forth to distribute concrete between the forms.
Source: Photo courtesy of Bob Harris, Decorative Concrete Institute.

The tools used to screed (or "strike off") concrete are:

- Wood straightedges. The wood needs to be straight and unwarped or unwanted crowns or belies will be imparted to the concrete surface.
- Metal (aluminum or magnesium) straightedges. They are available in lengths between 6 and 24 ft. These types of straightedges are more

Figure 10.23   Concrete rakes, come-alongs and square-ended shovels can be used to distribute the concrete evenly between the forms. (It would be best to have the wire mesh reinforcement secured in place with plastic chairs.)
Source: Photo courtesy of the Portland Cement Association.

Figure 10.24 Screeding the concrete with a wood straightedge.
Source: Photo courtesy of the Portland Cement Association.

desirable than wood, as they will not be bowed or warped, ensuring that the concrete will be screed to a straight plane. In addition, concrete will not stick to these metals as it does to wood (especially for air-entrained concrete mixes) making them easier to clean and maintain.

- Mechanical screeds (vibratory, oscillating and roller). These are usually used for large projects, often for concrete roadways.

Figure 10.25 A surplus of concrete should be kept ahead of the screed to prevent low spots or voids.
Source: Photo courtesy of the Portland Cement Association.

Figure 10.26 A large power screed moves along the top of the steel formwork. Concrete is being shoveled in front to keep a surplus of concrete ahead of the screed. The power screed levels and vibrates, consolidating the concrete as part of the same operation.
Source: Photo courtesy of the Portland Cement Association.

Finishing

Bullfloating or Darbying

After all surface water has been re-absorbed by the concrete or evaporated, the concrete the can then be smoothed to eliminate ridges, high or low points, fill voids and slightly imbed the coarser aggregates beneath the surface. This initial smoothing is accomplished by using a bullfloat or darby. A bullfloat is used for areas that are too large to reach with the shorter handled darby. The bullfloat handles can be extended with 4 to 10 ft long extensions, made from lightweight aluminum, magnesium or fiberglass, which screw into each other and allow for very long reaches. Magnesium floats with top reinforcement ribbing are strongest, resist distortion and minimize the waviness that can occur when using a bullfloat with handle extensions. Tilt action brackets can change the float pitch for better control.

Bullfloating or darbying must be completed before bleed water accumulates on the surface. Care must be taken not to overwork the concrete as this could result in a less durable surface. The preceding operations should level, shape, and smooth the surface and work up a slight amount of cement paste.

▶ Bullfloating or darbying should not close up or seal the surface, as it is important in this phase of finishing to continue to let water bleed out.

Be careful when using these tools not to close up or seal the surface of the concrete, which may cause blistering or scaling.

On most slabs, bullfloating or darbying is followed by one or more of the following finishing operations:

- Edging
- Jointing
- Floating
- Troweling
- Brooming

A slight hardening of the concrete is necessary before the start of any of these finishing operations. When the bleed-water sheen has evaporated and the concrete will sustain foot pressure with only about ¼ in. indentation, the surface is ready for continued finishing operations.

Floating and troweling the concrete before the bleeding process is completed may also trap bleed water under the finished surface producing a weakened zone or void under the finished surface. The use of low-slump concrete with an adequate cement content, air entrainment and properly graded fine aggregate will minimize bleeding and help ensure maintenance-free slabs.

▶ One of the principal causes of surface defects in concrete slabs is finishing while bleed water is on the surface. If bleed water is worked into the surface, the water-cement ratio is significantly increased which reduces strength, entrained-air content, and watertightness of the surface. Any finishing operation preformed on the surface of a concrete slab while bleed water is present can cause crazing, dusting, or scaling (PCA 2001).

Edging

Edging is required along all edge forms and isolation and construction joints on outdoor concrete slabs such as walks, drives, and patios. Edging consolidates, densifies and compacts concrete next to the form where floating and troweling are less effective, making it more durable and less vulnerable to scaling, chipping, and popouts. Edge tools used along the perimeter give the edge a slight radius with a smooth width.

The edging process begins with the concrete being cut away from the form with a pointed mason trowel to a depth of about 1 in. after any bleed water has disappeared from the surface. An edge tool is then run along the concrete while being held almost flat (the front edge slightly raised as to not gouge the concrete) imparting a smooth width and radius to the concrete edge.

Figure 10.27 Use of a darby to finish concrete surface.
Source: Photo courtesy of the Bob Harris, Decorative Concrete Institute.

Figure 10.28 Bullfloating to eliminate high or low spots and imbed aggregate.
Source: Photo courtesy of Bob Harris, Decorative Concrete Institute.

Edge tools come in various radii from ⅛ through 1 in. with depths from ⅜ to 1-½ in.; lengths from 6 to 10 in. long; and widths from 1-½ to 6 in. The variety of different edge tool choices can give the finished edge of the concrete a different look and some consideration should be given to incorporating specific size choices to complement the design intent.

Edge tools are made from steel, bronze or stainless steel. The heavy gauge stainless steel edger is considered to produce a smoother, denser edge. Some edgers are available with slightly curved ends which help prevent gouging the concrete while finishing. While most hand edgers are used by a construction crew worker kneeling next to the slab, there are walking edgers that allow a worker to finish the edge of the concrete while walking alongside.

Jointing

Control joints (also referred to as contraction joints or score lines) help to relieve the internal stresses of concrete pavement that may form when the slab contracts due to drying shrinkage or from temperature changes. Control joints create intentional weak spots within the pavement that serve to control cracking within the joint and minimize the cracking elsewhere along the surface of the slab. The control joints should be cut into the slab after bullfloating, in conjunction with the edging operation (unless the joints are to be sawcut at a later time).

Figure 10.29 Hand edging tool gives the edge of the pavement a radius and provides a smoother and denser edge that increases durability and prevents chipping.
Source: Photo courtesy of Bob Harris, Decorative Concrete Institute.

Figure 10.30a Jointing the concrete is accomplished by grooving tools (unless the slab will be sawcut later).
Source: Photo courtesy of the Portland Cement Association.

Figure 10.30b The longer handle allows the joint to be tooled without having to kneel on the fresh concrete.
Source: Photo courtesy of the Portland Cement Association.

The control joints can also be made by inserting premolded plastic strips (zip strips) but are more commonly made with a hand groover. When a hand groover is used to form control joints in exterior concrete slabs, the forms are marked to accurately locate the joints. In order to be effective, their depth should be at least $\frac{1}{4}$ of the overall thickness of the concrete pavement.

▶ Get more information on control joints under the Concrete Joints heading found later in this section.

Floating

After the concrete has been hand-edged and hand-jointed, it should be floated with a hand float or with a finishing machine using float blades. The purpose of floating is threefold:

- To embed aggregate particles just beneath the surface.
- To remove slight imperfections, humps, and voids, producing a flatter surface.
- To compact the slab and mortar at the surface in preparation for additional finishing operations.

▶ The concrete should not be overworked as this may bring an excess of water and fine material to the surface and result in subsequent surface defects.

Hand floats usually are made of fiberglass, magnesium, rubber or wood. The metal float reduces the amount of work required because drag is reduced as the float slides more readily over the concrete surface. A magnesium float is essential for hand-floating air-entrained concrete because a wood float tends to stick to and tear the concrete surface. The light metal float also forms a smoother surface than the wood float. Wood floats are available in a variety of different wood types, each producing a different surface texture. Rubber floats produce textured or slip-resistant finishes because they bring more sand to the surface.

The hand float should be held flat on the concrete surface and moved with a slight sawing motion in a sweeping arc to fill in holes, cut off lumps, and smooth ridges. When finishing large slabs, power floats can be used to reduce finishing time.

Floating produces a relatively even (but not smooth) texture that has good slip resistance and is often used as a final finish, especially for exterior slabs. Where a float finish is the desired final finish, it may be necessary to float the surface a second time after it has hardened a little more.

▶ Marks left by hand edgers and groovers are normally removed during floating unless the marks are desired for decorative purposes;

in such cases the edger and groover should be used again after final floating.

Troweling

Where a smooth, hard, dense surface is desired, floating should be followed by steel troweling. Troweling should not be done on a surface that has not been floated.

It is customary when hand-finishing large slabs to float and immediately trowel an area before moving the kneeboards. These operations should be delayed until the concrete has hardened sufficiently so that water and fine material are not brought to the surface. Too long a delay of course, will result in a surface that is too hard to float and trowel. The tendency, however, is to float and trowel the surface too soon.

► Premature floating and troweling can cause scaling, crazing, or dusting and a surface with reduced wear resistance.

Wait for the bleed water to evaporate. Bleed water is a result of the wet concrete settling, although with an entrained air mix, it doesn't settle much and therefore little water comes to the surface. Spreading dry cement on a wet surface to take up excess water is a bad practice and can cause crazing. Such wet spots should be avoided, if possible, by adjustments in aggregate gradation, mix

Figure 10.31 Hand floating the surface of the concrete pavement. A steel trowel produces a hard, smooth, dense surface.
Source: Photo courtesy of the Portland Cement Association.

proportions, and consistency. When wet spots do occur, finishing operations should be delayed until the water either evaporates or the water is removed with a soft rubber garden hose or squeegee. Care must be taken so that excess cement paste is not removed with the water.

Steel trowels look similar to hand floats, but the blades are thinner and made from either blue, stainless or high carbon steel and range from 3 to 5 in. wide by 10 to 24 in. long. For larger areas, a fresno can be used. A fresno is a steel trowel, 2 to 4 ft long, attached to a bull-float handle and therefore can be used without having to walk onto the slab. They allow large areas to be troweled relatively quickly but do not achieve the same level of compaction that is possible with a hand trowel. Some fresnos are available that cut small $1/4$-in.-deep, V-shaped grooves into the concrete for safety.

The first troweling may produce the desired surface free of defects. However, surface smoothness, density, and wear resistance can all be improved by additional trowelings. There should be a lapse of time between successive troweling to permit the concrete to become harder. As the surface stiffens, each successive troweling should be made with smaller trowels, using progressively more tilt and pressure on the trowel blade. The final pass should make a ringing sound as the trowel moves over the hardening surface.

▶ **When the concrete sticks to the trowel when it is lifted off the concrete, or concrete sticks to the finisher's kneeboards, too much sand in the mix or higher than necessary air entrainment are most likely the causes.**

A power trowel is fitted with smaller, individual steel trowel blades that are adjustable for tilt and pressure on the concrete surface. When the first troweling is done by machine, at least one additional troweling by hand should be done to remove small irregularities. If necessary, tooled edges and joints should be rerun after troweling to maintain uniformity and true lines.

Exterior concrete slabs are generally NOT troweled because:

- It can lead to a loss of entrained air caused by overworking the surface, and
- Troweled surfaces can be slippery when wet.

Unless the concrete is specified to receive a special decorative or stamped surface, finishing by floating and brooming should be sufficient for exterior concrete slabs. Some contractors like to trowel the slab before brooming in order to remove some of the lines created with the bullfloat. However, if the surface is troweled hard, it may be difficult to impart any texture to the surface with the broom. In some cases, a dampened broom may be helpful when brooming a concrete slab that has been troweled.

▶ When called for, troweling produces a hard, smooth, dense surface and should be done immediately after floating.

Brooming

Brooming should be performed before the concrete has thoroughly hardened, but it should be sufficiently hard to retain the scoring impression to produce a slip-resistant surface. Rough scoring can be achieved with a rake, a steel-wire broom, or a stiff, coarse, fiber broom; such coarse-textured brooming usually follows floating. If a finer texture is desired, the concrete should be floated to a smooth surface and then brushed with a soft-bristled broom.

Best results are obtained with brooms that are specially made for texturing concrete. Brooms are available in various widths and the block that holds the bristles can be made from wood, aluminum, or plastic. Bristle materials can be horsehair, polypropylene, or nylon and come in various stiffnesses and sizes to produce different textures. For extreme textures, wire combs are available to produce tined finishes.

Typically the broom should be run from one side of the concrete to the other, without stopping. With a standard broom, you should pull the broom toward you, then lift it and set it back on the far side to pull it across again. However, there are brooms that are available that you

Figure 10.32   A walk-behind power trowel.
Source: Photo courtesy of the Portland Cement Association.

can push or pull. There are also brooms that can be attached to bull-floats or fresnos as well as handleless brooms that are pulled back and forth with ropes. These are very useful where the slab to be broomed is so large that it would be difficult to push or pull a regular broom all the way across in one motion.

Typically, concrete slabs are broomed perpendicular to the direction of traffic and perpendicular to any slope. Although for drainage purposes, the broom finish should run parallel to the direction of water flow. By varying the direction of the broomed finish, the textured surface can provide a distinctive design characteristic to the concrete slab.

Curing and Protection

The strength of the concrete pavement is directly related to the successful completion of the hydration process (the chemical reaction between the cement and water). In order for the curing process to be successful, the newly poured concrete pavement must retain enough moisture to allow this process to continue for the 28 days that is necessary for the pavement to reach its compressive strength. Curing needs to begin immediately after finishing to minimize early drying shrinkage until the concrete is strong enough to resist shrinkage cracking.

This can be accomplished in several ways:

- Burlap fabric that is continually kept wet by sprinklers or soaker hoses provides an effective barrier to prevent moisture loss in the concrete pavement.
- Plastic sheets that are placed over a thoroughly watered concrete pavement surface can prevent moisture loss from the pavement. Plastic sheets should be overlapped and weighted down to completely seal the pavement beneath to be effective.
- A curing compound (compatible with the final finish of the concrete) can be sprayed over the entire surface of the pavement. These curing compounds create a barrier that seals the moisture in the concrete pavement. They often come in colors (that fade after 28 days) that make it easy to determine if the product has been applied thoroughly and evenly over the entire surface.

▶ For larger jobs, it may be more efficient to apply a curing agent sprayed from a hose connected to a tank.

Newly poured concrete pavements must be protected from any vehicular traffic for a minimum of 14 days and preferably for the full 28-day curing period. Construction should be sequenced or barriers erected that prevent any construction equipment from running over the new concrete pavements.

Figure 10.33a   Wet burlap fabric covering the new concrete pavement.
Source: Photo courtesy of the Portland Cement Association.

▶ For more information see the "Curing Concrete" topic under the Concrete section of this Field Guide.

Concrete Pavement Joints

Concrete is a material that contracts and expands based on moisture content and temperature variations. Joints are necessary in concrete to relieve the internal stresses of expansion and contraction as well as the

Figure 10.33b   Soaker hoses keeping the surface of the new concrete wet.
Source: Photo courtesy of the Portland Cement Association.

Figure 10.33c Plastic sheets weighted down with stone placed over the freshly laid concrete.
Source: Photo courtesy of the Portland Cement Association.

overall horizontal movement of the concrete slab. Contraction during the curing process is particularly significant as the newly placed concrete dries. This is one of the reasons that cracks in concrete often appear within the first several weeks of the placing of concrete pavement. Overall contraction and expansion will occur as temperature

Figure 10.34 Concrete curing agent being applied with a hand sprayer. Concrete curing agents have a pigment that allows a visual check to ensure complete coverage. The pigment is temporary and fades after a month.
Source: Photo courtesy of the Portland Cement Association.

variations occur, particularly where there are wide temperature variations between summer and winter.

There are four common types of concrete pavement joints:

- Control Joints
- Expansion Joints
- Isolation Joints
- Construction Joints

Control Joints

Control joints (also referred to as contraction joints or score lines) help to relieve the internal stresses of concrete pavement created when drying and thermal shrinkage produce tensile stresses that exceed the concrete's tensile strength. Control joints provide for movement in the plane of a slab and induce controlled cracking caused by drying and thermal shrinkage at pre-selected locations. Control joints create intentional weak spots within the pavement that serve to control cracking within the joint and minimize the cracking elsewhere along the surface of the slab. In order to be effective, their depth should be at least $1/4$ of the overall thickness of the concrete pavement. Control joints transfer loads perpendicular to the plane of a slab beneath the control joint by aggregate interlock with a width that is typically a $1/4$ in. (and should not exceed $1/3$ of an in.).

Control joints in concrete pavement can be made in several ways.

- Hand tooled
- Placing strips of preformed plastic joint material (zip strips)
- Saw cut

The hand groover is the concrete jointing tool that is used after the bullfloating of concrete, when the surface is set up enough to allow workers access to the surface without leaving marks (usually by using kneeboards to help distribute their weight over a larger area of the surface) but still soft enough to allow the jointing tool to be worked into the concrete to the full depth of the groove in the tool. This type of joint creates a smooth width (width varies depending on the tool) on each side of the groove and is a distinctive characteristic of this type of joint. The effective use of the hand groover is dependent upon the window of opportunity that exists between the concrete surface being hard enough to allow workers to begin the control jointing process and the point at which the concrete becomes too hard to allow the joint to be cut to the full depth of the tool.

Sawing of control joints must be coordinated with the setting time of the concrete. The timing depends on factors such as mix proportions,

Figure 10.35 Tooled control joint in concrete pavement with broom finish intersecting with an expansion joint.

Figure 10.36a Control joints can be sawcut with a hand circular or chop saw.
Source: Photo courtesy of the Portland Cement Association.

Figure 10.36b A more accurate straight cut can be obtained with this walk-behind saw that has a guide to follow the chalk line.
Source: Photo courtesy of the Portland Cement Association.

temperature, and type and hardness of aggregates. Generally, saw cut control joints can be cut with:

- An early entry saw, that can be used between 1 and 4 hours after the concrete has been finished.
- A wet-cut gas-powered concrete saw is typically used between 4 and 12 hours after the concrete has been finished, when the concrete has achieved a compressive strength of approximately 500 psi and the edges of the concrete will not ravel or tear during sawing.
- A dry-cut cut-off saw can be used for smaller slabs after 12 hours but never more than 24 hours after the concrete has been finished.

▶ Sawing should be completed before drying shrinkage stresses become large enough to produce cracking, preferably before the concrete cools. Saw cut control joints do not have the smooth width associated with a tooled joint and are very distinctive in appearance.

▶ When observing control joints being saw cut in the field, be sure to use a proper respirator—airborne silica is a serious health hazard, leading to silicosis. Also use eye and ear protection.

Expansion Joints

Expansion joints extend the full depth of the pavement and completely separate one concrete slab from the adjacent slab and should also be used wherever new concrete pavement meets an existing

Figure 10.37 It is easier to ensure a control joint is the required ¹/₄ depth of the pavement thickness with a sawcut joint than when the joint is hand tooled. *Source:* Photo courtesy of the Portland Cement Association.

structure such as a building, walls, or steps. Typically, these joints are filled with a preformed flexible material installed prior to the placing of the concrete that will allow the concrete slab to move laterally, causing this material to compress or expand with the corresponding movement of the concrete. Expansion joint material can be as thin as ¹/₄ in. or less, but ¹/₂ in. material is the most commonly used.

The typical joint filler materials are asphalt impregnated fiber boards, wood strips or a variety of plastic, rubber and metal types:

▪ The asphalt impregnated fiber board has been most commonly used and is generally sealed with an asphaltic based product. Both the sealer and fiber board have a tendency to dry, shrink, crack and lose their resiliency over time limiting their long-term effectiveness.

▪ Wood strips used as expansion joint filler need to be made of a decay-resistant species or be pressure treated with a wood preservative. They should have nails or screws driven into their face surface to provide anchoring into the concrete and ensuring that they remain flush with the finished grade of the pavement over time.

- Plastics, rubber and metal expansion joint material represent a wide range of different products, available in a variety of different shapes and sizes. The more popular expansion joint material of this type is a closed cell polyethylene material that is most commonly sealed with a urethane based sealer. Urethane based sealers come in a number of different colors that can be specified to match the color of the concrete pavement. The combination of this joint material and sealer retains its flexibility over time and is an excellent long-term choice for an effective expansion joint system.

Whatever type of expansion joint material used, it is important that the sealer used is compatible with all the materials it will be in contact with in order for it to be effective. Some manufacturers may recommend the use of a backer rod to be placed between the expansion joint material and sealer to prevent the sealer from adhering to the

Figure 10.38 Plastic cap fits over the polyethylene expansion joint material. The top of the cap is set level to the finished grade of the pavement. After the concrete has hardened, the small top square of plastic breaks off, leaving a void space of the correct size for the urethane based sealer. The remaining piece of the plastic cap provides a bond break between the sealer and expansion joint.

expansion joint material and the sides of the concrete pavement. Special caps can be used that fit on the expansion joint material (set flush with the proposed finished grade of the concrete) that break-away after the concrete has been placed and hardened. These break-away caps have a top section that is removed after the concrete has hardened. The use of this product ensures the proper depth from the top of slab for the installation of the expansion joint sealer. The cap piece that remains on the joint filler provides a bond break between the joint material and the sealer.

Isolation Joints

Isolation joints completely isolate the concrete pavement from any other structure that is not likely to move in the same way the concrete slab does from drying shrinkage, temperature fluctuations or settling. These structures can be walls, columns, pipes or any structure adjacent to or passing through the concrete slab. Isolation joints permit both horizontal and vertical differential movements at adjoining parts of a structure.

Isolation joints are formed by placing preformed expansion joint material around the structure to be isolated for the full depth of the concrete pavement that is to be poured. The isolation joint should be sealed in the same manner as the expansion joints.

Construction Joints

Construction joints are used where the placing of concrete pavement is to be stopped for a period of time. They are generally formed with keyways to lock adjacent pours of concrete together and minimize movement. Construction joints are typically formed with a thickened edge at the joint and may also include sleeved dowels that tie the slabs together. A true construction joint should bond new concrete to existing concrete and permit no movement. Deformed tiebars are often used in construction joints to restrict movement.

Because extra care is needed to make a true construction joint, they are usually designed and built to function as control joints by working them into the overall plan. A construction joint can also be used in cases of equipment breakdown, an unexpected shortage of materials, or bad weather. A liquid curing compound should be applied to the vertical face of the construction joint after removal of the form.

▶ If the slab will have no significant traffic crossing the joint, a plain butt joint, with no reinforcement crossing the joint, is acceptable. If there is to be traffic other than foot traffic, you will need to use some sort of load transfer device. Use internal vibration during concrete placement at the construction joint to assure proper consolidation along the edge and around any dowels or load transfer devices.

Load Transfer

Across construction joints in slabs that will have to carry heavy loads, a mechanical load transfer device (to transfer shear) may need to be used to keep the slabs vertically aligned. There are a variety of mechanical load transfer devices available, including dowels (both square and round), diamond-shaped load plates, and keyways. Keyways alone are not recommended as they often are not tight enough to be totally effective after the concrete initially shrinks.

Dowels are short, stainless or epoxy coated steel bars that help transfer loads from one slab to the next over a joint minimizing stress at the joint without restricting horizontal movement necessary for expansion and contraction. Dowels should be smooth. Rebars do not make good dowels. One half of the dowel, within the concrete on one side of the joint, should be sleeved or coated with a bond-breaking substance to prevent the concrete from bonding to the dowel in order to allow the slabs to move horizontally. Dowels must be aligned properly to be effective. Dowels must be perpendicular to the joint both vertically and horizontally. Misaligned dowels can lead to joint deterioration.

Sealing Joints

Expansion and isolation joints should be sealed. A sealer is soft, flexible and able to accommodate the concrete slab's expansion and contraction. The sealer's purpose is to bond to the concrete and prevent water, ice, and dirt from getting into the joint.

Figure 10.39a These dowels are held in place at the right height and spacing by a wire basket that is anchored in place with steel spikes to prevent shifting during the concrete pour.
Source: Photo courtesy of the Portland Cement Association.

Figure 10.39b Epoxy-coated dowels installed at a joint are typically between 1 to 1-$^1/_2$ in. in diameter. The exposed dowels will be sleeved or coated with a bond breaker to prevent the concrete of the adjacent slab from bonding to dowel.
Source: Photo courtesy of the Portland Cement Association.

Sealed joints should have a backer rod or bond breaker to prevent the sealer from adhering to the top of the expansion joint filler material. Expansion joint sealers are typically installed with a caulking gun.

Integrating Concrete Joints into the Design

While many construction drawings show areas that proposed pavement is to be installed, and the specifications may stipulate maximum or typical spacing for concrete joints, most plans don't have locations or joint spacing marked on them. It is important that these decisions are not left to the contractor's judgment or convenience.

The location of expansion joints should relate to major design elements and become extensions of those elements and strengthen the design intent and expression. Expansion joints are generally spaced every 20 to 30 ft apart. Again, the actual distance may be influenced by other site elements in the design. The important factor within these parameters is to choose spacing that relates to your design and not leave these important decisions to some typical spacing that may be called for in a general way in the specifications.

Control joints in pavements are visible elements in the site design and locating them in a purposeful way is the mark of a thoughtful design that appreciates the subtle design enhancements that the incorporation of this level of detail offers.

The spacing of control joints depend on:

- Slab thickness
- Shrinkage potential of the concrete
- Subgrade friction
- Environment
- The absence or presence of steel reinforcement.

Control joints are generally spaced between 4 and 6 ft apart. As mentioned above, the choice on which dimension to use may be influenced by other factors in the design. As a general rule, control joints should not be spaced (in feet) more than 2 to 3 times the concrete slab thickness (in inches). The concrete pavement panels created by contraction joints should be approximately square. Panels with excessive length-to-width ratios (more than 1-$\frac{1}{2}$ to 1) are likely to crack at an intermediate location.

To be most effective, it is best if contraction joints are straight and continuous rather than staggered, disjointed or offset from each other. Avoid panels that will be L-shaped or T-shaped. In joint layout design it is also important to remember that control joints should only terminate at a free edge, expansion joint or isolation joint. Control joints should never terminate at another control joint as cracking will be induced from the end of the terminated joint into the adjacent panel. This is sometimes referred to as sympathetic cracking.

Try to avoid "re-entrant" (inside) corners within the slab. These can be avoided by locating control joints going in both directions from a re-entrant corner. If an inside corner is unavoidable, you can also place a couple of pieces of rebar diagonally in the slab to strengthen the corner.

Plastic Shrinkage Cracks

Plastic shrinkage cracks sometimes occur in the surface of freshly mixed concrete soon after it has been placed, while it is being finished or shortly thereafter. Plastic shrinkage cracking is usually associated with hot-weather concreting. However, it can occur any time ambient conditions produce rapid evaporation of moisture from the concrete surface. These cracks occur when water evaporates from the surface faster than it can travel to the surface during the bleeding process. This creates rapid drying, shrinkage and tensile stresses in the surface that often result in short, irregular cracks. The following conditions, singly or collectively, increase evaporation of surface moisture and increase the possibility of plastic shrinkage cracking:

- Low or high air temperature
- High concrete temperature
- Low humidity
- High wind speed

One or more of the precautions listed below can minimize the occurrence of plastic shrinkage cracking. They should be considered while planning for hot-weather concrete construction or while dealing with the problem after construction has started. They are listed in the order in which they should be done during construction.

- Moisten concrete aggregates that are dry and absorptive.
- Keep the concrete temperature low by cooling aggregates and mixing water.
- Dampen the subgrade and fog forms prior to placing concrete.
- Erect temporary windbreaks to reduce wind velocity over the concrete surface.
- Erect temporary sunshades to reduce concrete surface temperatures.
- Protect the concrete with temporary coverings, such as polyethylene sheeting, during any appreciable delay between placing and finishing.
- Fog the slab immediately after placing and before finishing, taking care to prevent the accumulation of water that may reduce the quality of the cement paste in the slab surface.
- Add plastic fibers to the concrete mixture to help reduce plastic shrinkage crack formation. Fogging the concrete before and after final finishing is the most effective way to minimize evaporation and reduce plastic shrinkage cracking. Use of a fog spray will raise the relative humidity of the ambient air over the slab, thus reducing evaporation from the concrete. Fog nozzles atomize water using air pressure to create a fog blanket. They should not be confused with garden-hose nozzles, which leave an excess amount of water on the slab. Fogging should be continued until a suitable curing material such as a curing compound, wet burlap, or curing paper can be applied.

Other methods to prevent the rapid loss of moisture from the concrete surface include:

- Spray application of temporary moisture-retaining films (usually polymers); these compounds can be applied immediately after screeding to reduce water evaporation before final finishing operations and curing commence. These materials are floated and troweled into the surface during finishing and should have no adverse effect on the concrete or inhibit the adhesion of membrane-curing compounds.

- Reduction of time between placing and the start of curing by eliminating delays during construction.

If plastic shrinkage cracks should appear during finishing, striking each side of the crack with a float and refinishing can close the cracks. However, the cracking may reoccur unless the causes are corrected.

Special Surface Finishes

There are a number of decorative measures and finishes that can be used on concrete pavement for a variety of different effects. Patterns can be formed with divider strips or by distinctive scoring patterns. Textures can be produced with little effort and expense with floats, trowels, and brooms. More elaborate colors and textures can be achieved with special techniques such as adding color to the concrete, stamping the concrete with a decorative pattern or allowing the aggregate to be exposed on the surface, being among the most common methods of adding interest.

Exposed Aggregate Surfaces

An exposed-aggregate surface is obtained by placing concrete and then removing the outer "skin" of cement paste to uncover decorative coarse aggregate. Exposed aggregate surfaces can add a wide range of colors and textures to concrete pavement. There are a number of decorative aggregates to choose from depending on the finished look that is desired.

There are three basic methods for incorporating decorative aggregate into concrete slabs:

- Seeding the aggregate onto the surface of the slab immediately after the concrete has been placed, struck off, and bullfloated. This involves sprinkling the aggregate by hand or shovel uniformly onto the surface and then embedding it with a bullfloat or darby until it's completely covered by a thin layer of cement paste.
- Mixing the aggregate into the concrete mix at the ready mix plant. This method can be more expensive than seeding because it requires using greater quantities of decorative aggregate.
- Putting the aggregate into a thin topping course of concrete containing the decorative aggregate over a base slab of conventional concrete. The topping can range in thickness from 1 to 2 in., depending on the aggregate size. This method generally works best when smaller decorative aggregates are specified.

Exposing the Aggregate

There are several exposure methods contractors can choose from, depending on the look desired and size of the project, to expose the decorative aggregate. Only the top of the stone is exposed while the rest remains permanently embedded in the concrete. The general rule of thumb is to remove the surface mortar to a depth no more than one-third the diameter of the aggregate particle.

The decorative aggregate can be exposed by:

- Brushing and washing away the thin layer of surface mortar covering the aggregate by spraying with water and scrubbing with a broom until the aggregate is exposed to the desired depth as soon as the surface mortar can be removed without overexposing or dislodging the aggregate. Timing is critical, so this method is often better suited for small jobs rather than large ones.
- Using a chemical surface retarder sprayed onto the slab surface immediately after placing and finishing the concrete. This delays the set and allows the cement paste to be removed up to a day or so later, either by scrubbing or pressure washing. This flexibility makes this method especially suitable for large jobs or during hot weather.
- Abrasive blasting (either sandblasting or shotblasting) can be used to expose the aggregate after the concrete has set and hardened. The disadvantage of abrasive blasting is that it can fracture the aggregate and negatively affect its appearance.

▶ Waterblasting can also be used to texture the surface of hardened concrete, especially where local ordinances prohibit the use of sandblasting for environmental reasons. High-pressure water jets are used on surfaces that have or have not been treated with chemical retarders.

After the aggregate has been exposed and the concrete has hardened, the aggregate should be cleaned to remove any remaining concrete paste. The surface can then be sealed with a clear coating of acrylic resins (designed for exposed aggregate surfaces) that bring out the natural color of the aggregates and leave a wet look to the exposed aggregate surface. The sealer will help protect against spalling, dusting, efflorescence, freeze-thaw damage, stains, deicing salts and abrasion.

Colored Finishes

Color can be added to the concrete either by integrally mixing it with the concrete or by the dry-shake method:

- The integrally mixed color is mixed with the other ingredients of the mix prior to the concrete being placed. It produces a uniform

Figure 10.40   A water spray and broom combination used to expose the aggregate.
Source: Photo courtesy of the Portland Cement Association.

color throughout the concrete and the slab is the same color for its entire depth.

- In the dry-shake method, a prepackaged dry color material is cast onto the surface of a concrete slab. The dry-shake material is applied after the concrete has been screeded and darbied or bullfloated, excess moisture has evaporated from the surface, and preliminary

Figure 10.41   Exposed aggregate decorative finish.
Source: Photo courtesy of the Portland Cement Association.

floating has been done. Two-thirds of the dry material is shaken evenly by hand over the surface and thoroughly floated into the surface in a manner that evenly distributes the material. Immediately, the rest of the material is cast onto the surface and floated as before. The surface can then be troweled at the same time as a typical slab. For exterior surfaces that will be exposed to freezing and thawing, little or no troweling followed by brooming with a soft bristle concrete broom is usually sufficient. With this method, the color only is absorbed into the top layer of the concrete. This method requires some degree of skill to ensure a uniform color for the entire surface.

Patterned Concrete

Closely associated with the use of colored concrete, is patterned concrete. This is the method used to stamp geometric shapes, often resembling a unit paver shape and pattern, into the surface of the freshly floated concrete. Combined with colored concrete, this method can closely resemble the look of unit pavers with the advantages of a monolithic slab.

One typical method of installing patterned concrete is installed by using rigid mats made of polyurethane that produce the desired pavement pattern when they are firmly tamped down imparting its impression into the surface of the colored concrete. It is best to use a tamper with a urethane base or cast iron base coated with rubber to prevent tearing or marring of the texture mat.

Figure 10.42 Color is being broadcast onto the surface of the freshly floated concrete.
Source: Photo courtesy of Bob Harris, Decorative Concrete Institute.

A cure and seal product is often used with colored concrete and/or colored patterned concrete. Unlike regular curing compounds that completely seal the water in a slab, the specially designed cure and seal products allow a controlled amount of water to leave the concrete, which is important for good color development while still allowing enough water for hydration. The same product can then be used again after the concrete has completely cured to protect the concrete.

Expansion and isolation joints should be placed at the same recommended spacing as regular concrete. They can be coordinated to fall in line with straight-line patterns to make them less noticeable, in a way that will not detract from the unit paver type appearance that the patterned concrete is trying to achieve.

▶ Fiber reinforcement can be used to space control joints further apart, or when using a random pattern to help avoid shrinkage

Figure 10.43 One system of imparting the pattern of the mold onto the surface of the concrete. In this system, a plastic sheet is placed between the fresh concrete and the mold before striking the vertical pole and pressing the mold into the concrete.
Source: Photo courtesy of the Portland Cement Association.

Figure 10.44 This system utilizes specially designed rigid mats that are struck with a hand tamper, imparting the pattern to the concrete. The handles on the tops of the mats make for easy handling.
Source: Photo courtesy of Bob Harris, Decorative Concrete Institute.

surface cracks. Care should be taken where the pavement may be walked upon without shoes, as fibers (especially steel fibers), may stick up through the surface.

Porous Concrete Pavement

Porous concrete pavement (also referred to as pervious concrete, permeable concrete, no-fines concrete, gap-graded concrete, or

Figure 10.45 Hand tooling to complete the pattern is a common practice to continue the pattern where a full mat cannot fit.
Source: Photo courtesy of Bob Harris, Decorative Concrete Institute.

Figure 10.46 The finished patterned concrete is a monolithic replica of the individual paving units.
Source: Photo courtesy of Bob Harris, Decorative Concrete Institute.

enhanced-porosity concrete) is a pavement that allows water infiltration and reduces storm water runoff. In addition to the obvious advantages porous pavement provides for storm water management purposes, it also filters rainwater before it returns to the ground to recharge aquifers and provides air and water to the critical root zone of trees. Its use allows more efficient use of the land by eliminating the need for retention ponds, swales or other storm water devices, as well as reducing the burden on water treatment facilities.

Porous concrete is made with the same components as regular concrete: Portland cement, water and aggregate. However, the aggregate is single sized, there is no sand or fine aggregate to fill the voids between the coarser aggregates. This creates an interconnected system of voids that allows the water to permeate the pavement. It is a "zero" slump mixture with very low water content. The exact amount of water is critical as too little prevents proper curing and too much causes the cement paste to drain to the bottom.

Porous concrete requires some unique installation methods as follows:

- As is the case with regular concrete, it is important that the subgrade be moist (without free-standing water) prior to placement, in order to prevent water from being removed from the lower portion of the pavement too quickly. This is critically important for porous concrete because of its low water content and higher percentage of voids that can allow for rapid drying.

- The low water content may make discharge from the concrete mixer truck slower than regular concrete, however, it is recommended that the porous concrete be discharged completely within 1 hour (1-$\frac{1}{2}$ hours if a retarding or hydration-stabilizing admixture is used).
- The effects of high ambient temperatures and windy conditions will have a more pronounced effect on porous concrete than regular concrete (see the weather-related sections of the Concrete Chapter for more information).
- Placement of the porous concrete mix should be continuous, with spreading and strike off completed as soon as possible. Mechanical (vibrating) and manual screeds are commonly used, although manual screeds can cause tears in the surface if the mixture is too stiff.

▶ Care should be taken that the frequency of vibration is reduced to avoid over-compaction or closing off of the surface, resulting in blocked voids.

- For pavements, it is recommended to strike off about $\frac{1}{2}$ to $\frac{3}{4}$ in. above the forms to allow for later compaction.

▶ One technique to establish this desired strike off elevation, is to attach a temporary wood strip above the top form. These strips are removed after strike off and the concrete surface can then be consolidated to the required finished elevations of the top of the forms.

- The edges of the porous concrete pavement adjacent to the forms should be compacted using a steel, float, or similar tool to prevent raveling of the edges.
- Consolidation is generally accomplished by rolling over the concrete with a heavy steel roller, which compacts the concrete to the height of the forms. Because of rapid hardening and high evaporation rates, it is recommended that consolidation be completed within 15 minutes of placement.
- Control joints to prevent random cracking of the pavement can be spaced farther apart (20 ft or more) as the low water content of porous concrete results in much less shrinking than regular concrete pavement. The control joints are cut into the pavement using a roller, sometimes referred to as a "pizza cutter", to the required $\frac{1}{4}$ depth of the slab, as soon as consolidation has been completed.

▶ Porous concrete pavement is not always jointed, as random cracking is less noticeable because of its coarser surface texture and they don't affect the pavement's structural integrity.

Figure 10.47a Porous concrete is placed between the forms and leveled with a vibratory screed, slightly higher than the desired elevation.
Source: Photo courtesy of R. Banka.

- Porous concrete pavements are not floated and troweled because these finishing techniques can close the surface of the pavement, preventing water from flowing down through the voids below. The final finish is usually the consolidation with the steel roller.
- Proper curing is extremely critical for porous concrete pavement because of its initial low water content. Curing should begin within minutes of placing, compaction and jointing by fog misting the surface and covering with plastic sheeting or curing blankets that must remain in place for at least 7 days.

Porous concrete does require regular maintenance to keep the voids from getting clogged. This can best be performed with a commercial power sweeper that lifts sediment out of the voids so that the pavement retains its permeability.

Practices to Avoid

Reinforcement

- It is unacceptable to lay the reinforcing on the ground and then pull the mesh up with the claw end of a hammer as the concrete is being placed.
- Floating steel reinforcing bars into the wet concrete is not acceptable.
- Avoid adding water to the concrete mix at the project site in order to maintain the specified water-cement ratio.

Figure 10.47b Consolidation and compaction to the desired finished grade is accomplished by rolling over the concrete with a steel roller. Photo courtesy of R. Banka.

Figure 10.47c Control joints are cut into the porous pavement with a special joint roller, commonly referred to as a "pizza cutter". *Source:* Photo courtesy of R. Banka.

- Do not allow water to be sprinkled on the surface during finishing, this can cause spalling, scaling or crazing.
- Do not stagger control joints, this will encourage cracking at the tee intersections.

Figure 10.47d   As porous concrete will tend to lose its moisture more quickly compromising proper curing, all placement and finishing operations must be completed as quickly as possible, and the concrete covered with plastic sheeting that must remain in place at least 7 days.
Source: Photo courtesy of R. Banka.

Avoid Installing Concrete Pavement in Hot Weather

The chemical reaction that causes concrete to harder, hydration, happens faster when the concrete is hot. This may lead to higher early compressive strength but lower compressive strength after the 28-day curing period. On hot days when the concrete may be cooler than the ambient air temperature, then the objective is to keep the concrete cool for as long as possible and prevent the concrete from drying too quickly.

Some procedures to help meet these objectives if concrete pavement must be poured in hot weather are as follows:

- Wet down subgrade and forms thoroughly with cool water prior to placing the concrete.
- In very hot weather, place the concrete early in the morning or late in the afternoon.
- Get the concrete out of the truck and into the forms as quickly as possible. Concrete in the mixer will heat up.
- Hot weather can reduce slump, making the concrete harder to work. Use a superplasticizer to maintain slump, do not add water to the mix.
- Use sun shades to keep the sun from beating down on the newly poured concrete pavement.

- Keep all tools and equipment that will come in contact with the concrete out of the sun.
- Use an evaporation retarder after bullfloating to prevent evaporation of surface water, do not sprinkle additional water onto the surface while finishing.
- Use a curing compound with a white pigment or white curing blankets to reflect the sun's rays.

Avoid Installing Concrete Pavement in Cold Weather

The chemical reaction that causes concrete to harden, hydration, slows when the temperature of the concrete falls below 50°F and stops completely at temperatures below 40°F. In cold weather (generally considered to be anytime the temperature is or is expected to be below 40°F), the temperature of the concrete must be kept high enough to allow the concrete to harden enough that it will be able to resist the cold on its own, without having the water in the concrete freeze and fracture the bonds created between the aggregates. The general rule of thumb is that the concrete must reach a compressive strength of at least 500 psi, which will usually occur after the second day, if kept at a temperature that allows hydration to take place.

▶ Concrete should never be poured on a frozen subgrade. Frozen ground will settle when it thaws, cracking the concrete.

Some special techniques that can be employed if concrete pavement must be poured in cold weather are:

- Have the concrete ordered using hot water and heated aggregates.
- Use an early strength Portland cement or add extra cement to develop a 4,500 to 5,000 psi mix, to ensure reaching the desired 500 psi strength by the end of the second day.
- Use of an accelerator can speed the rate of hydration. Calcium chloride is common, but can lead to corrosion of steel reinforcement. Non-chloride is available but can be more expensive.
- Use insulated blankets over the finished concrete pavement, which need to be weighted down along the perimeter to prevent cold air getting underneath and from blowing away overnight. The insulating blankets will trap the heat generated as hydration takes place. Any protruding reinforcing bars should be covered as well.

▶ Do not add any on-site admixtures that have frozen; the chemicals may have separated.

Avoid Improper Use of Deicing Salts

The use of deicing salts should not harm concrete that is mixed, installed and cured properly. Their use does increase the number of freeze-thaw cycles the upper surface of the concrete pavement experiences that can cause internal pressures that can damage the surface of weak concrete surfaces. This is a common, but baseless, excuse given by contractors for initial spalling or scaling of concrete pavement that was most likely caused by improper installation.

There are four basic types of deicing salts:

- Sodium chloride (rock salt)—the most common and least expensive, it can melt ice in temperatures down to approximately 16°F. It releases the highest amounts of chloride ions that can pollute water bodies and corrode metal.
- Calcium chloride—can melt ice at temperatures well below zero. Concentrations can chemically attack concrete and can cause skin irritation.
- Potassium chloride—not as common and can melt ice at temperatures down to 15°F. Does not cause skin irritation and is less harmful for vegetation.
- Magnesium chloride—relatively new, melts ice at temperatures down to -13°F. It releases less chloride ions than sodium or calcium chloride and is less harmful for vegetation. However, it can cause corrosion of aluminum and steel over the long term.

▶ Do not use fertilizers as deicers for concrete pavement. The ammonium nitrate and ammonium sulfate they contain will attack and damage the concrete pavement surface.

Avoid Surface Crazing

Surface crazing are non-structural cracks that develop early and detract from the appearance of newly poured concrete pavements. Surface crazing can be avoided by:

- Not using a concrete mix that is too wet;
- Not floating or continuing finishing the concrete if there is bleed water on the surface;
- Not allowing the freshly poured concrete to quickly dry before the curing process begins.

▶ Sprinkling cement on the pavement during finishing to "soak up" bleed water on the surface is not acceptable and will contribute to surface crazing.

Concrete Steel Reinforcing

Description

Steel reinforcement for concrete consists of reinforcing bars and welded wire fabric. Bars are manufactured by hot-roll process as round rods with lugs, or deformations, which inhabit longitudinal movement of the bar in the surrounding concrete. Bar sizes are indicated by numbers. For sizes #2 through #8, the numbers are the number of eighths of an inch in the nominal diameter of the bars. Numbers 9, 10, and 11 are round and correspond to the former 1 in., 1 $\frac{1}{8}$ in., and 1 $\frac{1}{4}$ in. square sizes. Sizes #14 and #18 correspond to the former 1 $\frac{1}{2}$ in. and 2 in. square sizes. The nominal diameter of a deformed bar is equal to the actual diameter of a plain bar with the same weight per foot as the deformed bar. Epoxy-coated, zinc-coated (galvanized), and stainless steel reinforcing bars are used when corrosion protection is needed; stainless steel also has nonmagnetic properties. In some instances, a fiber-reinforced plastic (FRP) rebar is used for highly tensile strength and light weight, corrosion resistance, and dielectric (nonconductive) properties. FRP rebars are manufactured in the same sizes as steel rebars and also have deformations on the surface. Consult manufacturers for further information.

Welded wire fabric is used in thin slabs, shells, and other designs in which available space is too limited to give proper cover and clearance to deformed bars. Welded wire fabric, also called mesh, consists of cold drawn wire (smooth or deformed) in orthogonal patterns; it is resistance welded at all intersections.

Assessing Site Conditions

If it is anticipated that the reinforced concrete will be exposed to corrosive conditions, such as the use of road salt, an alternative of an epoxy-coated reinforcing steel should be considered.

The long-term effectiveness of epoxy-coated steel reinforcing is dependent upon reducing damage when handling, storing and placing the material in the field. Proper field techniques include:

- Inspect the material upon delivery at the site for any damage. When unloading, nylon or padded slings should be used, with spreader bars or additional straps for very long bundles to prevent abrasive contact that can damage the coating;

- Store close to the point of placement on wooden cribbing spaced close enough to avoid sagging, to keep the coated steel off the ground. The bundle should be covered with an opaque plastic sheet if it will be exposed to the elements for longer than a month;

- Use non-conductive or plastic bar supports to position the reinforcing in place. The reinforcing bars should always be lifted and carefully placed into supports, never dragged across the ground or other reinforcing bars;

- Tie wire should be coated and mechanical couplers should be epoxy coated and compatible with the epoxy-coated reinforcing;

- If necessary, cutting of epoxy-coated steel reinforcing should be done with power shears or a chop saw, never flame cut;

- Any and all damage to the epoxy coating (including cut ends) should be wire brushed and cleaned and then patched with a two-part epoxy material approved by the manufacturer and applied in accordance with all directions. Allow for a sufficient curing period, before the placing of concrete;

- Avoid damaging the coating with any equipment during the concrete installation. When consolidating the concrete, use a plastic or rubber vibrator head to avoid damaging the coating.

- Avoid worker or equipment traffic on the reinforcing after it has been set in place. Workers should step in the spaces between the grid and a runway constructed if necessary to deliver the concrete to where it is to be poured.

▶ Damage to the epoxy coating can result in rusting in that localized area that can cause early deterioration, mitigating any of the benefits of the epoxy coating.

Acceptable Practices

Placement of Steel Reinforcement

The design of reinforced concrete is dependent upon the proper placement of the steel reinforcement and keeping it in that position without shifting during the concrete pour. The construction detail drawings will show the type of reinforcement, size of reinforcement, position, lengths and any necessary bends.

Ensuring that the steel reinforcing remains in place is important in order:

- For the concrete to attain its desired design strength.
- For the steel reinforcement to be effective adding strength where it is most needed.

- To maintain the necessary cover of concrete to prevent corrosion of the reinforcing steel.
- To not interfere with the installation of posts or other elements that may require cored holes or anchoring bolts after the concrete has hardened.

Steel Reinforcement Supports

In order to position, secure and prevent shifting of the steel reinforcement, supports fabricated specifically for this purpose must be used. These supports can be specially formed concrete blocks (often referred to as "dobies", sometimes formed with a notch to hold the steel reinforcement), plastic chairs and steel wire. Plastic chairs are the most economical and are the most commonly used.

These supports are available to support specific sizes and types of steel reinforcement at the required heights and positions called for on the detail drawings. This level of specificity helps ensure that the detail design intent is carried out during the concrete forming process and that the reinforcing will not shift during the concrete pour.

Steel reinforcement supports are typically spaced 3 to 5 ft apart. The larger the diameter of the reinforcing bar, the farther apart the supports can be placed. For example, a #6 bar may need to be supported every 5 ft, whereas a #4 bar may need to be supported closer to every 3 ft. Welded wire fabric would need the supports closer, depending on the gauge of wire, in order to support the workers that need to work on top of the placed fabric during the concrete pour.

Although available, these type of specific supports are not commonly specified for vertical reinforcement. The bottom horizontal reinforcing bars are often supported by one of the standard type supports, while the top and intermediate horizontal bars are often secured by tying them to the form snap ties or other formwork supports. Vertical steel reinforcing is often secured by tying them to horizontal reinforcing bars near the top and bottom to keep the vertical bar from shifting.

Steel Reinforcement Tying Requirements

In order to securely hold steel reinforcement in place during the concrete forming process and during the concrete pour, they must be tied together using steel tie wire. In addition to using supports, the steel reinforcement may need to be secured to the supports with a tie wire to prevent shifting or having the reinforcing separate from the support. Vertical steel reinforcement is commonly secured to horizontal reinforcement bars by the use of steel tie wire.

Figure 10.48a Typical plastic rebar support.
Source: Edgeworth Construction Products www.edgeworthconstruction.com/projects/.

Tie wires are generally 16-gauge (or 14-gauge for heavy construction), fully annealed, black wire that is soft enough to twist easily. The wire is held on a reel attached to the worker's belt and a special tool is used to properly tie the wire. For epoxy-coated steel reinforcement, PVC ties should be used. Wire tie ends shall be twisted away from concrete surfaces (toward the interior of the concrete) to maintain necessary cover and prevent the wire tie from rusting.

Steel reinforcing needs to be tied often enough to make the assembly rigid and prevent any shifting during the concrete pour, usually every third or fourth intersection, unless otherwise specified in the contract documents. The number of tie wires do not contribute to the strength of the structure.

Splices

Generally, construction details will call for horizontal reinforcing bars to be continuous. Because steel reinforcing bars come in a variety of different but fixed lengths, long linear construction requires that these

Figure 10.48b Plastic supports are available to support a variety of different size reinforcing steel and heights to provide the specified concrete cover and placement to accommodate almost any concrete steel reinforcement requirement.
Source: Edgeworth Construction Products www.edgeworthconstruction.com/projects.

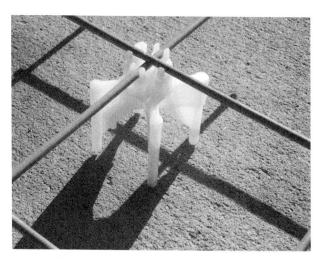

Figure 10.49 Plastic support specifically designed for the support of welded wire mesh steel reinforcement.

Figure 10.50 Contractors will often secure steel reinforcing to ties for formwork and then to each other as is the case with this wall under construction.

Figure 10.51 Concrete being poured from truck chute with steel reinforcing firmly secured in place and worker is able to consolidate concrete with a vibrator without disturbing positioning of reinforcing bars.
Source: Edgeworth Construction Products www.edgeworthconstruction.com/projects.

Figure 10.52 Concrete being poured from wheel barrow. Plastic supports are strong enough to support the wheel barrow filled with concrete with the load spread over a sheet of plywood.
Source: Edgeworth Construction Products www.edgeworthconstruction.com/projects.

individual lengths be joined together in a manner that will have them function as one long, continuous bar.

There are three methods of splicing different sections of bars together whenever continuous, horizontal steel reinforcement is called for. They are:

- Welded
- Mechanical
- Lap

Welded splices are not generally recommended and mechanical splices or couplers are usually recommended as an alternative. Mechanical splices are metal couplers that join two reinforcing bars together and transfer the tension or compression forces across the splice to be shared by the adjoining bars. However, the most common and preferred method used in general site work is the lap splice.

A lap splice is created by overlapping two pieces of steel reinforcement to form a continuous line and joining them using steel tie wire. The length of overlap is dependent upon the size of the reinforcement and spacing and should be a minimum of 12 in. or as noted in the plans, detail drawings or specifications.

Construction Tolerances

It is important to place an anchor steel reinforcement as close as possible as noted in the drawings and specifications. However, during the construction phase some variation is difficult to avoid. Of particular concern is maintaining the clear distance specified from the steel reinforcement to the surface of the concrete. The American Concrete Institute offers specific information on tolerances for placement but generally for clear distances to the surface, tolerances are measured by the fraction of an inch.

Practices to Avoid

- Do not run construction equipment across steel reinforcement bar or welded wire mesh supports. They are not designed to support heavy weight;
- Placing reinforcement atop a layer of fresh concrete and then pouring more on top is not an acceptable method for positioning. Neither is the practice of floating bars on top of fresh concrete and pushing them down into place;
- Adjusting the position of bars or welded wire reinforcement during the concrete pour should not be permitted. The all too common practice of laying steel reinforcing bars or welded wire mesh on the subgrade and then pulling it up with the claw end of a hammer or crowbar (called "hooking") during the concrete pour is not acceptable. Equally unacceptable is the practice of placing the reinforcement on top of the fresh concrete and pushing it in;
- Rebar must be properly supported/tied to maintain its position during the concrete pour by using approved tie wires and supporting devices. Rocks, wood blocks, bricks or other material not approved for the support of steel reinforcement should not be used;
- Some rust on rebar is acceptable but rebar must be free of loose or flaky rust, dirt, ice, oil or any other substance that might reduce or prevent it from fully bonding to the concrete;
- The cross-sectional area of the rebar must not be reduced in any way. Any rebar that has been compromised in this way should not be used;
- Field cutting of epoxy-coated reinforcing should be avoided but if necessary, cut ends should be patched with a two-part epoxy to match the existing coating;
- Never flame cut epoxy-coated steel reinforcing;
- Avoid traffic over epoxy-coated steel reinforcing to prevent damage to the coating;

Unit Pavers

Description

Unit pavers are a good choice for ground plane treatments for pedestrian and vehicular uses. Material choices for unit pavers include clay-fired brick, stone, asphalt and precast concrete. Brick, asphalt and concrete pavers are manufactured and sold in specific shapes, while stone pavers are usually cut to size for a given application. Unit pavers come in a variety of shapes and colors and can be assembled into an infinite number of patterns, adding richness and texture to any landscape.

Unit pavers can be utilized in four conditions:

- Pedestrian—walkways, plazas, patios or other public exterior spaces and not subject to vehicular loads.
- Vehicular—applications include roadways, driveways, walkways, plazas, patios or other exterior spaces that may or will receive vehicular traffic including maintenance or emergency vehicles.
- Porous includes paving that allows rainwater to percolate through the pavement openings or joints.
- Garden—residential uses not necessarily subject to ADA design guidelines.

It is important to select the appropriate unit paver type, size, finish, with a compatible base and joint system for a given application and use.

Table 10.1 Typical Paver/Base/Joint Compatibility

Type of Natural or Cut Stone Paver	Base Materials	Joint
Cobblestone	Flexible base	Swept joints
	Concrete base with mortar setting bed	Mortar joints
Flagstone (slate or bluestone)	Flexible base	Swept joints
	Concrete base with mortar setting bed	Mortar joints
Block units (Belgian block)	Flexible base	Swept joints
Pavers (thin format cut from stone)	Flexible base	Swept joints
.	Concrete base with mortar setting bed	Mortar joints

Continued

Table 10.1 *continued*

Premolded Paver Units	Base Material	Joint
Brick (clay)	Flexible base	Swept joints
	Asphalt or concrete base with bituminous setting bed	Swept joints
	Concrete base with mortar setting bed	Mortar joints
Tile pavers (clay $1/2$" - $5/8$" thick)	Concrete base with mortar setting bed	Mortar joints
Asphalt block pavers	Asphalt or concrete base with bituminous setting bed	Swept joints
Concrete pavers	Flexible base	Swept joints
	Asphalt or concrete base with bituminous setting bed	Swept joints
	Concrete base with mortar setting bed	Mortar joints

Source: Hopper, Landscape Architectural Graphic Standards. Copyright 2007, John Wiley & Sons, Inc.

Assessing Site Conditions

Evaluating Existing Unit Paver Installations

Unit pavers installed on a flexible base are easily taken up and re-installed if any subsurface utility repairs are necessary or if problems with the installation develop. Although some surface problems can develop over time, they are for the most part easily corrected.

Some problems that commonly affect unit pavers on a flexible base with suggested repairs are:

- Loss of joint sand by weather-related factors, vehicular traffic or some settling over time can be easily fixed by sweeping additional sand into the joints.
- Shifting of pavers creating uneven joints (too wide or too narrow) can cause problems. This can be caused by bedding sand or base displacement or loss of jointing sand. The problem area pavers can be removed, the problem addressed and the pavers can be re-installed with consistent joints aligned with the rest of the paving pattern.
- Pavers can sometimes exhibit cracks or break into smaller pieces, usually caused by heavy loads for one reason or another. The damaged pavers can be removed, the base and bedding sand checked for any problems, and then new pavers installed.

- Uneven settling of pavers or areas of pavers (sometimes resulting in a depression where water can pond or a bulge that protrudes upwards or a tripping hazard) can be caused by some settlement of the subgrade, sub-base, base or bedding sand course. The problem pavers should be removed and the layers below checked for problems ranging from expansive soils, organic materials, improper compaction, freeze/thaw damage, heavy loads or general settling of one or more layers supporting the pavers. Once the problem has been addressed, the foundation layers can be reconstructed and the pavers re-installed.

A real advantage to unit pavers on a flexible base is that they can be easily removed whenever subsurface repairs are necessary. After the repair is made, almost all the pavers can be re-installed and the area restored to its previous condition with little or no evidence of the disturbance that was made. To ensure a successful re-installation, a couple of feet of additional pavers around the excavation should be removed to allow for proper subgrade and base course compaction after the repair—the key to a successful paver re-installation.

▶ Sometimes with very tight installations, it may be necessary to break out one or two of the pavers. In these cases, some additional pavers may need to be purchased to make the re-installation complete.

Acceptable Practices

Unit Pavers on a Flexible Base

Layout
Prior to excavation to the required subgrade elevation, the work area should be marked out with stakes set out just beyond the planned excavation so that they will not be disturbed during the removal process. The use of string lines or grade markings on the stakes should be used to help guide the establishment of the subgrade at the proper elevation. The stakes should be checked throughout the excavation phase to ensure that they have not been disturbed and still represent the correct elevations.

Subgrade Preparation
Uniformity, in both soil composition and compaction, is the key to a good subgrade—one that will provide adequate support. Soft spots should be removed and replaced with good material, such as gravel or crushed rock. Soils that are susceptible to frost action (such as high silt soils found above the frostline and those containing

organic material) should be removed and replaced as much as practically feasible.

In some cases where soil resists good compaction or heavy loads are anticipated, soil stabilization may be specified in order to improve the characteristics of the soil. Soil stabilization is the process of blending and mixing materials with a soil to improve certain properties of the soil. The process may include the blending of soils to achieve a desired gradation or the mixing of lime, Portland cement, fly ash, or other commercially available additives that may alter the gradation, texture or plasticity, or act as a binder for stabilization of the subgrade. (See Concrete Pavements—Subgrade Preparation)

▶ **Although subgrade soil does not always require analysis by a soils engineer, it is advisable for pavements that will be subject to vehicular traffic.**

Utility trenches or other excavations that extend deeper than the prepared subgrade must be brought back up to the required subgrade elevation by backfilling and compacting in 6-in.-thick layers (lifts). If suitable, the material removed during the utility installation can be used to backfill; if not, approved clean fill should be brought in as required.

After excavation, any necessary soil replacement and/or stabilization, the subgrade must be rough graded and compacted. The subgrade should be graded parallel to the proposed finished grade. Compaction of sand and gravel soils is best accomplished by the use of a smooth drum roller (walk-behind or ride-on) or for smaller areas, rammers or vibratory plate compactors. Fine grained soils and clay are better compacted with a sheepsfoot roller (see Concrete—Sub-base). The moisture content and compacted density of the subgrade soil should be checked against the requirements of the specifications (Proctor test) before continuing with the installation (see Concrete Pavement—Subgrade Preparation).

Geotextile Fabric

Geotextile fabric, woven or unwoven (as recommended by the manufacturer), can be used as a separation layer to prevent fine grained soils from the subgrade from migrating up and contaminating the base course. Although not required for every installation, it is advisable when the subgrade consists of very finely graded silty soils, clay or other conditions where the soil could remain saturated and be subject to freeze/thaw cycles (or when recommended by an engineer).

▶ **The geotextile fabric should be laid as flat as possible, without wrinkles. Care should be taken during the laying of the base course to prevent trucks or other construction equipment from running over the fabric resulting in wrinkles or folds.**

Figure 10.53 Compacting the subgrade with a rammer.
Source: Photo courtesy of Unilock.

Figure 10.54a A plate vibrator is very good for compacting small areas of sand and gravel.

Figure 10.54b A small compacting roller is an effective machine for compacting subgrades of smaller sites.
Source: Photo courtesy of ICPI.

Another important function of a geotextile installation is to prevent the loss of perimeter bedding sand along the edge restraints that can cause the uneven settling of pavers. The loss of bedding sand along these edges can be prevented by the use of a 12 to 18-in. strip of geotextile that is placed along the base course and folded up along the edge restraint to just below the finished grade of the paver. This will effectively prevent any loss of sand through the edge restraint or down into the base course.

Sub-base and Base Course

After compaction of the subgrade (and laying of a geotextile if required), a compacted granular sub-base and/or base course can be installed. Typically, a sub-base is installed to support the base course above in conditions that call for thicker aggregate bases (such as vehicular roads or areas susceptible to freeze/thaw cycles). The sub-base is generally a larger and less expensive aggregate. The base course is the layer directly under the bedding sand and is generally a higher quality more finely graded angular aggregate. It is placed above the sub-base or directly on the subgrade depending on the thickness of the specified aggregate base course.

In areas with well drained soils (poor soil conditions can require thicker base courses), pedestrian areas should be constructed with a minimum base course depth of 4 in. and residential driveways with a minimum base course depth of 6 in. It is common for streets and other areas where heavy vehicular use is anticipated to use an aggregate base course depth of 8 to 10 in. For these thicker base courses, a sub-base layer can be used, however it is recommended that the more finely graded base course be a minimum depth of 6 in. For vehicular uses it is important that applicable codes and standards are met and a civil engineer be consulted to determine the appropriate sub-base and/or base course depths.

▶ **Frozen base course aggregates should not be used. Base course aggregate should never be placed on a frozen subgrade.**

Proper compaction of the base course is critical to minimizing movement or uneven settling of the unit pavers, particularly along edges and against existing structures. The sub-base and/or base courses should be compacted in 4 to 6-in. uniform lifts to ensure a consistent density. The thickness of the lifts should not exceed the compaction capacity of the equipment being used.

▶ **Although not required for an aggregate base or asphalt stabilized base, a geotextile fabric should be used over a cement stabilized base to prevent the migration of bedding sand into cracks which can develop as the cement stabilized base cures. The geotextile fabric should be turned up along the edge to prevent loss of bedding sand along the edge restraint or existing structure.**

Bedding Sand Placement

After the proper installation of the base course, the bedding sand of specified gradation (and conforming to ASTM C 33) is spread loosely over the area and screeded to a uniform depth of between 1 to 1-$\frac{1}{2}$ in. Screed rails set upon the base course at the required elevations and slope or the edge restraints themselves, if set at the required elevation and slope prior to the installation of the pavers, can be used to guide the screeding process. String lines and grade stakes should be used to set the screed rails so that they are parallel and true to line, grade and required slope. The bedding sand can then be screeded by pulling a straight piece of 2 x 4 or even better, an aluminum screed bar along the screed rails, keeping a constant level of sand in front of the screed bar, filling any voids or irregularities as they appear and re-screeding if necessary.

A bedding course of less than 1 in. may not provide enough depth for interlocking pavers to "lock up" and more than 1-$\frac{1}{2}$ in. will not provide the required stable base for the pavers. The screeded level of the sand should set the pavers up to $\frac{1}{4}$ in. higher than the desired finished elevation to allow for some change in elevation during vibration and typically expected minor settlement over time.

A loss of bedding sand can occur at the perimeter of the paver area adjacent to the edge restraint and edges along existing structures. The loss of bedding sand in these areas can be prevented by the use of a 12-in. strip of geotextile that is placed along the base course and folded up along the edge restraint to just below the finished grade of the paver.

▶ Although bedding sand on large projects may involve use of large power screeds, most unit paver installation still involves setting screen rails set to the proper grade and slope.

▶ Bedding sand should not be used to compensate for irregularities in the base course. Any irregularities must be corrected before placing the bedding sand.

Installing the Pavers

Unit pavers are generally installed by hand, although they can be installed mechanically on larger areas (mechanical clamps can install a square yard of pavers at one time, greatly increasing the area of pavers that can be laid in a day). They can be installed in various patterns, usually as specified on the drawings or based on the shape(s) of the pavers.

Figure 10.55 Bedding sand is laid between the rails and a straight edge pulled across to level the bedding sand.
Source: Photo courtesy of Unilock.

Figure 10.56 In this installation a pull screed is used to level the bedding sand between the guide rails.
Source: Photo courtesy of Pave Tech Inc.

Chalk lines snapped onto the bedding sand or string lines should be used to help in maintaining straight joint lines and the integrity of the pattern. Unless a specific joint spacing is specified, pavers are generally installed hand tight. Some pavers are manufactured with spacers to ensure uniform joints between pavers and leave a distinctive space between them to be later filled with jointing sand.

▶ Pallets of pavers should be spread out in locations as close to the area where they are to be installed, rather than one central location, to make placement a more efficient operation.

The installation of the pavers should start at one end along the hard edge of an existing structure or from an edge restraint, and proceed out from this starting point in one direction. Existing structures are often not straight or square, although they may appear to be, do not depend upon them to determine the line of your pattern or joints. Always use a string line that is carefully measured and checked often during the paver installation process.

▶ When installing edge restraints or working with complex patterns, it is important to leave a little extra space to be able to fit the pavers in the desired pattern without cutting. Leaving an extra quarter inch space between restraints for every 5 or 6 ft of paver pattern will allow for slight variances that can be expected within

Figure 10.57 Placing the unit pavers with typical interlocking concrete pavement system components. String lines help keep the pattern straight.
Source: Photo courtesy of PICP.

Figure 10.58 Mechanical setting of permeable pavers on large projects.
Source: Photo courtesy of PICP.

normal construction tolerances. Having to cut an $1/8$ of an in. off a long line of unit pavers to make them fit is a difficult and time-consuming task that leaves a very unfinished edge compared to the smooth full paver edges. If there is a space of a $1/4$ to $1/8$ in. or so left between the last paver course and the edge restraint, the space can be filled with joint sand or the last couple of paver courses can be shifted slightly to fit better against the edge.

Although the cutting of pavers should be kept to a minimum, it is difficult to avoid completely. A masonry diamond saw should be used to cut pavers, if required, to provide a clean, smooth cut. Other methods do not produce as sharp and accurate of a cut. The cutting of pavers should be done on an ongoing basis once paver placement has begun, to infill gaps in the pattern and prevent any horizontal shifting during the placement process.

Small cut pieces of paver along the edge restraint can be a problem. By including a perimeter soldier course edge, any cut pieces are kept from the edge restraint or adjacent pavement edge. The soldier course helps to hold the smaller pieces in place.

A Herringbone pattern installed at either 45 or 90 degrees to the direction of traffic is the most effective pattern for street applications, as it resists shifting from lateral forces created by vehicle tires turning and breaking as well as offers the most load-bearing capacity. Long linear patterns in the direction of traffic, such as running bond, are least effective and should be avoided.

After the pavers have been placed, the area should be compacted by two passes with a plate vibrator to set the pavers in place. Special plate attachments that lessen the chance of damaging the pavers are available. After initial compaction, any damaged pavers should be removed and replaced. Joint sand should then be broadcast over the paver surface, swept into the joints and the pavers vibrated again. This process may need to be repeated two or three times until the joints are full. This process should be completed at the end of each day for all pavers that have been installed and the leading edge protected against disturbance, ready for the next day's work.

Although the same sand as used for the bedding course can be swept into the joints, a finer graded joint sand (conforming to ASTM C 144) makes the joint sweeping process easier. Polymeric jointing sands, a blend of sand and polymers, is an alternative that provides resistance to insect infestation, weed growth and weather-related erosion of the jointing material. It is swept into the joints dry and hardens after being moistened.

Edge Restraints

Edge restraints are essential to provide resistance to lateral forces and to prevent pavers from shifting. Edge restraints are also used at changes in the paver pattern and where there is a change in slope. Edge restraints can be made from concrete, stone, steel aluminum and plastic, in addition, buildings or other existing structures can also function as an edge restraint. Edge restraints installed at the proper elevation can be used as a guide during the screeding of the bedding sand.

▶ Compaction around cast iron utility structures can be difficult. The installation of a concrete band around the structure as a transition to the field of pavers is a good alternative solution.

Manufactured edge restraints specifically made for use with unit pavers are available in steel, aluminum and plastic. They are generally held in place by spikes that are driven into the base course. Edge restraints with "L shaped" designs offer greater stability. These types of edge restraints come in different thicknesses for light residential use or heavy vehicular use.

Some manufactured edge restraints lend themselves to being installed after the installation of the setting bed and pavers. Where there is room, this allows the edge restraint to be installed after a complete paving pattern (like a basketweave), eliminating the need to cut any pavers. For other patterns, and particularly for curved perimeters, the pavers can be extended beyond the perimeter, marked with a chalk line and then neatly saw cut, resulting in a perfect edge for the restraint to be installed up against.

Edge restraints can be made from precast concrete or cut natural stone. Extending down the bottom of the base course, they can be set on the subgrade or in a pocket of wet mortar. Poured-in-place concrete curbs can also be used as an edge restraint. Provision should be made for excess water to drain through the curbs, either at joints or by adding weep holes. At all joints or weep holes a geotextile should be used to prevent loss of bedding sand.

▶ The base course should extend beyond the edge restraint by the same dimension as its thickness, providing firm anchoring for any edge restraint spikes and creating a stable edge condition.

Final Inspection and Maintenance

After installation is complete the entire paver area should be swept clean and any excess sand removed from the surface. The area can then be checked to see that the surface is uniform in slope ensuring positive drainage, with no bulges or depressions. The jointing sand should completely fill the joints.

Although not required, a sealer can be applied to some unit pavers that enhance their aesthetic appearance by keeping that "new" paver look and prevent stains from being absorbed into the pavers themselves. Any stains that do need to be removed should be removed with materials that are approved by the paver manufacturer. Another option available are joint sand stabilizers that are used to prevent the loss of joint sand over time. If these are not used, joint sand may need to be replenished from time to time as loss is discovered.

Unit Pavers on an Asphalt or Concrete Base

Unit pavers can be installed on an asphalt base (semi-rigid) or a concrete base (rigid base) (refer to the chapters on asphalt pavement and concrete pavement). It is particularly important for these installations that the base material, setting bed and joint treatment are all compatible:

Semi-rigid base

- Pavers can be installed on a bituminous setting bed with mortarless, sand swept joints.

Rigid base

- Pavers can be installed on a bituminous setting bed with mortarless, sand swept joints.
- Pavers can be installed on a mortar setting bed with mortar joints.
- Pavers can be installed on a sand setting bed with mortarless joints.

Bituminous Setting Bed

A bituminous setting bed is a blended mixture of 93% sand and 7% asphalt cement that is heated to 300 degrees F and delivered to the site hot. The bituminous setting bed material and pavers should be installed as follows:

- The bituminous setting bed material is laid onto the asphalt or concrete base and spread between screed rails set to provide a typical setting bed depth of $3/4$ in. after compaction.
- Low points and voids should be filled with fresh bituminous setting bed material ahead of the screed bar to provide a uniform surface.
- Screed rails should be removed and the resulting void filled with fresh bituminous setting bed material.
- Bituminous setting bed should be compacted with a roller compactor to produce a smooth surface while the material is still hot. Any low spots or depressions should be filled and re-rolled.
- After the bituminous setting bed has cooled, a neoprene modified adhesive should be applied to the surface with a notched trowel.
- When adhesive has dried but is still tacky to the touch, pavers can be placed.

- Pavers should be placed hand tight, checking alignment of pattern continually as pavers are laid.
- After pavers have been placed, joints can be filled by sweeping with jointing sand.

Sand stabilized by mixing cement with dry joint sand is not compatible with a bituminous setting bed installation.

The size of the area that a bituminous setting bed material should be laid at one time, is a factor of how long it takes to screed and still be able to compact while still hot.

When Portland cement concrete is used as a base for a bituminous setting-bed application, do not allow the use of curing compounds that prevent the asphalt from bonding to the concrete.

Mortar Setting Bed

Pavers set in a mortar bed produce a rigid pavement that is only compatible with a rigid pavement of concrete as a base (see section on Concrete Pavement). After the concrete base has cured for 10 – 14 days, the pavers can be installed as follows:

- The concrete surface should be cleaned and dampened (surface should not be wet) prior to the laying of the mortar setting bed.
- The cement mortar setting bed material should be laid onto the concrete base and troweled to provide a typical setting bed depth of approximately ¾ in.

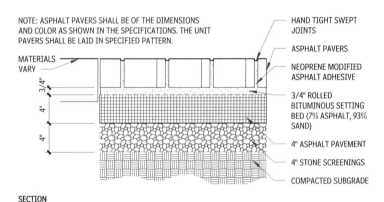

NOTE: ASPHALT PAVERS SHALL BE OF THE DIMENSIONS AND COLOR AS SHOWN IN THE SPECIFICATIONS. THE UNIT PAVERS SHALL BE LAID IN SPECIFIED PATTERN.

MATERIALS VARY

HAND TIGHT SWEPT JOINTS

ASPHALT PAVERS

NEOPRENE MODIFIED ASPHALT ADHESIVE

3/4" ROLLED BITUMINOUS SETTING BED (7% ASPHALT, 93% SAND)

4" ASPHALT PAVEMENT

4" STONE SCREENINGS

COMPACTED SUBGRADE

SECTION

ASPHALT PAVERS ON ASPHALT BASE

Figure 10.59 A detail example of a unit paver, in this case asphalt block, installed on bituminous setting bed.
Source: Hopper, Landscape Architectural Graphic Standards. Copyright 2007, John Wiley & Sons, Inc.

- Mortar setting bed should be placed approximately 2 ft ahead of the laying of the pavers in a continuous process.
- The pavers should be buttered with mortar on the bottom and edges and then set into the mortar setting bed.
- Pavers should be placed hand tight or with joint spacing as specified before mortar setting bed begins to set, checking alignment of pattern continually as pavers are laid.

▶ For thin format pavers, a bond coat is applied to the concrete pavement surface prior to applying thin mortar setting bed, and the pavers.

- For full mortar joints between pavers, cement, lime and sand are mixed so that the joint material flows easily into the joints. When the mortar begins to set, the joints can be finished by tooling with a concave jointer.
- Joints need to be completely filled to prevent moisture from penetrating into the joint.
- The mortar for joints can be ordered in colors to match the color of the unit pavers.
- Latex additives are often used in the mortar mix to improve bonding with the base slab and to the pavers.
- Polymer additives are also added to the grout mix to increase freeze-thaw resistance by making the grout more impervious to water.
- Care taken during the jointing process can minimize cleaning the surface of the pavers from excess mortar. Some excess mortar can be removed by pulling wet burlap bags over the surface. For more extensive cleaning, special solutions may be necessary.

▶ Some pavers can be ordered coated with paraffin or wax to prevent grout from adhering to the surface of the paver and allowing for steam cleaning of the pavers after joint mortar has cured.

- Edge restraints are not required for pavers that are mortared in place but they are sometimes used for aesthetic reasons.

Expansion Joints

Expansion joints are required for paver installations on a mortar setting bed. Expansion joints need to be installed in the following situations:

- Expansion joints should always be included in the unit paver installation wherever expansion joints occur in the concrete base.
- Wherever pavers meet existing curbs, walls, steps or other permanent structure.

MORTAR JOINT (MAXIMUM WIDTH 1")

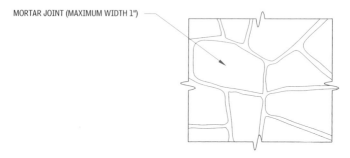

PLAN

1" MORTAR SETTING BED

2" FIELD STONE (MINIMUM 9", MAXIMUM 24" IRREGULAR SHAPE

CONCRETE SLAB W/ REINFORCEMENT 4" THICKNESS

FULL DEPTH 1/2" EXPANSION JOINT W/STAINLESS STEEL DOWEL (DIA. x 18" LENGTH) @ 24" O.C. PLASTIC SLEEVE @ ONE END

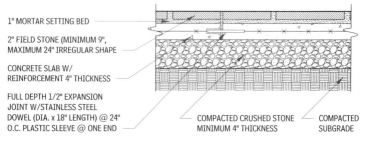

COMPACTED CRUSHED STONE MINIMUM 4" THICKNESS

COMPACTED SUBGRADE

SECTION

Figure 10.60 Unit pavers, in this example fieldstone, installed on a mortar setting bed.
Source: Hopper, Landscape Architectural Graphic Standards. Copyright 2007, John Wiley & Sons, Inc.

- At right angle turns.
- Around posts, utilities or other penetrations through the paver surface.

Unit Pavers Over Existing or New Asphalt or Concrete Base

Unit pavers can be installed on a sand setting bed over new asphalt or concrete pavements or used as an overlay on existing asphalt or concrete pavements. After determination of structural requirements, the unit pavers can be installed as follows:

- If pavers are being installed over existing pavements, cracks, joints or other damage should be repaired.
- Although storm water should not penetrate through the sealed joints to the sand setting bed, drain holes can be formed in new concrete or drilled in existing pavements (minimum 2 in. diameter) approximately 10 ft on center and at all low points as an added precaution to prevent the accumulation of water under the pavers. The drain holes should be filled with an open graded aggregate.

- A geotextile fabric should be laid across the pavement to prevent any loss of bedding sand through the drain holes, joints or damaged areas of the pavement base.
- A sand bedding course can be laid on the geotextile, up to 1 in. on new pavements. On existing pavements the bedding sand can be laid up to a depth of 4 in., in order to meet the required finished grade elevation. Where additional depth is required, an asphalt overlay should be used before the bedding sand is placed.
- The sand bedding course should be screeded to the correct depth, the pavers laid handtight and jointing sand swept into the joints (as described earlier in this section).
- In this type of installation, it is recommended to use a polymeric jointing sand to minimize the amount of water that can penetrate to the sand setting bed.
- Expansion joints are not necessary with this type of installation except where expansion joints exist in the pavement base. In these cases, the expansion joint must be carried up through the paver surface. No pavers should ever straddle across an expansion joint.
- An edge restraint is required in these types of mortarless installations. Any of the edge restraints listed earlier in the chapter can be used. However, for vehicular applications, precast or poured-in-place concrete or granite curbs should be used in order to prevent the pavers from shifting.

Permeable Unit Pavers

There are two basic types of permeable unit pavers:

- Small units that allow water to pass through their joints that are filled with open graded aggregate.
- Open grids made from plastic or concrete that have large voids that are most commonly filled with aggregate or topsoil and planted with turf.

Both of these permeable unit paver types rely on aggregate bases to support heavy loads and to store storm water until it has time to infiltrate into the subgrade. The installation of permeable unit pavers has some significant differences compared to regular unit pavers.

Subgrade Preparation

Compaction of the subgrade reduces the infiltration rate that is critical to a permeable paver installation. Therefore, it is important that the subgrade be compacted no more than necessary to support anticipated loads. For pedestrian traffic, this may mean little or no compaction at all. The input of a civil or geotechnical engineer is critical in balancing the necessary level of compaction and the required infiltration rates.

Figure 10.61a   Joint filling stone laid out over pavers prior to sweeping into the joints. Voids between the stones can clearly be seen.
Source: Photo courtesy of PICP.

Figure 10.61b   Permeable pavers with slightly open joints that are filled with No. 8 or 9 stone, allowing water to infiltrate to the stone drainage layers below.

Figure 10.61c   Open concrete grid paver used for slope stabilization.
Source: Photo courtesy of Russell Adsit, FASLA.

▶ Heavy construction equipment can cause unintentional subgrade compaction. They should be kept off of areas that are to receive permeable unit pavers.

After excavation and removal and replacement of any soft, spongy, or other deleterious materials:

- The subgrade should be graded parallel to the proposed finished grade.
- Large areas are best compacted by the use of a smooth drum roller (walk-behind or ride-on) and for smaller areas, vibratory plate compactors or jumping jacks.

▶ Special attention should be given to compacting the soil around utilities and along building edges, curbs, walls or other structures, as these areas are inherently susceptible to settling.

- After compaction, the subgrade surface should not deviate more than ³/₈ of an inch from the specified finished grades and when measured with a 39 in. straight edge in any direction.
- The moisture content and compacted density of the subgrade soil should be checked against the requirements of the specifications (Proctor test) before continuing with the installation (see Concrete Pavement—Subgrade Preparation).

Geotextile, Sub-base and Base Courses

After compaction of the subgrade, a geotextile fabric should be placed on the subgrade and up the sides of the excavated area, and secured in place to prevent shifting, folds or wrinkling. The geotextile fabric should be overlapped a minimum of 12 in. to provide effective separation of the subgrade from the sub-base or base course, and 24 in. in the direction of drainage, based on the slope of the subgrade.

After the installation of the geotextile, a compacted granular subbase and/or base course consisting of open graded aggregate can be installed. If required, perforated drainage pipe should be installed and protected from damage prior to the installation of the sub-base or base course.

Typically, a sub-base is installed to support the base course in conditions that call for thicker aggregate bases (such as vehicular roads or areas susceptible to freeze/thaw cycles). The sub-base is generally a larger and less expensive aggregate. The base course is installed on top of the sub-base layer and is generally a higher quality more finely graded angular aggregate. It can be placed directly on the subgrade if a sub-base is not required.

The thickness of these courses are based on:

- The required storage capacity (a product of the percentage of void spaces), as these courses function as a temporary reservoir until the storm water can infiltrate into the subgrade.
- The permeability, susceptibility to frost and strength of the subgrade.
- Anticipated loads (pedestrian or vehicular).

The sub-base layer is typically an open-graded aggregate conforming to ASTM No. 2. The sub-base is generally a minimum of 6 in. thick after compaction. For greater depths, the sub-base aggregate should be spread and compacted in uniform lifts of between 4 to 6 in.

The base layer is typically an open-graded aggregate conforming to ASTM No. 57. The base course is generally a minimum of 4 in. thick after compaction, however, it can be laid thicker and substitute for the sub-base. For thicker applications, it should be spread and compacted in uniform lifts of between 4 to 6 in. The surface of the prepared base should not deviate more than $3/8$ of an inch when measured with a 10-ft-long straight edge in any direction.

▶ Installation of No. 57 stone over a compacted subgrade provides a transition between the subgrade and bedding course, interlocking all stone layers and providing storm water storage capacity.

Figure 10.62 Installation of sub-base material on geotextile.
Source: Photo courtesy of PICP.

▶ The aggregate will compact best when moistened. A vibratory roller can be used initially to consolidate the lifts but the final compaction passes should be made with a static roller (10 ton).

▶ Where extra strength is required the sub-base and base courses can be stabilized with asphalt or cement prior to installation. Care needs to be taken to use just enough asphalt or cement to coat the aggregate without excess filling the voids that are critical to the permeability system.

Bedding Course

After the sub-base and base have been compacted, a bedding course of ASTM No. 8 or No. 9 stone can be spread and screeded to a thickness of 1-$\frac{1}{2}$ to 2 in. The moistened stone serves as a choker course into the No. 57 base course. The bedding course should have less than 1% of material being able to pass through a #8 sieve.

For open grid permeable pavements where the voids will be filled with topsoil a setting bed of sharp particled concrete sand should be used, screeded to a uniform depth of 1 to 1-$\frac{1}{2}$ in. Where voids are to be filled with aggregate, the same aggregate should be used for the setting bed to increase permeability.

Installing the Pavers

- After the bedding course has been screeded the permeable pavers can be placed:

- The permeable pavers are placed directly on the stone bedding course.
- Pavers should be cut with a masonry saw so that pavers fit snuggly against the edge restraints, but no cut resulting in less than one-third of a whole paver is acceptable.
- After placement of the pavers, the joints are filled with No. 8 or No. 9 stone.
- The paver area should be swept clean and compacted with a plate vibrator.
- The joints should be re-filled with stone and vibrated again. The process should be repeated until there is no further settling of the joint stone.
- Proof rolling with a rubber tired roller may be necessary for pavements where vehicular loads are anticipated.

▶ Urethane or rubber pads are available for plate vibrators that will minimize any damage to the pavers during the final vibration passes.

For open grid permeable pavements, compaction should be with a vibratory plate vibrator with 3500–5000 pound force. The specified gravel or topsoil should be swept into the openings to within ¾ of an inch of the surface. Where turf is specified the grass seed can be placed into the topsoil within the voids. The open grid pavers should be vibrated again and any additional gravel or topsoil added to bring the level in the voids back to ¾ of an inch.

▶ The addition of topsoil on the seed after initial vibration to bring the level of the topsoil back up, will help the turf seed germinate. After the turf in the voids is established, it will need the same maintenance and care of a regular turf lawn (watering, fertilizer, mowing, etc.). Snow removal is possible if the plow blade is set slightly above the surface of the open grid pavers.

Open Grid Pavers for Erosion Control and Stabilization
Open grid pavers can be used to stabilize embankments up to 2:1 slopes. They are installed by:

- Starting at the bottom of the slope, placing the open grid pavers on the graded and compacted embankment.
- Staking every third row of pavers with steel spikes to secure them to the slope.
- Filling the voids with topsoil and the specified vegetation that, once established, will provide a green and stable slope.

▶ Open grid pavers can also be used in the same manner to stabilize drainage ditches preventing erosion while allowing for a green vegetated appearance that allows permeability and conveyance of storm water.

Unit Pavers Over Structure or Roofs

There is increased interest in using unit pavers over structure or on roofs. They are commonly installed over structural decking or roofs that are waterproofed and pitch toward a roof drain. The compatibility of the type of unit paver and the method of installation with the insulation, protection board, waterproofing membrane and drainage system of the roof is absolutely critical and should be confirmed with the applicable manufacturers before proceeding.

Unit pavers can provide a number of positive improvements over a traditional roof surface including:

- Serves as an attractive pavement and design element for pedestrian use of the structural deck space or roof as an amenity.
- Supports vehicular use and protects the roofing materials against damage by vehicles.

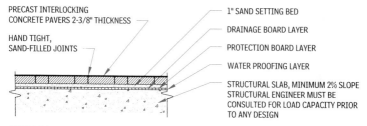

PRECAST INTERLOCKING CONCRETE PAVERS 2-3/8" THICKNESS

HAND TIGHT, SAND-FILLED JOINTS

1" SAND SETTING BED

DRAINAGE BOARD LAYER

PROTECTION BOARD LAYER

WATER PROOFING LAYER

STRUCTURAL SLAB, MINIMUM 2% SLOPE STRUCTURAL ENGINEER MUST BE CONSULTED FOR LOAD CAPACITY PRIOR TO ANY DESIGN

INTERLOCKING CONCRETE PAVERS ON STRUCTURE (PEDESTRIAN)

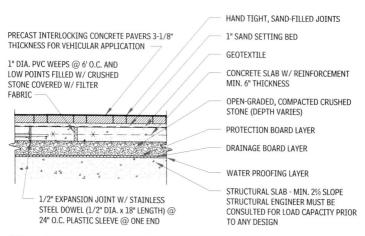

PRECAST INTERLOCKING CONCRETE PAVERS 3-1/8" THICKNESS FOR VEHICULAR APPLICATION

1" DIA. PVC WEEPS @ 6' O.C. AND LOW POINTS FILLED W/ CRUSHED STONE COVERED W/ FILTER FABRIC

HAND TIGHT, SAND-FILLED JOINTS

1" SAND SETTING BED

GEOTEXTILE

CONCRETE SLAB W/ REINFORCEMENT MIN. 6" THICKNESS

OPEN-GRADED, COMPACTED CRUSHED STONE (DEPTH VARIES)

PROTECTION BOARD LAYER

DRAINAGE BOARD LAYER

WATER PROOFING LAYER

STRUCTURAL SLAB - MIN. 2% SLOPE STRUCTURAL ENGINEER MUST BE CONSULTED FOR LOAD CAPACITY PRIOR TO ANY DESIGN

1/2" EXPANSION JOINT W/ STAINLESS STEEL DOWEL (1/2" DIA. x 18" LENGTH) @ 24" O.C. PLASTIC SLEEVE @ ONE END

INTERLOCKING CONCRETE PAVERS ON STRUCTURE (VEHICULAR)

Figure 10.63 Typical sections of pavers on structure.

- Provides necessary ballast to protect the roof from damage that high winds can inflict.
- The use of a lighter color unit paver can reduce the negative contribution a dark roof makes to the urban heat island effect and be integrated with a green roof approach.
- The additional layer of a unit paver reduces the impact of weather-related deterioration on the roofing or structural decking materials.

▶ **A structural engineer should be consulted to determine whether the structure can support the additional weight of the unit pavers as well as the anticipated use.**

A unit paver or a concrete slab can be used over a structure either over a setting bed or on a pedestal system. Unit pavers can be used for either pedestrian or vehicular use. The larger slab units are generally used for pedestrian use areas only. Concrete slab units that are installed on pedestals have open joints that allow water to pass through down to the roof below. The pedestals have protection to prevent damage to the waterproof membrane of the roof.

Installing the Unit Pavers or Paving Slabs

Unit pavers or paving slabs can be installed over a structural deck or roof in one of the following ways:

- Pedestal installation involves placing the paving slabs on plastic or fiberglass pedestals that support the corners of the paving slabs. The paving slabs are installed level by adjusting the pedestals (by the pedestal leveling system or by shimming), until all paving slabs are set level.
- Another pedestal type system is the use of 8-in. square by 2-in.-thick extruded polystyrene blocks stacked and glued together to achieve the desired elevation. The top block may need to be trimmed to achieve the exact elevation and the bottom block grooved as to not impede water flow. The blocks are glued to a polystyrene insulation board that is installed over the waterproofing membrane.
- Unit pavers and paving slabs up to 12 in. square can be set on a sand setting bed. Similar to an installation on grade, the bedding sand is screeded over the geotextile drainage mat to a thickness of approximately 1 in.

▶ **Geotextile fabric should be wrapped around all drains, vents, and other roof penetrations as well as turned up at ends along parapet walls to prevent any migration of the sand setting bed.**

- Unit pavers can be set on a bituminous setting bed installed on an asphalt impregnated protection board. An asphalt primer is applied to the protection board and the bituminous setting bed is screeded and compacted. A neoprene adhesive is applied and the pavers set into place after a dry skin forms over the adhesive. Joint sand or a stabilized joint sand is swept into the joints. Compatibility between the waterproofing membrane, protection board, bituminous setting bed material, neoprene adhesive and joint sand is critical.

- The least common installation of unit pavers or slabs is on a mortar setting bed. Although installed in a manner similar to on-grade installations, the tendency to deteriorate more quickly, susceptibility to weather-related damage as well as the high difficulty associated with removal for any types of roof repair, make it an undesirable choice.

Roof joints that allow sections of the roof to move independently must be respected with the paver pattern above. These roof joints should be treated as edges, with edge restraints to hold the pavers in place without any pavers straddling the joint. The space between the edge restraints should be sealed.

▶ **Aesthetically, it is best to work any roof joints into the paving pattern instead of having them occur haphazardly in the field of pavers, clearly visible by the cut pavers and broken pavement pattern.**

When the parapet walls are separated from the roof deck by an expansion joint, an expansion joint should also be used between pavers installed on a sand setting bed and parapet wall. Expansion joints would not be necessary if the wall is sitting on the same roof deck as the pavers.

Roof drains should have openings below the paver surface to allow water to flow from a sand bedding course or from along the surface of the bituminous setting bed. Geotextile fabric should protect all openings to prevent clogging by sand or the bituminous setting bed.

▶ **Unlike on-grade installations, pavers cannot necessarily be stored on pallets on a roof during installation. The roof may not be able to support the concentrated weight of the pavers. The guidance of a structural engineer regarding the placing of any materials and equipment on the roof during the installation is critical.**

Practices to Avoid

- Soil backfill is never a suitable edge restraint, and edge restraints should never be installed on top of the bedding sand.
- Some older specifications allow the use of crusher screenings, but this practice is discouraged, especially under trafficked pavements.

Some crusher screenings may, however, be used, provided that the gradation of the screenings is similar to the specified gradation. Caution should be exercised with screenings, as they may contain an excess of particles passing the 75-μm sieve size, and too many flat and elongated particles. This is not recommended for typical paver installations.

- Begin cutting infill pavers as soon as the installation is far enough ahead to allow room for cutting, thereby reducing the potential for lateral creep.
- Small pieces (less than ¹/₃ of a paver) shall be avoided as much as possible.
- There are two types of cutting tools, the guillotine type cutter and the diamond blade power saw. The guillotine type cutter does not cut as neatly or as accurately and is therefore less desirable. The diamond saw allows completion of sharper, more accurate cuts.
- Pavers should be cut to a size that will allow ample spacing for joint sand, and not to fit tight, which could lead to edge chipping later.
- Filter cloth generally is not required across the entire surface of an aggregate base, nor should it be placed on top of the bedding sand.
- Timber is not recommended for an edge restraint because it warps and eventually rots.
- A sand bedding course should never be used with permeable pavers because it lacks the necessary permeability.
- Open grid pavers with turf are intended as overflow parking or access for emergency vehicles. When installed where cars will be parked on consecutive days the voids should be filled with gravel, as the grass will not tolerate the shade or heat of the engines very well.
- Vehicular traffic on open grid pavers with topsoil and turf installed in the voids should be avoided until turf is established.
- De-icing salts should not be used on open grid pavers where the voids are filled with turf.
- Deficiencies in the elevation or slope of the base course should not be corrected by using additional bedding course material.

References

OTHER RESOURCES:

- American Institute of Architects. Architectural Graphic Standards, 11th ed. Hoboken, NJ: John Wiley & Sons, 2007.
- Federal Highway Administration. Distress Identification Manual for the Long-Term Pavement Performance Program. FHWA-RD-03-031.
- Landscape Architectural Graphic Standards, First Edition, Hoboken, NJ: John Wiley & Sons, 2007.

Chapter 11

Curbs and Gutters

Curbs and Edges

Curbs and Edges

Description

Curbing has both functional and aesthetic purposes in the landscape. Functionally, curbs and gutters help direct storm water, serve as a vehicular traffic control device, as a base for fences and railings and separate incompatible uses (e.g., vehicular traffic and pedestrians). Aesthetically, curbing defines the edges in the landscape that serve as transitions from one type of space to another.

Concrete and asphalt are the most frequently used curbing materials due to their low cost and flexibility to form. Single-unit materials such as stone, brick, steel, and wood are also commonly used materials for curbing. There are several types of curb configurations, from simple vertical curbs to combination vertical curb and gutter to a mountable rolled curb and gutter.

Assessing Site Conditions

The intensity and type of use dictates the material and design of the curb.

Concrete curbs have the following characteristics and design criteria:

- Concrete curbs are tough, durable, long-lasting, and can be relatively inexpensive to install;
- The size and configuration of concrete curbs depends on anticipated traffic load, strength, and bearing capacity of the subsoil, climatic conditions, and compressive strength of the supporting aggregate materials;
- Concrete curbs can be molded into various shapes and forms over long distances, and are suitable for complicated curbing layouts;
- The minimum compressive strength of concrete curbing is 3200 psi at 28 days. Higher compressive-strength concrete should be specified in heavy-use areas;
- Steel-reinforcing specifications vary for each construction situation. Check all local building codes before specifying size and spacing of steel reinforcement;
- Install expansion joints every 25 to 30 linear feet on center;
- Concrete curbs can be steel faced for additional strength and durability.

Granite and stone curbing have the following characteristics and design criteria:

- Granite curbs are tough, durable, and long-lasting, but can be expensive to install;
- Granite curbing is used in high-traffic areas with high vehicular loads;
- Granite does not deteriorate from the use of salts or chemicals that are commonly used in snow conditions;
- Individual granite block stones are used for medium- and lower-intensity traffic areas;
- The finish surface can be either split-face or sawn and polished, depending on aesthetic preference.

Asphalt curbs have the following characteristics and design criteria:

- Asphalt curbs have a medium durability and can be relatively inexpensive to install;
- The size and configuration of asphalt curbs depend on anticipated traffic load, strength, and bearing capacity of the subsoil, climatic conditions, and compressive strength of the supporting aggregate materials;
- Asphalt curbs can be molded into various shapes and forms over long distances and are suitable for complicated curbing layouts;
- Asphalt curbs are susceptible to deformation when struck with heavy loads, therefore they should be reinforced with a compacted solid granular material, backfilled behind the curb;
- Asphalt curbs are typically used for edging and directing storm water and are not recommended as wheel stops.

Brick curbing has the following characteristics and design criteria:

- Brick curbing has a medium durability and can be relatively inexpensive to install;
- Specify high-quality, severe weather (SW) grade bricks in colder climates where freeze/thaw cycles are prevalent. Hollow-core bricks should not be used for curbing applications;
- Reinforce brick curbs with a concrete sub-base or mortar setting bed;
- Mortar is used to fill vertical joints between individual bricks;
- Use brick with higher compressive strength in high vehicular traffic areas.

Wood curbing has the following characteristics and design criteria:

- Wood curbing has fair durability and can be relatively inexpensive to install;

- Use pressure-treated lumber or wood with natural resistance to decay and rot;
- Drill pilot holes through wood members and install vertical metal stakes up to 24 in. deep 36 to 48 in. on center;
- Backfill against wood curbing with mortar or compacted soil to secure curb in place;
- Install wood curb on 4- to 6-in. gravel sub-base;
- Wood curbing is used primarily as an edging device and is not recommended for use as wheel stops.

Metal edging has the following characteristics and design criteria:

- Metal edging has a good durability and can be relatively inexpensive to install;
- Metal edging is available in many thicknesses, ranging from $\frac{1}{8}$ to $\frac{1}{4}$ in. Thicker edging is used in heavier traffic situations;
- Metal edging can be specified in various widths, ranging from 4 to 6 in., depending on design intent and function;
- Install support stakes every 30 in. on center or as directed by manufacturer;
- Metal edging should be made of a noncorrosive metal or be coated to withstand corrosive weathering processes.

Acceptable Practices

Concrete
Cast-In-Place

On many construction projects, concrete curbs are formed using traditional wood forms. The trench for the curb is dug to allow for the forms to be placed for the full depth of the curb. The bottom of the trench should be compacted before forms are placed. Because the curb trench is typically rather narrow, a rammer is usually used to compact the earth.

Typically, a cast-in-place concrete curb will have steel reinforcement at the top and bottom of the curbs, which must be anchored in place to prevent shifting during the concrete pour (see Steel Reinforcement section). Reinforcing should always be continuous through the corners. Steel reinforcing is stopped $1\text{-}\frac{1}{2}$ to 2 in. from the expansion joint, they do not pass through the joint, which would lock the two sections of curb together and completely negate the purpose of the expansion joint. Dowels are typically used at the expansion joint, with one end fitted with a pipe sleeve to keep the curb aligned and at the same time allow the curb to freely expand and contract horizontally.

Figure 11.1   The curb formwork extends for the full depth of the curb.

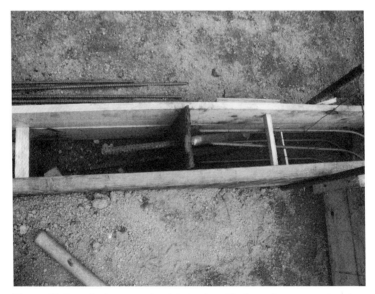

Figure 11.2a   At the expansion joint, a dowel is sleeved on one end and the steel reinforcing bars stop short of the expansion joint. Prior to pouring the concrete, the dowels and sleeves and steel reinforcing bars will be secured in place. It is important that the dowels are aligned to allow horizontal movement for expansion and contraction.

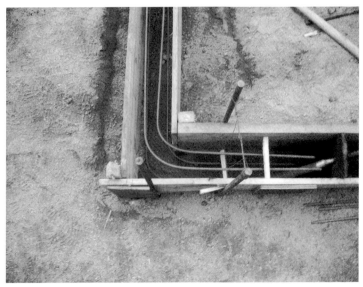

Figure 11.2b Reinforcing bars need to be continuous through corners.

Figure 11.3 A PVC pipe is often used as a sleeve over a dowel that is fixed into the curb prior to the installation of an expansion joint and the pouring of the next section of the curb.

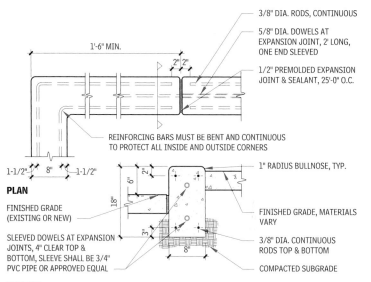

3/8" DIA. RODS, CONTINUOUS

5/8" DIA. DOWELS AT
EXPANSION JOINT, 2' LONG,
ONE END SLEEVED

1'-6" MIN.

2" 2"

1/2" PREMOLDED EXPANSION
JOINT & SEALANT, 25'-0" O.C.

REINFORCING BARS MUST BE BENT AND CONTINUOUS
TO PROTECT ALL INSIDE AND OUTSIDE CORNERS

1-1/2"   8"   1-1/2"

PLAN

6"

2"

18"

3"

1" RADIUS BULLNOSE, TYP.

FINISHED GRADE
(EXISTING OR NEW)

FINISHED GRADE, MATERIALS
VARY

SLEEVED DOWELS AT EXPANSION
JOINTS, 4" CLEAR TOP &
BOTTOM, SLEEVE SHALL BE 3/4"
PVC PIPE OR APPROVED EQUAL

8"

3/8" DIA. CONTINUOUS
RODS TOP & BOTTOM

COMPACTED SUBGRADE

SECTION

6" REVEAL CONCRETE CURB

Figure 11.4   Detail drawing of a concrete curb with 6-inch reveal.

The forms need to be firmly secured in place to prevent bowing during the pour. Spacers, spreaders, outside staking and diagonal bracing are all used to keep the form secure and resistant to the force the concrete imparts to the forms during the pour. The wood forms should be coated with a form release agent to allow them to be stripped cleanly from the concrete without damaging the surface. The formwork for curved curb sections are constructed from thinner pieces of wood and therefore need to be braced and anchored at much closer intervals than long straight runs that utilize thicker lumber.

▶ Because thinner lumber is used for the curved sections of curb, care needs to be taken at the point at which they meet the thicker lumber of the straight sections in order to ensure a smooth transition.

As the concrete is poured into the forms, an internal vibrator should be used to consolidate the concrete. Typically the top of the curb will be given a troweled finish. After the forms are removed, the curb can be rubbed with a stone to eliminate rough spots or blemishes. Plastering the curb with a cement water mix should never be allowed.

For curbs that may be subject to regular impacts of cars and trucks, such as street curbs in commercial areas, steel faced curbs can be installed. The steel plate has anchors that secure it to the concrete curb as it is poured.

Figure 11.5 Formwork is braced from the outside and spread from the inside to keep the forms stable as the concrete is poured.

Figure 11.6 The formwork for curved sections are constructed from thinner lumber. Note the extra support at the joints in the form boards.

Figure 11.7   The formwork for curves need to be supported at closer intervals and fit to the tangent straight forms for a seamless and smooth transition.

Manufactured curb and combination curb and gutter forms are available for straight and radius cast-in-place installations. They are constructed of heavy duty steel (10 to 12 gauge) with provisions for anchoring stakes and connecting flanges. The forms are available with holes for dowels at expansion joints. Flexible forms for curbs are available with closely spaced stake pockets that can be used to create any size radius down to about 5 ft. These re-usable forms can be set quickly and efficiently by the work crew, saving time and labor costs.

Curb Machine
Concrete curb machines, electric or gas powered, form concrete curbs or combination concrete curb and gutters by forcing concrete through the desired shaped mold, as the machine moves along (sometimes referred to as "slipform" or "formless" pavers). They can compact, vibrate and finish the concrete as it is installed. Although the curb machines form a very consistent finish to the concrete, some minor touch-up can be expected.

They are available in different sizes that are appropriate for any size project. These curb machines generally have self-feeding hoppers with an auger system that feeds the machine with a consistent flow of concrete typically allowing the laying of more than 10 linear feet of curb per minute.

Figure 11.8 Concrete is being worked into the concrete curb forms using square point shovels and screeded with a board cut to give the top of the curb the desired shape.
Source: Photo courtesy of Portland Cement Association.

Some contractors offer extruded concrete curbs and edging with color and stamped patterns to resemble stone or brick.

▶ The different shaped curb molds, tool patterns and concrete colors can create a variety of border appearances.

Precast
Precast concrete curbs and combination curbs and gutters can save on installation time, although may cost more than cast-in-place curbs. They are manufactured in a controlled setting generally using

Figure 11.9   Special curved trowel is used to give the inside and outside radii a smooth finish.
Source: Photo courtesy of Portland Cement Association.

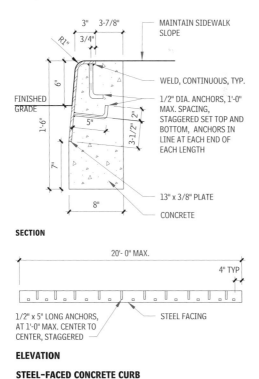

Figure 11.10   Detail drawing of a steel faced concrete curb showing steel anchors that secure the plate into the concrete as it is poured.

Figure 11.11 Steel faced concrete curb with a break between the steel plates at the concrete curb expansion joint

between a 4,000 to 5,000 psi, low slump, air-entrained concrete mixture. They are available with steel reinforcement and provision for steel dowels at the joints between sections. They come in a variety of different shapes, sizes, transition pieces and radii. They are typically installed on an aggregate base or mortar bed over a compacted subgrade.

Granite and Stone

Stone curb is durable with a natural beauty, typically granite or bluestone. Limestone and sandstone curbs are also available, but being softer are not as durable and can be chipped or damaged when subjected to heavy vehicular use.

Stone curbs are generally installed on an aggregate base or mortar bed over a compacted subgrade. They can also be installed on a concrete base with a mortar setting bed. They come in straight sections up to 10 feet long, various shapes, dimensions, edge details and

Figure 11.12 Concrete is fed into the curb machine as it follows the line and grade of the new curb being installed.
Source: Photo courtesy of Portland Cement Association.

finishes. They are available with standard radii for curved sections and various joints for corners as well as accommodations for storm water inlets and catch basins.

Smaller, individual granite blocks are often used as a curb or edging in residential design. These units are usually set in a mortar bed with mortar joints between them.

Reconstructed stone, created from graded stone and a dense concrete mixture and formed by intense pressure, is an alternative to natural stone. The reconstructed stone has the desirable qualities that you would want in a street or landscape curb, high compressive strength, low water absorption rates and salt resistance. It is available in a range of sizes, radii, transitions, colors, aggregates, finishes and shapes.

▶ When a decision is made during the design phase to use a precast concrete, granite or stone curb, the availability of different sizes,

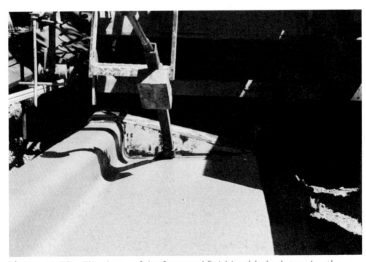

Figure 11.13 The shape of the form and finishing blade determine the shape of the curb and gutter.
Source: Photo courtesy of Portland Cement Association.

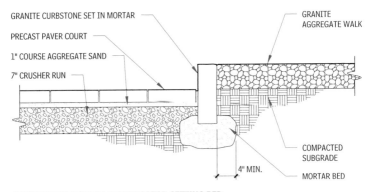

GRANITE CURBSTONE SET IN MORTAR

PRECAST PAVER COURT

1" COURSE AGGREGATE SAND

7" CRUSHER RUN

GRANITE AGGREGATE WALK

COMPACTED SUBGRADE

MORTAR BED

4" MIN.

GRANITE COBBLE CURB WITH MORTAR SETTING BED

Figure 11.14 Detail drawing of a granite curb installed in a mortar setting bed.

shapes and radii should be researched early on and those dimensions incorporated into the design to avoid costly custom work.

Asphalt

Asphalt curbs are typically extruded from a machine, with inside and outside corners needing to be formed and finished by hand. Asphalt curbs are often formed by hand for residential installations.

The asphalt curb is laid directly on the surface of the pavement. A tack coat should be used to bond the asphalt curb to the pavement. The

Figure 11.15 Asphalt curb being installed.
Source: Photo courtesy of Richard Dinkela II, Creve Coeur Paving http://ccpstl.com/.

asphalt curb can be installed on the top course of asphalt or on top of the binder course with the top course paved up to it. In all cases, the asphalt curb must be backfilled to provide stability.

Figure 11.16a Asphalt curbs can be extruded in a number of different shapes by using different molds, in this case an angled asphalt curb.
Source: Photo courtesy of Richard Dinkela II, Creve Coeur Paving http://ccpstl.com/.

Figure 11.16b Using a different shaped form, a more rounded asphalt curb is being installed.
Source: Photo courtesy of Richard Dinkela II, Creve Coeur Paving http://ccpstl.com/.

Brick

Brick curbing for roads or heavy pedestrian use are usually installed on a concrete sub base with a 1-in. mortar setting bed with mortar joints between the bricks. The bricks are set with a half brick below the level of the pavement to lock them in. Bullnose bricks can be used to give the brick curb a rounded edge.

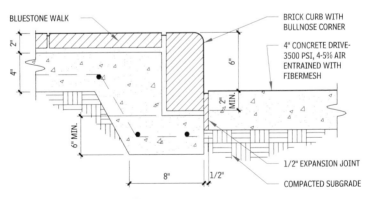

BRICK CURB ON CONCRETE BASE

Figure 11.17 Detail drawing of a brick curb with bullnose set on a 1-in. mortar setting bed on a concrete base.

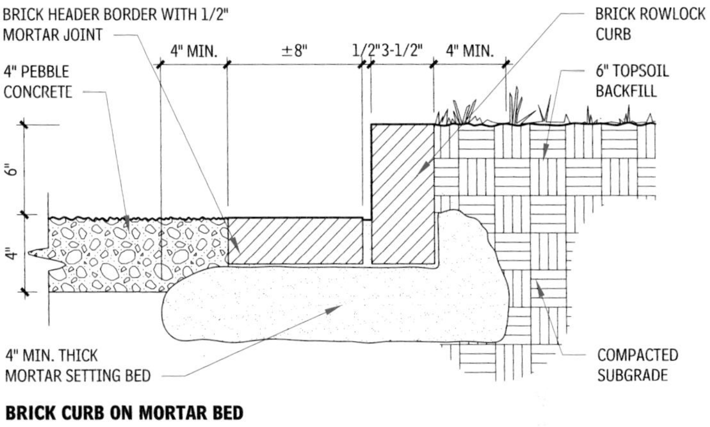

BRICK HEADER BORDER WITH 1/2"
MORTAR JOINT

4" MIN.   ±8"   1/2"3-1/2"   4" MIN.

4" PEBBLE
CONCRETE

6"

4"

BRICK ROWLOCK
CURB

6" TOPSOIL
BACKFILL

4" MIN. THICK
MORTAR SETTING BED

COMPACTED
SUBGRADE

BRICK CURB ON MORTAR BED

Figure 11.18   Detail drawing of a brick curb and border installed in a mortar setting bed.

For light duty and residential use, brick curb or edging can be set directly into a thick mortar setting bed, with mortared joints between the bricks.

Wood

Pressure treated or wood that naturally resists decay and rot can be used as wood curb. They are generally created with larger sized members such as 4 by 4, 6 by 6, or 8 by 8 in. They are anchored in place by driving a steel stake (up to 24 in.) through pilot holes centered in the wood curb or secured with a steel stake or a tapered pressure treated wood stake behind the wood curb. Spikes or stakes should be installed every 3–4 ft on center. A cleat can be installed between

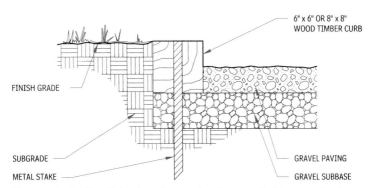

6" x 6" OR 8" x 8"
WOOD TIMBER CURB

FINISH GRADE

SUBGRADE

METAL STAKE

GRAVEL PAVING

GRAVEL SUBBASE

Figure 11.19   Detail drawing of a wood curb secured with a metal stake.
Source: Hopper, Landscape Architectural Graphic Standards. Copyright 2007, John Wiley & Sons, Inc.

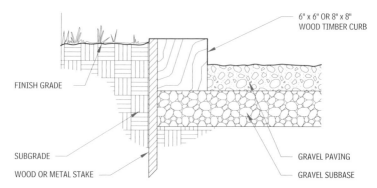

6" x 6" OR 8" x 8"
WOOD TIMBER CURB

FINISH GRADE

SUBGRADE

WOOD OR METAL STAKE

GRAVEL PAVING

GRAVEL SUBBASE

Figure 11.20 Detail drawing of a wood curb secured with a wood or metal stake attached from behind.
Source: Hopper, Landscape Architectural Graphic Standards. Copyright 2007, John Wiley & Sons, Inc.

Figure 11.21 Wood edge secured with vertical wood stakes behind with a wood cleat joining the two pieces of wood at the joint.

lengths of wood curb to keep wood curb pieces aligned and add strength at the joints. The cleat can be made of metal or another piece of wood, such as a 2 by 4 in., nailed or screwed to the wood curbing. Wood curbing is best installed on a gravel base.

Plastic lumber made from post-consumer and post-industrial waste (including soda and milk bottles, plastic grocery bags, etc.) is available from many manufacturers dyed to look like natural wood, in a wide variety of sizes, up to a 12 by 12 in. Plastic wood offers several advantages over natural wood. It is generally resistant to rot, mildew and insect infestation, making it desirable for curbs. Plastic lumber sometimes requires the use of special connectors and hardware and this should be checked with the manufacturer.

Metal

Metal edging can be made of steel or aluminum.

Steel edging comes in thicknesses from $1/8$ to $1/4$ in. with the thicker edging more suitable for heavier duty applications. They are available in 4-, 5-, and 6-in. widths in standard 10-ft-long sections. The end of each section is shaped with double spike pockets to overlap with the next section and be locked together with the tapered spikes. Tree rings between $2\text{-}1/2$ to 6-ft diameters are also available. Steel edging is available in powder coated or unpainted galvanized steel. Tapered spikes (available 12–24 in. long) are driven through pockets in the steel edging to anchor it in place. Special sections (short sections, corner stakes, end pieces) make working with steel edging easy.

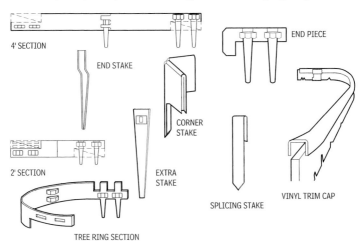

Figure 11.22   Steel edge components.
Source: www.colmet.com.

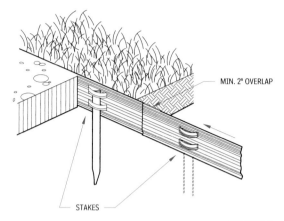

MIN. 2" OVERLAP

STAKES

DIAGRAM A

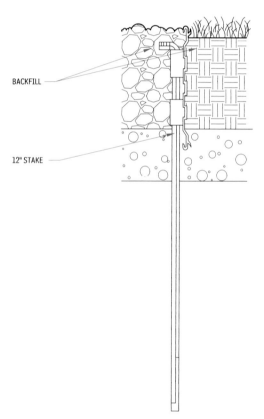

BACKFILL

12" STAKE

DIAGRAM B

Figure 11.23 Aluminum edge staking options.
Source: www.permaloc.com.

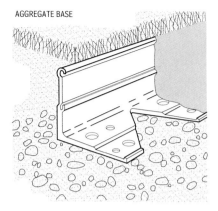

AGGREGATE BASE

DIAGRAM A

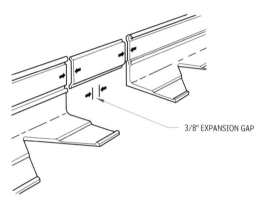

3/8" EXPANSION GAP

DIAGRAM B

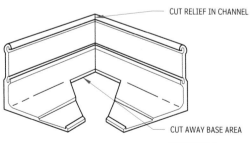

CUT RELIEF IN CHANNEL

CUT AWAY BASE AREA

DIAGRAM C

Figure 11.24 Aluminum edge for asphalt pavement secured with spikes into the aggregate base with detail of joint connection (to allow for aluminum expansion from heat of asphalt) and how edging is cut to form corners. *Source:* www.permaloc.com.

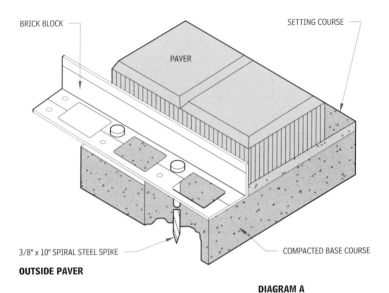

BRICK BLOCK

SETTING COURSE

PAVER

3/8" x 10" SPIRAL STEEL SPIKE

COMPACTED BASE COURSE

OUTSIDE PAVER

DIAGRAM A

QUICK CLIP ™
CONNECTION SYSTEM

DIAGRAM B

Figure 11.25 Aluminum edge for paver installation. Note that the edge restraint is secured to the compacted base course and retains both the setting course and the paver.
Source: www.permaloc.com.

Aluminum edging is available in thicknesses from $^1/_8$ to $^3/_{16}$ in. The thinner material is very good for light duty residential curvilinear edging. The thicker material is better suited to heavy duty and straight installations. They are available in widths from 3 to 12 in. and in several different colors. The ends of each section are designed to snap into the adjacent section, and the edging is held in place by 18-in.-long, heavy duty aluminum stakes driven through pockets in the edging. Corners and angles can be formed by cutting part way through the bottom of the edging and bending to the desired angle.

The installation for metal edging requires that the area be trenched a bit deeper than required to set the top edge at the desired height. The metal edge is set in place and secured at the correct height with the metal stakes. For long curvilinear edges, connecting several sections together before staking may make it easier to achieve a smooth flowing curve. Backfill and compact on both sides of the metal edging evenly to avoid shifting the edge out of line or distorting the curve.

Practices to Avoid

Avoid designs that require custom curbs. When a design anticipates using a precast, machine laid or natural stone curb, it is best to check on the standard sizes available during design development, particularly when designing with a radius. It is always more economical, in terms of money and time, to work with standard shapes, sizes and dimensions than to have a custom design made.

References

ALSO IN THIS BOOK:

- Asphaltic Concrete
- Concrete
- Concrete Steel Reinforcing
- Pressure Treated Wood
- Unit Pavers
- Wood Alternatives
- Wood General

OTHER RESOURCES:

- Landscape Architectural Graphic Standards, First Edition, Hoboken, NJ: John Wiley & Sons, 2007.

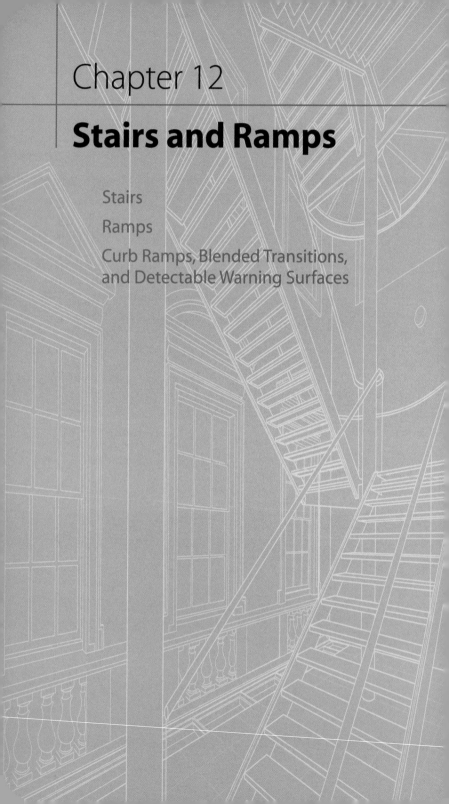

Chapter 12

Stairs and Ramps

Stairs

Description

Stairs should be designed to promote safe, efficient, easy, and comfortable vertical transitions. Specifically, dimensional design decisions should focus on proper riser-tread ratios, overall widths, consecutive length of run, and landing frequency, to ease negotiating vertical change and to increase safety in exterior circulation routes. Proper material choices and construction methods should also be considered in the context of safety.

Assessing Site Conditions

Safety considerations include the following:

- Stairways should be visually "announced" with material changes, textural changes, lighting, planting and/or railings.
- Stair treads should be specified to contain a rough to medium textured finish, to decrease the risk of slipping during poor weather. Natural stone treads should have textured finishes rather than polished surface treatments. Concrete should be specified to have a medium broom finish.
- All treads should be sloped toward the nose to avoid pooling storm water, a minimum of 1% (sometimes expressed as $1/8$ in. per ft) and a maximum of 2% ($1/4$ in. per ft).

Acceptable Practices

Overview

To avoid becoming a dangerous tripping hazard, treads and risers within a consecutive run of stairs should be uniform in size within close tolerances ($1/4$ in.). Stairs within a single run should be constructed out of similar materials and construction techniques.

In order to ensure that riser heights and tread lengths are constructed uniformly, the construction grading plan should specify a number of "equal risers" with a bottom of step and top of step elevation indicated. The construction detail should indicate "equal risers" and "equal treads" with the desired slope toward the nosing. This places the responsibility of constructing the stairs uniformly on the contractor. Too often,

Figure 12.1   Uneven risers can be a tripping hazard. In this photo, the top riser is significantly higher than the bottom riser. The correct approach would be to construct two equal risers. Uneven risers coupled with a valve cover at the bottom and handrails that do not have the required extension beyond the bottom tread are a bad combination of factors all in one stair.

exact riser heights are specified (even though this needs to be calculated to determine that the number of risers specified will be within the minimum and maximum heights), and the contractor builds the stairs with every riser to that exact height, except for one, because the grade change is not evenly divisible by the specified height of the riser. This can happen very easily because of slightly different top and bottom of step elevations in the field or by not calculating the slope toward the nosing as part of the riser height elevation change.

▶ There are too many variables in the field that can affect stair uniformity during construction. Let the drawings specify your specific intent, not the specific dimensions.

The top of stair and bottom of stair elevations along a stairway should maintain a constant level along the edge of the upper and lower treads. The grade leading to the stair should be modified in cross-slope situations, to ensure a level condition at the top and bottom of a stairway.

There may be occasions where the slope of the pavement is too great or the stair length too long to modify the pavement leading to the stair. Although not desirable, in those situations it may be necessary to have a riser that varies in height between the legal maximum and

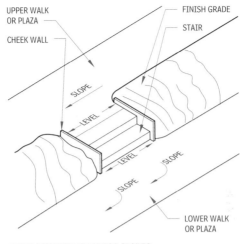

UPPER WALK OR PLAZA

FINISH GRADE

CHEEK WALL

STAIR

SLOPE

LEVEL

LEVEL

SLOPE

SLOPE

SLOPE

LOWER WALK OR PLAZA

STAIR LEVELING AT CROSS SLOPES

Figure 12.2   Stair leveling at cross slopes.
Source: Hopper, Landscape Architectural Graphic Standards. Copyright ©2007 by John Wiley & Sons, Inc. Reprinted by permission of John Wiley & Sons, Inc.

minimum riser heights. Disappearing risers that vary until they become level with the pavement should be avoided—they are a tripping hazard.

Figure 12.3   A long run of stairs and a sloping sidewalk create disappearing risers that as they become closer to flush with the pavement, create a tripping hazard.

Figure 12.4   A long run of stairs can be broken up by site elements, like a planter, to keep a variable riser height between acceptable limits. On this sloping sidewalk the first risers vary between a minimum and maximum height. Before these risers exceed those limits, the stair run is broken by the planters eliminating risers that disappear or would be too tall.

The most commonly accepted equation for the comfortable proportioning of exterior stairs is:

$2R+T=24$ to 26in.

where:

R = riser height

T = tread length

This ratio tends to work with the average stride of average-height people and creates a regular rhythm or cadence for ascending and descending grade changes.

A low riser height allows a person's foot to comfortably travel a longer distance horizontally; therefore, the tread length is longer. As the riser height increases, a person's foot comfortably travels less horizontally, therefore, as the riser height increases, there is a corresponding decrease in tread length.

Stair Risers

The preferred riser height for outdoor stairs is 6 in. For purely functional situations, a riser height of 7 in. is used and is accepted by

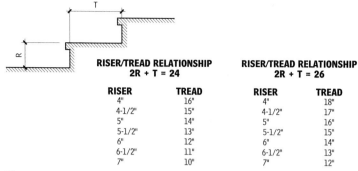

RISER/TREAD RELATIONSHIP 2R + T = 24		RISER/TREAD RELATIONSHIP 2R + T = 26	
RISER	**TREAD**	**RISER**	**TREAD**
4"	16"	4"	18"
4-1/2"	15"	4-1/2"	17"
5"	14"	5"	16"
5-1/2"	13"	5-1/2"	15"
6"	12"	6"	14"
6-1/2"	11"	6-1/2"	13"
7"	10"	7"	12"

Figure 12.5 Typical riser/tread relationships.
Source: Hopper, Landscape Architectural Graphic Standards. Copyright ©2007 by John Wiley & Sons, Inc. Reprinted by permission of John Wiley & Sons, Inc.

American's with Disabilities (ADA) Standards. The minimum riser height for outdoor situations is 4 in. Riser heights are measured from top of nosing to top of nosing.

Riser slopes typically fall between 60 and 90 degrees from horizontal. Riser slopes less than 60 degrees or more than 90 degrees are considered trip hazards and should be avoided to prevent accidents. All riser angles in a single run of stairs should be identical to each other. All stair risers should comply with the ADA Standards.

Stair Treads

The minimum tread length is 10 in. measured from riser to riser of two consecutive stairs. The maximum tread length is 18 in. and is typically used with a shallow riser. Wider treads offer more fluid transitions between grade levels and are more accommodating when used for sitting purposes. Masonry or natural stone treads should be a minimum of 2 in. thick to add visual and structural strength to stairways.

To avoid potential slipping hazards, standing water on stair treads should be allowed to drain off under natural conditions. This is accomplished by sloping treads toward the nose of each tread.

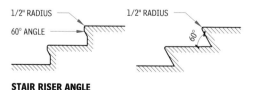

STAIR RISER ANGLE

Figure 12.6 Typical stair riser angles.
Source: Hopper, Landscape Architectural Graphic Standards. Copyright ©2007 by John Wiley & Sons, Inc. Reprinted by permission of John Wiley & Sons, Inc.

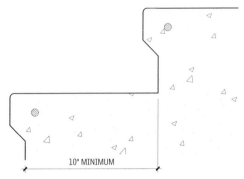

10" MINIMUM

Figure 12.7   Minimum tread length is measured from riser to riser.
Source: Hopper, Landscape Architectural Graphic Standards. Copyright ©2007 by John Wiley & Sons, Inc. Reprinted by permission of John Wiley & Sons, Inc.

▶ Sheet runoff from areas adjacent to the stairs should not be allowed to cascade over steps from above, especially in colder climates where freezing is possible.

Stair Nosings

Improper nosing design on stair treads is often the cause of tripping accidents. Poured-in-place concrete stair nosings should not have abrupt edges and should not project outward more than 1-½ in. beyond the base of the riser. The nosing itself should have a ½-in.

Figure 12.8   Minimum thickness for masonry treads is 2 in.

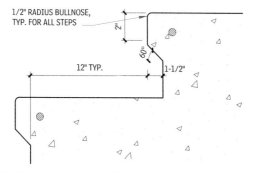

Figure 12.9 Typical stair nosing dimensions.
Source: Hopper, Landscape Architectural Graphic Standards. Copyright ©2007 by John Wiley & Sons, Inc. Reprinted by permission of John Wiley & Sons, Inc.

maximum radius or 45-degree bevel. Brick and other stone masonry stairs should not project outward more than $\frac{1}{2}$ in. beyond the base of the riser.

Shadow lines are often included within exterior stairways for aesthetic reasons and to visually mark riser locations. If improperly designed, shadow lines can be trip hazards if they are large enough to catch the toes of pedestrians. Shadow lines should have a maximum of 1-$\frac{1}{2}$ in. or 60-degree batter from face of riser. For stairways that will be used at night, install proper lighting to illuminate the shadow line.

Landings

Grade changes can serve as psychological barriers and decrease a pedestrian's incentive to proceed up or down a grade change. Elevations of consecutive landings in a single run of steps should be separated by no more than 5 ft so that a person of average height can see the ground plane of the next higher landing.

▶ Landing heights located above visual sight lines make the height of stairs appear more of an obstacle.

Landings should be long enough to allow a regular rhythm of move-ment (average human stride length) between runs of stairs. The typical

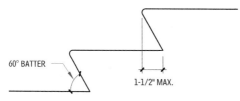

Figure 12.10 Shadow line maximum dimensions.
Source: Hopper, Landscape Architectural Graphic Standards. Copyright ©2007 by John Wiley & Sons, Inc. Reprinted by permission of John Wiley & Sons, Inc.

Figure 12.11 Precast tread with radius, angled batter to the face of the riser and textured tread for increased traction.

length for a landing is 5 ft, which allows a minimum of three strides on the landing. Longer landings are usually in multiples of 5-ft intervals (e.g., 5 ft, 10 ft, 15 ft, etc.).

Figure 12.12 Cast-in-place concrete steps with broom finish and textured nosing with radius.

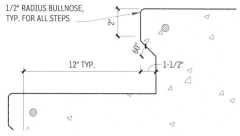

1/2" RADIUS BULLNOSE, TYP. FOR ALL STEPS

2"

60°

12" TYP.

1-1/2"

Figure 12.13 Landing heights should allow a visual sight line to the landing. *Source:* Hopper, Landscape Architectural Graphic Standards. Copyright ©2007 by John Wiley & Sons, Inc. Reprinted by permission of John Wiley & Sons, Inc.

In situations where a large grade change occurs, stairs should have a minimum of one landing for every 9 to 11 risers to alleviate fatigue. Landings should occur at regular intervals along the vertical route by dividing the overall vertical change into equal segments. Generally, odd numbers of stairs, paired with regular sequenced landings, is the optimal stairway configuration for physical comfort.

Landings that provide a level platform at a door entry have specific dimension guidelines set forth in ADAAG. These dimensions are based on the direction of approach, location of the hinge/door latch and direction of the door swing.

Figure 12.14 Landings allowing visual sight lines are more inviting and the stairs appear less formidable an obstacle. This stair has three groups of steps with 9 risers, and the landing at eye level makes the entire stair less imposing.

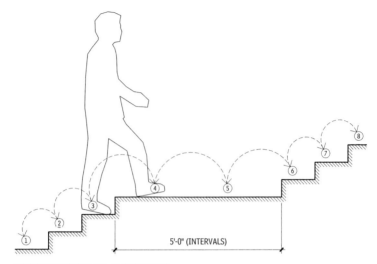

LANDING LENGTHS (5'-0" INTERVALS)

Figure 12.15 Landing lengths should allow for a regular rhythm of equal strides.
Source: Hopper, Landscape Architectural Graphic Standards. Copyright ©2007 by John Wiley & Sons, Inc. Reprinted by permission of John Wiley & Sons, Inc.

Stair Handrails

Building code requirements often govern handrail design, typically necessitating that stairs have continuous handrails on both sides. In stairways wider than 60 in., intermediate handrails are desirable (although not necessarily mandatory) so that all portions of the overall width of the stairs are within 2 ft 6 in. of a handrail.

▶ Local building codes can vary; it is important to check them for stair requirements.

Handrails must extend at least 12 in. beyond the top and 12 in. plus one tread width beyond the bottom of the steps, and be parallel with the floor or ground plane. The height of a handrail's gripping surface must conform to the applicable standards. Some national standards specify that the height of the handrails should be between 30 and 34 in., measured to the top of the rail (Uniform Federal Accessibility Standards (UFAS)). Other national standards specify that the top of the handrail be measured between 34 and 38 in. above stair nosings (American National Standards Institute (ANSI)). It is important to check which standards apply to the application at hand. A handrail that measures 34 in. to the top of the rail would meet all recognized standards.

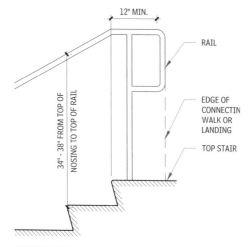

RAILING EXTENSION AT TOP

Figure 12.16 Handrail extension at top of stairs. Edge of handrail extension should not extend perpendicular into the direction of travel of the connecting walk or landing. Handrails are always measured from the nosing to the top of rail.
Source: Hopper, Landscape Architectural Graphic Standards. Copyright ©2007 by John Wiley & Sons, Inc. Reprinted by permission of John Wiley & Sons, Inc.

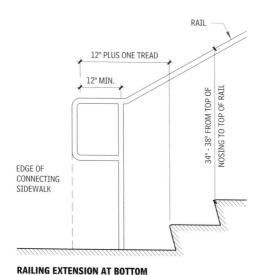

RAILING EXTENSION AT BOTTOM

Figure 12.17 Handrail extension at bottom of stairs. Edge of handrail extension should not extend perpendicular into the direction of travel of the connecting walk or landing.
Source: Hopper, Landscape Architectural Graphic Standards. Copyright ©2007 by John Wiley & Sons, Inc. Reprinted by permission of John Wiley & Sons, Inc.

▶ Handrails are generally made from multiple pieces of pipe. An internal sleeve is used to join the sections of pipe together and a small space is left between them to allow for expansion and contraction of the handrail.

Ends of handrails must be either rounded or returned smoothly to floor, wall, or post. Handrails must have a circular cross section with an outside diameter of at least 1-$\frac{1}{4}$ in., and not greater than 2 in. (although the UFAS maximum diameter is 1-$\frac{1}{2}$ in.). The clear space between the handrail and a cheekwall must be 1-$\frac{1}{2}$ in. (Further information regarding stair railings can be obtained from the American's with Disability Act (ADA) and in the Americans with Disabilities Act Accessibility Guidelines (ADAAG).)

Poured-In-Place Concrete Stairs

Poured-in-place concrete stairs should have the following construction characteristics:

- A footing should be no less than 6 in. thick for stairways. If constructed in colder climates, an air-entrained additive is recommended. Concrete footings should have a minimum compressive strength of 3200 psi at 28 days. Use a higher compressive-strength concrete when greater traffic loads are expected.
- The toe of concrete footings should be constructed below the frost line to prevent heaving.
- Steel reinforcing specifications vary for each construction situation. Check all local building codes before specifying size and spacing of steel reinforcement. In high traffic areas, nosing rebar is recommended.
- All treads should be slip-resistant with a medium broom finish.
- Expansion joints are needed at the base and top of the footing. Expansion joints are also needed on each side of the steps when these are constructed adjacent to cheekwalls, buildings, or other fixed objects. Seal expansion joints with a compatible joint sealing compound to prevent moisture infiltration.
- A compacted gravel or compacted soil (95 percent standard Proctor Test) sub-base should be incorporated under all concrete footings.
- Concrete stairs should be formed using similar materials to ensure uniformity in size and configuration.

Masonry Stairs

In addition to the applicable characteristics for poured-in-place concrete stairs for the base, masonry stairs should have the following characteristics:

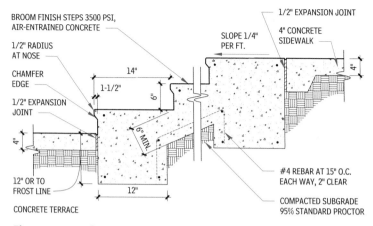

BROOM FINISH STEPS 3500 PSI,
AIR-ENTRAINED CONCRETE

1/2" RADIUS
AT NOSE

CHAMFER
EDGE

1/2" EXPANSION
JOINT

14"

1-1/2"

6"

6" MIN.

4"

12" OR TO
FROST LINE

12"

CONCRETE TERRACE

1/2" EXPANSION JOINT

SLOPE 1/4"
PER FT.

4" CONCRETE
SIDEWALK

4"

#4 REBAR AT 15" O.C.
EACH WAY, 2" CLEAR

COMPACTED SUBGRADE
95% STANDARD PROCTOR

Figure 12.18 Concrete steps.
Source: Hopper, Landscape Architectural Graphic Standards. Copyright ©2007 by John Wiley
& Sons, Inc. Reprinted by permission of John Wiley & Sons, Inc.

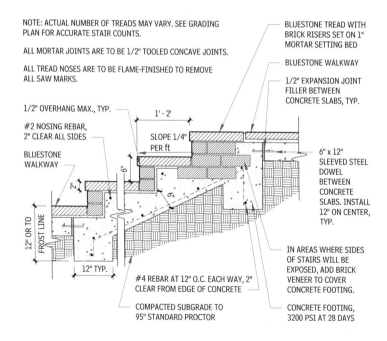

NOTE: ACTUAL NUMBER OF TREADS MAY VARY. SEE GRADING
PLAN FOR ACCURATE STAIR COUNTS.

ALL MORTAR JOINTS ARE TO BE 1/2" TOOLED CONCAVE JOINTS.

ALL TREAD NOSES ARE TO BE FLAME-FINISHED TO REMOVE
ALL SAW MARKS.

1/2" OVERHANG MAX., TYP.

#2 NOSING REBAR,
2" CLEAR ALL SIDES

BLUESTONE
WALKWAY

2"

1' - 2'

SLOPE 1/4"
PER ft

6"

6"

12" OR TO
FROST LINE

12" TYP.

#4 REBAR AT 12" O.C. EACH WAY, 2"
CLEAR FROM EDGE OF CONCRETE

COMPACTED SUBGRADE TO
95" STANDARD PROCTOR

BLUESTONE TREAD WITH
BRICK RISERS SET ON 1"
MORTAR SETTING BED

BLUESTONE WALKWAY

1/2" EXPANSION JOINT
FILLER BETWEEN
CONCRETE SLABS, TYP.

6" x 12"
SLEEVED STEEL
DOWEL
BETWEEN
CONCRETE
SLABS. INSTALL
12" ON CENTER,
TYP.

IN AREAS WHERE SIDES
OF STAIRS WILL BE
EXPOSED, ADD BRICK
VENEER TO COVER
CONCRETE FOOTING.

CONCRETE FOOTING,
3200 PSI AT 28 DAYS

Figure 12.19 Stone treads with brick risers.
Source: Hopper, Landscape Architectural Graphic Standards. Copyright ©2007 by John Wiley
& Sons, Inc. Reprinted by permission of John Wiley & Sons, Inc.

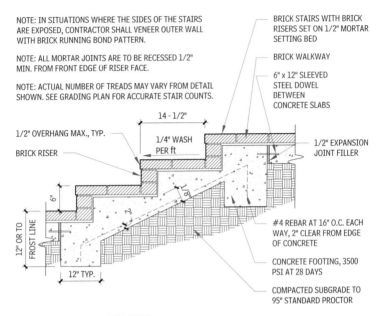

NOTE: IN SITUATIONS WHERE THE SIDES OF THE STAIRS ARE EXPOSED, CONTRACTOR SHALL VENEER OUTER WALL WITH BRICK RUNNING BOND PATTERN.

NOTE: ALL MORTAR JOINTS ARE TO BE RECESSED 1/2" MIN. FROM FRONT EDGE OF RISER FACE.

NOTE: ACTUAL NUMBER OF TREADS MAY VARY FROM DETAIL SHOWN. SEE GRADING PLAN FOR ACCURATE STAIR COUNTS.

BRICK STAIRS WITH BRICK RISERS SET ON 1/2" MORTAR SETTING BED

BRICK WALKWAY

6" x 12" SLEEVED STEEL DOWEL BETWEEN CONCRETE SLABS

14 - 1/2"

1/2" OVERHANG MAX., TYP.

1/4" WASH PER ft

BRICK RISER

1/2" EXPANSION JOINT FILLER

6"

12" OR TO FROST LINE

12" TYP.

#4 REBAR AT 16" O.C. EACH WAY, 2" CLEAR FROM EDGE OF CONCRETE

CONCRETE FOOTING, 3500 PSI AT 28 DAYS

COMPACTED SUBGRADE TO 95" STANDARD PROCTOR

BRICK TREADS WITH BRICK RISER

Figure 12.20   Brick treads and risers.
Source: Hopper, Landscape Architectural Graphic Standards. Copyright ©2007 by John Wiley & Sons, Inc. Reprinted by permission of John Wiley & Sons, Inc.

- Tread stones should have a minimum thickness of 2 in. and should slope ¼ in. per ft toward the nose.
- Tread surface finishes should be sufficiently textured to avoid becoming slippery when wet.

Wood Timber Stairs

Wood timber stairs should have the following characteristics:

- Various sizes of wood timber (4 in. by 4 in., 6 in. by 6 in., 8 in. by 8 in.) can be used in various configurations to create risers between 4 and 7 in. However, used alone, a 6-by-6-in. timber (nominal dimension of 5-½ in. square) is an ideal riser height.
- Wood material should be naturally weather-resistant or pressure-treated to prevent rotting.
- Timbers can be held in place by drilling vertical holes (24 to 48 in. on center) and inserting a 30-to-36-in. galvanized or corrosion-resistant bar.
- Side edges of timber stairs must be held in place by an edge restraint to prevent erosion of sub-base and surface material.

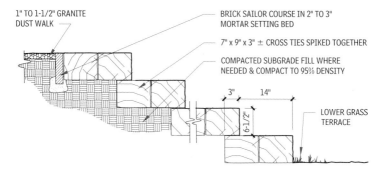

Figure 12.21 Landscape tie steps.
Source: Hopper, Landscape Architectural Graphic Standards. Copyright ©2007 by John Wiley & Sons, Inc. Reprinted by permission of John Wiley & Sons, Inc.

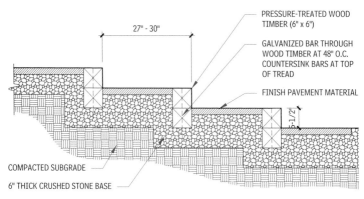

Figure 12.22 Wood timber ramp stairs with masonry treads.
Source: Hopper, Landscape Architectural Graphic Standards. Copyright ©2007 by John Wiley & Sons, Inc. Reprinted by permission of John Wiley & Sons, Inc.

Practices to Avoid

The requirements for steps and handrails are fairly straightforward. However, there are common mistakes that are made, either in the design phase or during construction. Some of the most common mistakes to avoid are:

- Single-step stairways are trip hazards and should not be specified. A minimum of two steps should be used in any single consecutive run of stairs. Three stairs are preferred to ensure visual legibility at level changes.
- Handrail extensions on stairs should not project into the direction of pedestrian traffic. This is often a case of enough space not being allocated to the handrail extension after the top riser.

Figure 12.23 A single riser off this platform at the bottom of a long run of stairs is a hazard. Notice how the handrail on the right changes slope even though the platform is level.

- At the bottom of stairs the handrail must extend 1 tread length at the same slope as the steps and then change slope to extend a minimum of 1 ft horizontal, keeping the rail at a constant height from the beginning of the handrail, all the way up the stairs.
- The ends of handrails must be either rounded or returned smoothly to floor, wall, or post.
- During construction it is very important to make sure that the treads and landings have the proper slope for positive drainage. Both stairs and landings should be sloped away from the building.

▶ **Water that is held on the treads because of the incorrect slope provides for a slippery condition that can be made worse in areas that may be subjected to freezing temperatures.**

- Risers less than 4 in. in height are considered trip hazards and should be avoided.
- Open riser faces are not permitted under the Americans with Disabilities Act Accessibility Guidelines (ADAAG) specifications. They can be significant trip hazards when used in outdoor situations.

Figure 12.24 In this instance, additional space should have been provided from the edge of the top riser so that the handrail would extend no farther than the line of the fence. In addition to the necessary one ft extension beyond the top riser, the radius of the handrail and its return to the post would also need to be figured in the calculation to determine the correct distance from the top riser.

Figure 12.25 This handrail would appear at first glance to have the correct handrail extension. However, the slope of the handrail changes to horizontal at the bottom riser, without sloping for a tread length, which results in the handrail being significantly higher at the extension than the rest of the stair run.

Figure 12.26 This center rail meets the handrail requirements. But the wall mounted handrail at both the top and bottom of the stair, does not have a rounded end, nor does it return to the floor, wall or post.

Figure 12.27 These stairs are not pitched toward the nosing and each of the treads hold water. The stairs and the landing are also pitched toward the building. Although ADAAG requires a handrail to be installed on each side of the stair, there is only one handrail and that handrail ends at the first riser with no extension. The railing slope changes to horizontal before the first riser, making the handrail uncomfortably high at the bottom of the stairs above the allowable maximum height.

Ramps

Description

Any part of an accessible route in the public domain with a slope greater than 1:20 (5 percent) is considered a ramp and must conform to ADA design guidelines. Ramps should be constructed of paving material the same thickness and type as adjacent surfaces, unless visual cues are desired to differentiate elevation changes. In such cases, use both visual and textural cues to warn pedestrians of the ramp and upcoming change in elevation. The finish surface of any ramp should be coarse enough to prevent accidental slippage when the pavement is wet. Adequate lighting should be provided during nighttime hours. Further information regarding ramp safety and design standards can be obtained from the Americans with Disability Act (ADA).

The three major national standards commonly referenced are the Americans with Disability Act Accessibility Guidelines (ADAAG); the Uniform Federal Accessibility Standards (UFAS); and the American National Standards Institute (ANSI). Although all three share many of the same standards there are some differences (edge protection heights and railing heights are two examples), therefore the applicable standard for a specific project should be followed (for example, a Federal government project would likely need to follow UFAS requirements). For most differences, there is an overlap that can be incorporated into the design that will meet all three standards (for example a railing height of 34 in. would meet the 30 to 34 in. UFAS standard and would also meet the 34 to 38 in. ANSI and ADAAG standards).

Although most states and municipalities defer to the major national standards, there may be slight deviations or differences in interpretation. Therefore, in addition to these national standards and guidelines, local laws and regulations related to accessibility should always be checked.

Assessing Site Conditions

The following existing conditions need to be assessed and confirmed with accurate dimension and elevation information:

- What is the overall elevation change that the proposed ramp will need to accommodate?
- Is there a slope to the pavement at either the top or bottom that might influence where the ramp should be located to minimize the

difference in elevation between the top and bottom of the ramp, thus requiring a shorter run?

- What will be the best layout for the ramp that will allow users to enter, exit and travel a similar route as those who use the stairs?
- Are there any obstacles (such as light poles, manholes, drains, building protrusions, etc.) that may pose a conflict with the proposed ramp?
- If the ramp is to be constructed to the entrance of a building, is there sufficient space for a landing, has the direction of the door swing and hinge side been taken into account to determine the correct dimension and shape of the landing?
- If a ramp will need to extend into the sidewalk, are there applicable building codes that need to be taken into account?
- The existing conditions and ramp design must take into account the requirement for handrail extensions at the top and bottom of the ramp, and those handrail extensions should not project out perpendicular to the direction of pedestrian traffic.

Acceptable Practices

General

All ramps must comply with the Americans with Disability Act (ADA) and the Americans with Disability Act Accessibility Guidelines (ADAAG). In addition, there may be local ordinances that contain guidelines that must be complied with. There are some very basic principles that must be considered during the design and construction phases which are critically important for compliance. All too often a ramp is constructed that does not comply with the guidelines and cannot be corrected without removing the work that has been done and starting over again. Many of the ramps that do not comply have problems with landings or handrails that have been designed or constructed incorrectly. The following sections will highlight some of these basic principles that need to be checked carefully and give examples of the types of common problems that need to be avoided.

Ramp Slope

As much as existing grade will allow, the least possible slope should be used for any ramp. In situations where the slope equals or exceeds 5%, ramps are necessary and must conform to ADA and all other applicable standards. The maximum slope must be 1:12 (8.33%) for a maximum rise of 30 in. that equals a horizontal distance of

30 ft, where a landing would be required. A ramp that slopes between 5% and 6.25% can have a 40 ft horizontal distance between landings.

▶ Curved ramps although allowable must meet all ramp criteria. For slope this means that the shortest distance along the curve (the inside radius) must be calculated for the slope percentage and the longest distance (the outside radius) for the distance between landings.

Be aware that there are construction tolerances in the field that are normal and must be taken into account. In order to ensure that the entire ramp conforms to an 8.33% maximum it would be advisable to design the ramp with a maximum of an 8% slope or less. Any slight variations in slope that might develop along a small segment of the ramp run will then not likely exceed the 8.33% maximum allowed.

Cross slopes on ramp landings are necessary to provide adequate drainage to prevent water from pooling on the surface. The cross slope of ramp surfaces must be no greater than 1:50, or 2%. Ramp surfaces must be stable, compact, and otherwise slip-resistant. For concrete ramps this usually is accomplished by applying a broom finish to the concrete surface, perpendicular to the direction of pedestrian traffic.

Ramp Clear Width

A ramp's clear width is the dimension that specifies the overall ramp opening that is free from protruding objects. Ramp clear widths are determined according to the type and intensity of use. One-way pedestrian travel requires a minimum clear width of 36 in., and two-way travel requires a clear minimum width of 5 ft. It is important to consider the distance between handrails for the clear width if they project into the ramp's travel zone.

Figure 12.28 Maximum and minimum slopes for ramps.
Source: Hopper, Landscape Architectural Graphic Standards. Copyright ©2007 by John Wiley & Sons, Inc. Reprinted by permission of John Wiley & Sons, Inc.

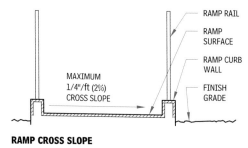

RAMP CROSS SLOPE

Figure 12.29 Ramp cross slopes should be a maximum of 2%. On the ramp surface a cross slope allows water to drain along one edge of the ramp surface instead of sheet draining down the entire ramp surface. On landings, a cross slope prevents ponding and allows any water to continue draining down to the bottom of the ramp.

Source: Hopper, Landscape Architectural Graphic Standards. Copyright ©2007 by John Wiley & Sons, Inc. Reprinted by permission of John Wiley & Sons, Inc.

Ramp Landings

Ramp landings are areas of transition that signal the beginning and ending of grade changes along steep circulation routes. Ramps should have level landings at the top and bottom of each ramp segment. Ramps longer than 30 ft should have a landing in between each 30-in. ramp rise segment to allow for pauses when negotiating long slopes. (Refer to the Americans with Disabilities Act Accessibility Guidelines (ADAAG) for a comprehensive compilation of dimensional criteria, as well as to all applicable state and local codes.) According to the Americans with Disabilities Act, all landings should have the following features:

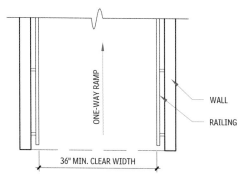

ONE-WAY RAMP CLEAR WIDTH

Figure 12.30 One-way pedestrian travel requires a clear width of 36 in. Note that the 36 in. is measured from edge of handrail to edge of handrail, not from wall edge to wall edge. It is not uncommon to have a contractor measure the wall to wall dimension and build the walls 36 in. apart. With the installation of the railings, the ramp no longer has the required clear width.

Source: Hopper, Landscape Architectural Graphic Standards. Copyright ©2007 by John Wiley & Sons, Inc. Reprinted by permission of John Wiley & Sons, Inc.

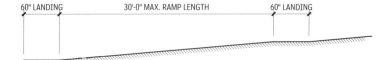

RAMP LANDING FREQUENCY

Figure 12.31 Ramps require landings at a maximum rise of 30 in. which for the most common ramps that slope between 6.25% and 8.33% would be every 30 horizontal ft.
Source: Hopper, Landscape Architectural Graphic Standards. Copyright ©2007 by John Wiley & Sons, Inc. Reprinted by permission of John Wiley & Sons, Inc.

- Landings should be at least as wide as the ramp leading to it;
- Landings should have a minimum clear length of 60 in. from the end of the ramp;
- Landings should have a minimum clear dimension of 60 by 60 in. if the ramps change direction;
- Landings shall have a 2% maximum cross slope for drainage purposes.

▶ For ramp runs that extend just over the 30-ft threshold required for a landing, it is advisable to locate the landing in the middle of the run as opposed to near one end or the other.

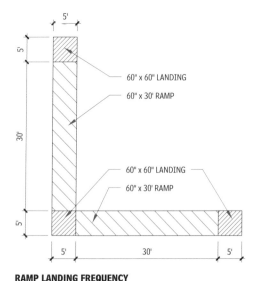

RAMP LANDING FREQUENCY

Figure 12.32 Ramps require landings wherever there is a change in direction.
Source: Hopper, Landscape Architectural Graphic Standards. Copyright ©2007 by John Wiley & Sons, Inc. Reprinted by permission of John Wiley & Sons, Inc.

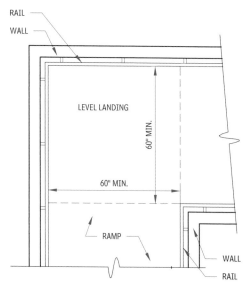

MINIMUM CLEAR WIDTH AT LANDINGS WITH 90° TURN

Figure 12.33 Landings require a clear width of 5 ft (square) at changes in direction. For switchback ramps the 5-ft-square clear widths can overlap.

Source: Hopper, Landscape Architectural Graphic Standards. Copyright ©2007 by John Wiley & Sons, Inc. Reprinted by permission of John Wiley & Sons, Inc.

Ramp Edge Protection

Ramps and landings where the edges drop off to a lower finish grade should have curbs, walls, railings, or other vertically projecting elements to prevent people from slipping and falling off the ramp edge. Edge protection should be a minimum of 2 in. for Federal projects subject to the Uniform Federal Accessibility Standards (UFAS) or minimum of 4 in. for other projects, in accordance with the American National Standards Institute (ANSI) in height (use applicable standard).

Edge protection is often provided by the supporting curb or cheek-wall that is adjacent to the ramp surface, also providing anchoring for the railing. Edge protection can also be provided by a continuous horizontal plate attached to the length of the railing at the bottom.

Handrails at Ramps

If a ramp run has a rise greater than 6 in. or a horizontal projection greater than 72 in., it should have handrails on each side. Handrails are not required on curb ramps at street intersections. (Refer to the Americans with Disabilities Act Accessibility Guidelines (ADAAG) for a comprehensive compilation of dimensional criteria and to all applicable

Figure 12.34 This 5-ft-square landing at the bottom of the ramp allows a person in a wheelchair the opportunity to easily change direction to either go up the ramp or stop and turn at the bottom to enter the walkway. Note that the edge protection is in place along the entire perimeter of the landing; the horizontal handrail extensions allow a person to grasp the rail either before going up the slope or after getting onto the level landing; the handrail extensions do not project into the 5-ft opening of the landing.

state and local codes.) According to the Americans with Disabilities Act, all handrails must have the following features:

- Handrails must be provided along both sides of ramp segments. The inside handrail on switchback or dogleg ramps must always be continuous;
- If handrails are not continuous, they must extend at least 12 in. (305 mm) beyond the top and bottom of the ramp segment and be parallel with the floor or ground surface;
- The clear space between the handrail and the wall must be 1½ in. (38 mm). This is not a minimum or maximum, it is an absolute dimension that allows someone using a wheelchair to rest their arm on the railing without it being caught between the rail and wall;
- Gripping surfaces must be continuous;
- Handrail diameters shall have a circular cross section of between 1-¼ to 2 in. to meet the ANSI standards or 1-¼ to 1-½ in. to meet ADAAG and UFAS.

▶ When specifying the material and size to be used for a railing remember that pipe is specified by its inside diameter and tubing is specified by its outside diameter. Therefore a 1-in. Schedule

Figure 12.35 Edge protection is provided by extending the top of the supporting curb to a height above the ramp surface to meet the edge protection requirement on the left and by the wall on the right. The distance between the handrail and the wall should be 1-¹/₂".

40 pipe used for a handrail would have an outside diameter of approximately 1-³/₈ in. (1 in. plus the wall thickness of a Schedule 40 pipe). A 1-¹/₂ in. tube would have an outside diameter of 1-¹/₂in. and the thickness of the tube would need to be specified.

- Top of handrail gripping surfaces must be mounted between 30 and 34 in. (UFAS) and between 34 and 38 in. (ADAAG and ANSI) above ramp surfaces;

▶ A railing that measures 34 in. to the top of the rail will meet UFAS, ADAAG and ANSI standards.

- Ends of handrails must be either rounded or returned smoothly to floor, wall, or post;
- Handrails must not rotate within their fittings.

▶ Many ramps that would be considered non-compliant with ADA standards do not have the required 12-in. horizontal handrail extensions beyond the slope of the ramp at the bottom and/or top.

Wood Ramp Construction

All wood ramp construction should have the following characteristics:

- All wood board materials should be pressure-treated or be cut from naturally rot-resistant wood (cedar, redwood, etc.);

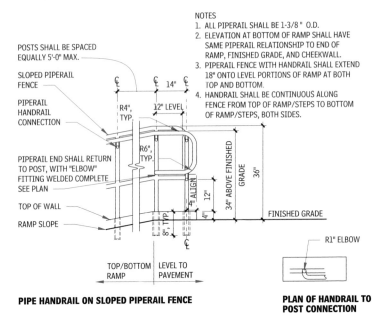

PIPE HANDRAIL ON SLOPED PIPERAIL FENCE

PLAN OF HANDRAIL TO POST CONNECTION

Figure 12.36 This design detail example of a 1-$\frac{3}{8}$ in. outside diameter handrail attached to a pipe rail barrier is measured 34 in. from the top of the gripping surface to the ramp surface; it extends onto the level surface at the top of the ramp 12 in. and then an additional 6 in. for the radius that returns the handrail back to the post where it is attached; a note is included that this same handrail extension is required at the bottom of the ramp.
Source: Hopper, Landscape Architectural Graphic Standards. Copyright ©2007 by John Wiley & Sons, Inc. Reprinted by permission of John Wiley & Sons, Inc.

- All metal fasteners should be hot-dip-galvanized or contain a corrosion-resistant finish;
- All wood post footings should be installed below frost line depth
- Beam and joist sizes and lengths vary depending on structural load and length of span

Concrete Ramp Construction

All concrete ramp construction should have the following characteristics:

- Steel reinforcing specifications vary for each construction situation. Check all local building codes before specifying size and spacing of steel reinforcement;
- All ramp surfaces should be slip-resistant with a medium broom finish, perpendicular to the direction of travel;
- Expansion joints are needed at the base and top of the ramp. Expansion joints are also needed on each side of the ramp when

Figure 12.37 Horizontal handrail extension 1 ft beyond sloping portion of surface at the bottom of the ramp.

these are constructed adjacent to cheekwalls, buildings, or other fixed objects. Seal expansion joints with a compatible joint-sealing compound to prevent moisture infiltration. A compacted gravel or compacted soil (95% standard Proctor Test) sub-base should be incorporated under all concrete ramps;

- Transitions from ramp surfaces to adjacent walks, gutters, or streets should be smooth, flush connections that are free from abrupt changes.

Masonry Ramp Construction

All masonry ramp construction should have the following characteristics:

- Masonry ramps should be constructed of paving material the same thickness and type as adjacent surfaces, unless visual or textural cues are desired to differentiate elevation changes. In such cases, use both visual and textural cues to warn pedestrians of the ramp and upcoming change in elevation;
- Steel reinforcing specifications vary for each construction situation. Check all local building codes before specifying size and spacing of steel reinforcement;
- Expansion joints are needed at the base and top of the ramp. Expansion joints are also needed on each side of the ramp when these are constructed adjacent to cheekwalls, buildings, or other

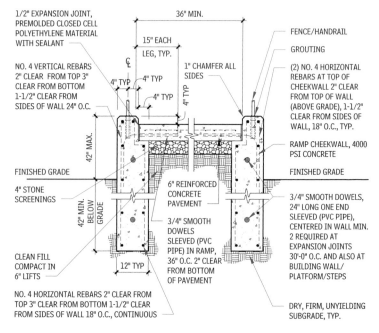

Figure 12.38 Typical concrete ramp detail with two cheekwalls.
Source: Hopper, Landscape Architectural Graphic Standards. Copyright ©2007 by John Wiley & Sons, Inc. Reprinted by permission of John Wiley & Sons, Inc.

fixed objects. Seal expansion joints with a compatible joint-sealing compound to prevent moisture infiltration. A compacted gravel or compacted soil (95% standard Proctor) sub-base should be incorporated under all ramps;

- Transitions from ramp surfaces to adjacent walks, gutters, or streets should be smooth, flush connections that are free from abrupt changes.

Practices to Avoid

There are many conditions that can make a ramp non-compliant with the standards, that could be easily avoidable during the evaluation of the existing conditions and design phase as well as situations that can be addressed during the construction phase that can avoid costly removal and replacement of construction completed incorrectly.

- One of the most common mistakes to avoid that can make a ramp non-compliant is the lack of the correct horizontal handrail extensions beyond the sloping portion of the ramp at both the top and

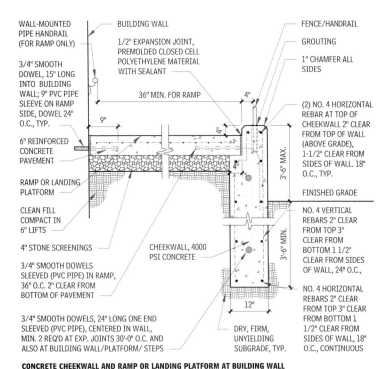

WALL-MOUNTED PIPE HANDRAIL (FOR RAMP ONLY)

BUILDING WALL

FENCE/HANDRAIL

GROUTING

3/4" SMOOTH DOWEL, 15" LONG INTO BUILDING WALL; 9" PVC PIPE SLEEVE ON RAMP SIDE, DOWEL 24" O.C., TYP.

1/2" EXPANSION JOINT, PREMOLDED CLOSED CELL POLYETHYLENE MATERIAL WITH SEALANT

1" CHAMFER ALL SIDES

36" MIN. FOR RAMP

4"

9"

4"

(2) NO. 4 HORIZONTAL REBAR AT TOP OF CHEEKWALL 2" CLEAR FROM TOP OF WALL (ABOVE GRADE), 1-1/2" CLEAR FROM SIDES OF WALL. 18" O.C., TYP.

6" REINFORCED CONCRETE PAVEMENT

4"

3'-6" MAX.

RAMP OR LANDING PLATFORM

FINISHED GRADE

CLEAN FILL COMPACT IN 6" LIFTS

NO. 4 VERTICAL REBARS 2" CLEAR FROM TOP 3" CLEAR FROM BOTTOM 1 1/2" CLEAR FROM SIDES OF WALL, 24" O.C.,

4" STONE SCREENINGS

CHEEKWALL, 4000 PSI CONCRETE

3'-6" MIN.

3/4" SMOOTH DOWELS SLEEVED (PVC PIPE) IN RAMP, 36" O.C. 2" CLEAR FROM BOTTOM OF PAVEMENT

NO. 4 HORIZONTAL REBARS 2" CLEAR FROM TOP 3" CLEAR FROM BOTTOM 1 1/2" CLEAR FROM SIDES OF WALL, 18" O.C., CONTINUOUS

12"

3/4" SMOOTH DOWELS, 24" LONG ONE END SLEEVED (PVC PIPE), CENTERED IN WALL, MIN. 2 REQ'D AT EXP. JOINTS 30'-0" O.C. AND ALSO AT BUILDING WALL/PLATFORM/ STEPS

DRY, FIRM, UNYIELDING SUBGRADE, TYP.

CONCRETE CHEEKWALL AND RAMP OR LANDING PLATFORM AT BUILDING WALL

Figure 12.39 Concrete with cheekwall and ramp along building wall. It is very important in these types of situations to take into account the wall-mounted handrail when calculating the clear width and the distance the cheekwall must be constructed to allow for the required width.
Source: Hopper, Landscape Architectural Graphic Standards. Copyright ©2007 by John Wiley & Sons, Inc. Reprinted by permission of John Wiley & Sons, Inc.

bottom and including a handrail on both sides of the ramp. During the existing conditions evaluation and design phase, it is important to incorporate the required space needed into the design and then clearly show this on the contract drawings.

- Many ramps do not comply with ADA standards because they do not have the required horizontal handrail extensions at the top and/or bottom. In some cases, modifying the handrails to meet the requirement is not possible because extending the handrails would project them into a pedestrian circulation path, interfere with the required clear width, reduce the size of the required landing or would interfere with entering or exiting out a door.
- In order for horizontal handrails to be most useful for those in a wheelchair, the extension of the handrails should be in the same direction of travel as the ramp, allowing a wheelchair user the opportunity to grasp the handrail prior to starting down (or up) the ramp.

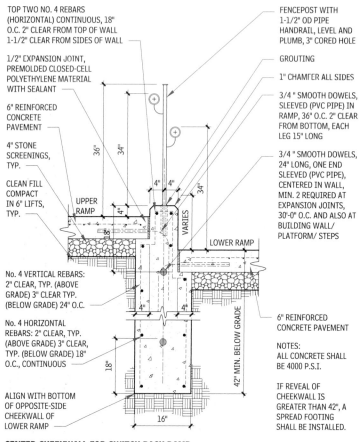

TOP TWO NO. 4 REBARS
(HORIZONTAL) CONTINUOUS, 18"
O.C. 2" CLEAR FROM TOP OF WALL
1-1/2" CLEAR FROM SIDES OF WALL

1/2" EXPANSION JOINT,
PREMOLDED CLOSED-CELL
POLYETHYLENE MATERIAL
WITH SEALANT

6" REINFORCED
CONCRETE
PAVEMENT

4" STONE
SCREENINGS,
TYP.

CLEAN FILL
COMPACT
IN 6" LIFTS,
TYP.

UPPER
RAMP

No. 4 VERTICAL REBARS:
2" CLEAR, TYP. (ABOVE
GRADE) 3" CLEAR TYP.
(BELOW GRADE) 24" O.C.

No. 4 HORIZONTAL
REBARS: 2" CLEAR, TYP.
(ABOVE GRADE) 3" CLEAR,
TYP. (BELOW GRADE) 18"
O.C., CONTINUOUS

ALIGN WITH BOTTOM
OF OPPOSITE-SIDE
CHEEKWALL OF
LOWER RAMP

FENCEPOST WITH
1-1/2" OD PIPE
HANDRAIL, LEVEL AND
PLUMB, 3" CORED HOLE

GROUTING

1" CHAMFER ALL SIDES

3/4 " SMOOTH DOWELS,
SLEEVED (PVC PIPE) IN
RAMP, 36" O.C. 2" CLEAR
FROM BOTTOM, EACH
LEG 15" LONG

3/4 " SMOOTH DOWELS,
24" LONG, ONE END
SLEEVED (PVC PIPE),
CENTERED IN WALL,
MIN. 2 REQUIRED AT
EXPANSION JOINTS,
30'-0" O.C. AND ALSO AT
BUILDING WALL/
PLATFORM/ STEPS

LOWER RAMP

6" REINFORCED
CONCRETE PAVEMENT

NOTES:
ALL CONCRETE SHALL
BE 4000 P.S.I.

IF REVEAL OF
CHEEKWALL IS
GREATER THAN 42", A
SPREAD FOOTING
SHALL BE INSTALLED.

VARIES

42" MIN. BELOW GRADE

CENTER CHEEKWALL FOR SWITCH BACK RAMP

Figure 12.40 Center cheekwall for a switchback ramp.
Source: Hopper, Landscape Architectural Graphic Standards. Copyright ©2007 by John Wiley & Sons, Inc. Reprinted by permission of John Wiley & Sons, Inc.

- Checking the construction at critical steps along the way is important. Inspecting the work after it is completed, if done incorrectly, often times cannot be modified and needs to be removed and redone.
- Temporary ramps should be constructed to meet all applicable standards. As is often the case, temporary measures can end up remaining in place for quite a bit longer than intended, often becoming a permanent installation. There should be no assumptions made that because prefabricated ramps are available that they meet these standards.

Figure 12.41 The common choice of using painted galvanized pipe, even when prepared, primed and painted properly, will wear and chip with heavy use. It might be best to leave the handrail with its galvanized finish, or if a color is desired, consider another choice such as an anodized or powder-coated metal for the handrail. Stainless steel and aluminum are also good choices for unpainted handrails that will continue to look good even with heavy use.

Figure 12.42 Seen from a distance the peeling and chipping paint from the handrail is not very attractive. Neither is that lack of required horizontal handrail extensions on the bottom of both the stair and ramp. Note that if the ramp and stair had the correct handrail extensions, the opening to the level platform at the bottom of the ramp would not meet the required 5'- ft dimension.

Figure 12.43 This prefabricated ramp has the required edge protection but not the required horizontal handrail extensions.

Figure 12.44 This prefabricated ramp does not have the required horizontal handrail extensions at the top or the bottom of the ramp nor does it have the required edge protection. The horizontal steel plate has a gap between the bottom of the steel plate and the ramp surface making it non-compliant. A more serious problem exists at the top of the ramp where the lack of a proper sized landing (note the location of the door hinge which puts the latch side of the door at the top step of the stair with little clearance from the edge of the door) puts a wheelchair user at serious risk of falling down the stairs as that person tries to negotiate to or from the entrance door and the top of the ramp. Unfortunately, this looks to be a permanent solution to making this entrance accessible.

Figure 12.45 Viewed from this angle it is clear that without the required horizontal handrail extensions and the close proximity of the latch side of the door to the top step of the stair this is a hazardous situation. The configuration and relationship between the entrance door, the door swing, the top of steps and top of ramp should have been more clearly thought out. Just because something can be done with prefabricated ramps and stairs does not make it right or safe. It is important that components meeting all ramp requirements be chosen and that they be configured in a way that is tailored to the unique conditions of where they are to be installed.

Curb Ramps, Blended Transitions and Detectable Warning Surfaces

Description

Curb ramps are small, short ramps that provide accessible transitions at street curbs and other short elevation changes. Curb ramps should be provided wherever an accessible route crosses a curbed street or intersection.

Blended transitions are connections between the pedestrian access route and the level of the street or crosswalk that have a running slope of 1:20 or less (5% or less). Level landings, gently sloped transitions, and raised crosswalks fall into this category.

A Detectable Warning Surface is defined by ADAAG as "a standardized surface feature built in or applied to walking surfaces or other elements to warn visually impaired people of hazards on a circulation path".

Detectable warnings were required in 1991 by the Americans with Disabilities Act Accessible Guideline (ADAAG) (regulatory standards) for hazardous vehicular ways, transit platform edges, and curb ramps. In 1994 a suspension was placed on requiring detectable warnings at curb ramps and hazardous vehicular ways, but not for transit platform edges.

During the time the suspension was in effect (ending on July 26, 2001), research was conducted to evaluate how effective the different methods being used were at providing a detectable warning. The results of this research were that grooves, striations, and exposed aggregate were not detectable in the sidewalk and roadway environment because of the similarities to other surface textures and defects.

It was determined that truncated domes are the only alternative to provide an effective detectable warning. Their unique design is easily identified by sound on cane contact and underfoot. The required contrasting color makes it visually detectable from the surrounding surface.

▶ The original ADA design standard for truncated domes is found in ADAAG (4.29.2). After the research was conducted, a new design recommendation was made for the dimension and placement of the domes on curb ramps. Both FHWA and the U.S. Access Board are encouraging the use of the new design over the original.

Assessing Site Conditions

Curb ramps should be provided wherever an accessible route crosses a curb. The least possible slope should be used. The maximum rise for a curb ramp is 6 in. If work is being done adjacent to an existing curb ramp that is not fully compliant with current requirements (this may include sidewalk replacement or road reconstruction or resurfacing), the existing curb should be modified or a curb ramp that meets all requirements (if technically feasible) should be constructed at the same time as the other work is being done.

Detectable warnings are required on the surfaces of curb ramps, hazardous drop-offs, along the perimeter of reflecting pools and wherever pedestrian routes blend with vehicular ways in order to alert people with vision impairments to these approaching situations.

▶ At the time of this writing, ADAAG and draft guidelines on public rights-of-way to supplement ADAAG are being reviewed and updated. In the following acceptable practices the current ADAAG and new draft guidelines are both noted where applicable. The new guidelines represent experience and research completed since the ADAAG were first issued in 1991, and may represent a more effective approach to accessibility. If feasible, they may be incorporated into the design, as they generally comply with and improve upon the original ADAAG. The latest guidelines should always be checked, as updates to the original ADAAG are planned.

Acceptable Practices

Slope

The most recent draft guidelines that are being recommended for new construction require perpendicular curb ramps to have a running slope that cuts through or is built up to the curb at right angles or meets the gutter grade break at right angles. Parallel curb ramps shall have a running slope that is in-line with the direction of sidewalk travel. The running slope for both shall be 5% minimum (1:20) and 8.33% maximum (1:12). However, the required slope range shall not require the ramp length to exceed 15 ft. The cross slope at intersections shall be 2% maximum. The cross slope at midblock crossings shall be permitted to be warped to meet street or highway grade.

For a perpendicular curb ramp, a landing 4 ft by 4 ft minimum shall be provided at the top of the curb ramp and shall be permitted to overlap other landings and clear space. For a parallel curb ramp, a landing 4 ft by 4 ft minimum shall be provided at the bottom of the ramp run and shall be permitted to overlap other landings and clear floor or ground space.

Running slope and cross slopes at intersections shall be 2% maximum. The counter slope of the gutter or street at the foot of a curb ramp, landing, or blended transition shall be 5% maximum. Running and cross slope at midblock crossings shall be permitted to be warped to meet street or highway grade. Where a parallel curb ramp does not occupy the entire width of a sidewalk, drop-offs at diverging segments shall be protected.

Blended transitions shall have a 5% maximum running slope and a 2% maximum cross slope.

For modifications of existing construction, ADAAG currently has additional provisions. If space limitations prohibit the use of a 1:12 slope or less, curb ramps to be constructed on existing sites or in existing buildings or facilities can be built with the following slopes and rises:

- A slope between 1:10 and 1:12 is allowed for a maximum rise of 6 in. (150 mm);
- A slope between 1:8 and 1:10 is allowed for a maximum rise of 3 in. (75 mm);
- Slopes steeper than 1:8 are not allowed.

▶ Transitions from ramp surfaces to adjacent walks or streets should be smooth, flush connections that are free from abrupt changes.

Sides of Curb Ramps

If a curb ramp is located where pedestrians must walk across the ramp, or where it is not protected by handrails or guardrails, it shall have flared sides; the maximum slope of the flare shall be 1:10. Curb ramps with returned curbs may be used where pedestrians would not normally walk across the ramp.

Width

The current ADAAG requires a minimum width of a curb ramp to be 36 in. (915 mm), exclusive of flared sides. The new draft guidelines require the clear width of landings, blended transitions, and curb ramps, excluding flares, to be 4 ft minimum.

The new draft guidelines also require, beyond the curb face, a clear space of 4 ft by 4 ft minimum to be provided within the width of the crosswalk and wholly outside the parallel vehicle travel lane.

Curb ramps shall be located or protected to prevent their obstruction by parked vehicles. Built-up curb ramps shall be located so that they do not project into vehicular traffic lanes.

Surface

The surface of curb ramps, landings and blended transitions shall be stable, firm and slip resistant. Gratings, access covers, and other appurtenances shall not be located on curb ramps, landings, blended transitions, and gutters within the pedestrian access route.

The original ADAAG required a curb ramp to have a detectable warning that extends the full width and depth of the curb ramp. Both FHWA and the U.S. Access Board are encouraging the use of the new design over the original. The new draft guidelines require the following:

- Detectable warnings shall consist of raised truncated domes in a detectable warning surface with a base diameter of 23 mm (0.9 in.) minimum to 36 mm (1.4 in.) maximum, a top diameter of 50% of the base diameter minimum to 65% of the base diameter maximum, and a height of 5 mm (0.2 in.);
- Truncated domes in a detectable warning surface shall have a center-to-center spacing of 41 mm (1.6 in.) minimum and 61 mm (2.4 in.) maximum, and a base-to-base spacing of 17 mm (0.65 in.) minimum, measured between the most adjacent domes;
- Detectable warning surfaces shall contrast visually with adjacent gutter, street or highway, or walkway surfaces, either light-on-dark or dark-on-light;
- The material used to provide contrast shall be an integral part of the walking surface. Detectable warnings used on interior surfaces shall differ from adjoining walking surfaces in resiliency or sound-on-cane contact;
- One corner of the detectable warning must be within 8 in. of the grade break; no other point on the leading edge of the detectable warning may be more than 5 ft from the grade break.
- Detectable warning surfaces shall extend 610 mm (24 in.) minimum in the direction of travel and the full width of the curb ramp (exclusive of flares), the landing, or the blended transition;
- For perpendicular curb ramps, where both ends of the bottom grade break are 5 ft or less from the back of curb, the detectable warning shall be located on the ramp surface at the bottom grade break. Where either end of the bottom grade break is more than 5 ft from the back of curb, the detectable warning shall be located on the lower landing.

For landings and blended transitions, the detectable warning shall be located on the landing or blended transition at the back of curb.

The rows of truncated domes in a detectable warning surface shall be aligned to be perpendicular or radial to the grade break between the ramp, landing, or blended transition and the street.

For rail crossings, the detectable warning surface shall be located so that the edge nearest the rail crossing is 6 ft minimum and 15 ft maximum from the centerline of the nearest rail. The rows of truncated domes in a detectable warning surface shall be aligned to be parallel with the direction of wheelchair travel.

▶ **The revised specifications are responsive to concerns that had been raised about the impact of the truncated dome surface on wheelchair maneuvering. The draft revised specifications, which permit wider dome spacing, an in-line grid pattern, and smaller surface coverage at curb ramps (24 in. instead of the full ramp length, set back from the curbline) will improve usability of surfaces without affecting detectability.**

There are many manufacturers that supply detectable warning surfaces of different materials with varying installation procedures. It is important that the manufacturer's installation directions are followed, and the resulting slopes and distances checked after installation to ensure compliance with the requirements.

Figure 12.46   Research concluded that grooves, striations, and exposed aggregate were not detectable in the sidewalk and roadway environment because of the similarities to other surface textures and defects.

Figure 12.47 The FHWA and U.S. Access Board encourage the use of truncated domes as the only effective detectable warning surface.

Practices to Avoid

Avoid designing or constructing curb ramps, landings or blended transitions that do not meet the legal requirements. As many of these requirements are currently in review with planned updates forthcoming, a review of the requirements prior to the start of construction is an important step to confirm that no changes have taken place since the design was completed.

Local municipalities will sometimes have additional or slightly different requirements for accessibility. In addition to the national standards, check applicable local codes and regulations to ensure compliance.

References

OTHER RESOURCES:

- ADA Accessibility Guidelines (ADAAG) - 1991, amended through 2002.
- American National Standards Institute - ANSI A117.1-2003, Accessible and Usable Buildings and Facilities Standards.
- Federal Highway Administration, Revised Draft Guidelines for Accessible Public Rights of Way, 2005.
- Uniform Federal Accessibility Standards, 1984.

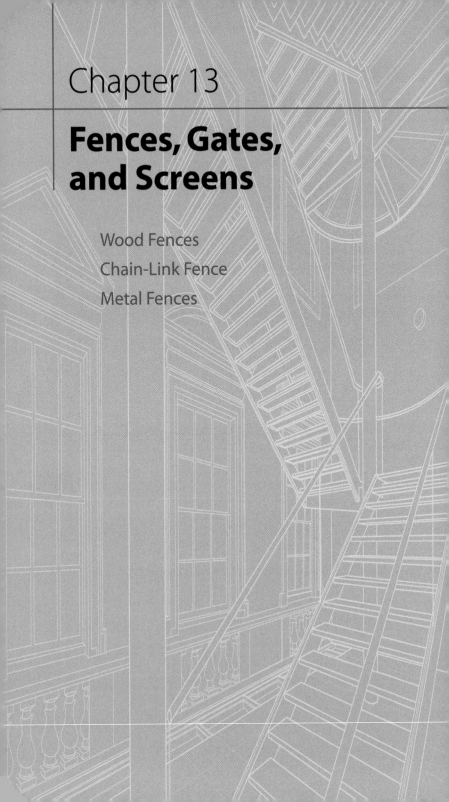

Chapter 13

Fences, Gates, and Screens

Wood Fences

Description

Wood fences have a long history of defining and dividing spaces, expressing and defending ownership, and creating sense of enclosure and privacy. Wood fences combine posts with rails, pickets or panels in a variety of different styles that can complement most any context.

Assessing Site Conditions

The two primary considerations for wood fence and gate design involve:

- Layout, and deciding where on-site the fence can and should go. If the fence is a boundary fence, its layout and height will be limited by property line setbacks.
- Degree of opacity of the fence design. Will the fence be a privacy wall, define the edges of the property, or create a barrier?

Both the layout and detailing of the fence can be designed to resist and dissipate the lateral forces of wind, extending the life of the structure. A straight, solid run of any fencing will be the weakest form, as it is solely reliant on the posts for wind resistance. Almost any deviation from the straight line increases resistance to lateral forces. A fence can be a visual screen and still allow wind to pass through. Proper detailing can extend the longevity of the materials by avoiding water entrapment. Function, aesthetics, topography, wind patterns, and costs are all factors in the layout and design for opacity.

Fences can be designed using prefabricated panels and posts, standard dimensioned lumber, or customized ornaments. This tremendous range of styles and types of wood fences, with variations in the shape and orientation of pickets, posts, balustrades, and rails, continues to evolve, but the basic construction methods remain similar for all.

Acceptable Practices

Posts

The structural integrity of any fence begins with the posts, the vertical members that connect the horizontal rails and any boards they carry down to the footing or earth. The post size is determined by the height and width of the fence panels, the combined weight of the materials used, and the character desired. In most applications with a height of 6 ft or less, and with a rail width of 8 ft or less, 4 x 4 posts are adequate for stability. If the fence is higher than 6 ft, 6 x 6 timbers are recommended for corner or end posts. If heavy gates are to be mounted, the posts should be increased to 6 x 6 or greater.

The post may be embedded into the earth, using only pressure-treated wood rated for ground contact or a naturally resistant species. The preferred installation is attachment to a concrete footing with a galvanized or stainless-steel post anchor. The footing top should be sloped to drain water away from the end grain of the post.

The footing should extend 2 to 3 in. beyond the anchor in all directions to ensure proper embedment. The depth should extend at least 2 in. below frost level and rest on compacted bearing soils. The depth also accommodates resistance to the forces of wind, weight, and any anticipated impacts. If the fence is mounted on a continuous footing or masonry wall, the post anchors are preset into the footing or wall cap, and the posts are bolted to the anchor.

Post Caps and Finials

The exposed end grain of a fence post is most susceptible to rotting. Fence caps, which are often used to shed water away from the top of the post, are often made out of redwood, cedar, cypress, mahogany, or treated wood, although metals, particularly copper, are also used. The caps should extend beyond the face of the post and be either pitched or sloped on all sides to facilitate the shedding of water. A drip groove

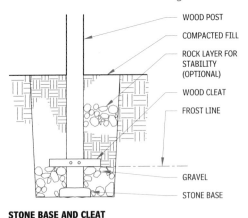

WOOD POST
COMPACTED FILL
ROCK LAYER FOR STABILITY (OPTIONAL)
WOOD CLEAT
FROST LINE
GRAVEL
STONE BASE

STONE BASE AND CLEAT

Figure 13.1   Embedded post detail—stone base and cleat gravel keeps water from collecting around end grain of post.
Source: Hopper. Landscape Architectural Graphic Standards, First Edition, Hoboken, NJ: John Wiley & Sons, 2007.

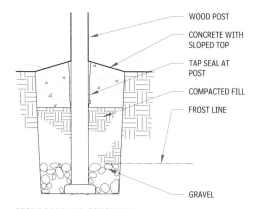

WOOD POST

CONCRETE WITH SLOPED TOP

TAP SEAL AT POST

COMPACTED FILL

FROST LINE

GRAVEL

STONE BASE AND CONCRETE CAP

Figure 13.2   Embedded post detail—stone base and concrete cap sloped away from post to direct water to sides.
Source: Hopper. Landscape Architectural Graphic Standards, First Edition, Hoboken, NJ: John Wiley & Sons, 2007.

saw cut on the underside of the cap, between the face of the cap and the face of the post, will prevent water from migrating around the edge of the cap and into the end grain of the post.

Horizontal Rails

The horizontal rails stabilize the posts from lateral movement and provide a structural frame for attaching vertical balusters, pickets, boards,

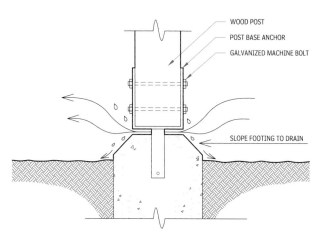

WOOD POST

POST BASE ANCHOR

GALVANIZED MACHINE BOLT

SLOPE FOOTING TO DRAIN

Figure 13.3   Typical post footing detail. Edges are rounded or chamfered to shed water. The raised post anchor prevents moisture buildup and facilitates air circulation.
Source: Hopper, Landscape Architectural Graphic Standards. Copyright 2007, John Wiley & Sons, Inc.

or lattice panels. The number of rails used depends on the height of the fence, style of design, and span between posts. With the exception of the single-rail fence (often referred to as a kick rail or guardrail), a minimum of two rails, top and bottom, are required. At heights above 4 ft, or if the vertical boards are narrow in proportion to the height, a third, or middle, rail can be added to provide additional attachment points to prevent cupping, twisting, or sagging.

Two details are commonly used to connect the rail to the post: either a recessed or a mechanical connection. An advantage of recessed connections, lap joints, dados, or mortise and tenons, where the post is sculpted to receive the rail, is that one-half of the weight of the span of material is transferred to and supported by each of the posts. Often, the notching of the post requires a cut that is deeper than the penetrating preservative, and these recessed joints and any prebored holes should receive an application of preservative before the rail is attached. When mechanical connectors such as fence brackets are employed, some of the weight of the rails and boards are transferred to the post, but significant forces, now actually shear forces, are carried by the connector. This system, though widely used, tends to negate the purpose of the post by relying on the fastener.

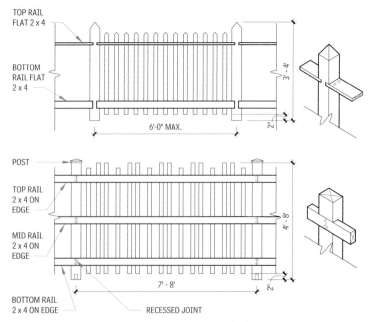

Figure 13.4 Typical two-rail fence panel used for fences up to 4 ft in height. Also shown is a three-rail fence panel which is useful for fences up to 8 ft in height.
Source: Hopper. Landscape Architectural Graphic Standards, First Edition, Hoboken, NJ: John Wiley & Sons, 2007.

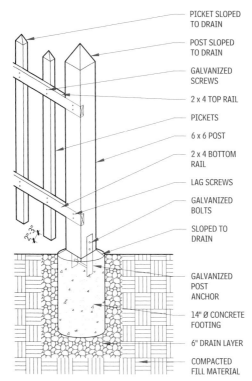

PICKET SLOPED
TO DRAIN

POST SLOPED
TO DRAIN

GALVANIZED
SCREWS

2 x 4 TOP RAIL

PICKETS

6 x 6 POST

2 x 4 BOTTOM
RAIL

LAG SCREWS

GALVANIZED
BOLTS

SLOPED TO
DRAIN

GALVANIZED
POST
ANCHOR

14" Ø CONCRETE
FOOTING

6" DRAIN LAYER

COMPACTED
FILL MATERIAL

Figure 13.5   Post footing connection with recessed rail connection.
Source: Hopper. Landscape Architectural Graphic Standards, First Edition, Hoboken, NJ: John Wiley & Sons, 2007.

Pickets, Balusters, and Boards

Many fences have vertical elements, and the most common of these are pickets, typically 1 x 2s, 1 x 4s, or 2 x 2s. These are commonly attached to the rails with galvanized nails or screws. Highly crafted fences may have pickets doweled through the rails. The top ends of the pickets may be cut to drain or shaped to create ornamental features. The infill can be designed as a prefabricated system in which the pickets and rails are preassembled as a panel and then inserted into the posts.

Balusters are vertical members that are set between the top and bottom rails. They range in height and thickness and are, in some cases, especially by historic precedent, very elaborate, turned pieces. For the attachment of simple balusters, such as 2 x 2s, a channel can be routed into the top rail to receive the balusters, and the bottoms can be set on a pitched bottom rail or rail cap and mechanically fastened. Other methods include boring or carving recesses into the rails to receive the

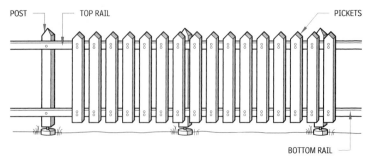

Figure 13.6 The classic picket fence can create a high proportion or visual openness by increasing the distance between pickets.
Source: Hopper, Landscape Architectural Graphic Standards. Copyright 2007, John Wiley & Sons, Inc.

balusters, or attaching a pair of horizontal members under the top rail to sandwich the top end of the balusters. The latter is not recommended on the lower rails as it will trap water.

Boards can be effectively used on smaller fences, but their width is maximized frequently in taller fences intended for privacy. The simplest, solid-board fences, using 1 x 4 or 1 x 6 vertical boards placed side to side and mechanically attached to the rails, are the least expensive but often the least interesting as well. To add visual interest, the edges of the boards are sometimes cut to create a row or field of voids in shapes such as diamonds.

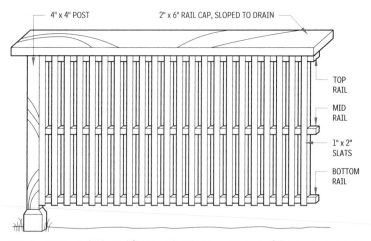

Figure 13.7 Solid board fence with rails on end is one of the most common and least costly fences.
Source: Hopper, Landscape Architectural Graphic Standards. Copyright 2007, John Wiley & Sons, Inc.

Figure 13.8 Board fence with small diamonds cut along upper portion of fence.

Transparent fences can be used where privacy is not the intent; the split-rail historic fence is an example. If transparency and security are desired, wire mesh can be attached to the post and rails.

Solid, slatted, and picket fences are, in principle, extensions of the post and rail, adding vertical members that increase the density and visual privacy of the fence. In the louvered style, 2 x 4 or 2 x 6 vertical boards are set into angles slotted into the top and bottom rails. This alignment allows visibility from an oblique angle and provides air circulation, while offering a large degree of privacy. Maximizing density are the solid fences, including vertical tongue-and-groove or ship-lapped boards; solid panels; and shadow box, where the boards alternate on each side of the rails; and board and batten.

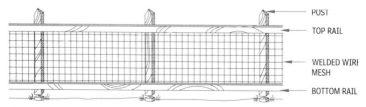

POST

TOP RAIL

WELDED WIRE MESH

BOTTOM RAIL

Figure 13.9 Wire mesh screen fence. Virtually transparent, the wire mesh screen fence used to restrict physical access is not intended for visual privacy.
Source: Hopper, Landscape Architectural Graphic Standards. Copyright 2007, John Wiley & Sons, Inc.

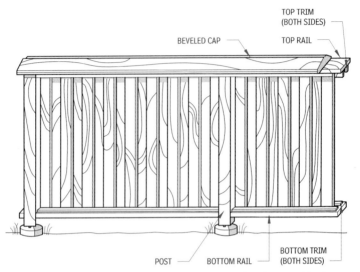

Figure 13.10 In the shadow box, the boards are offset front and back between the rails. The boards must be 2x if the midrail is eliminated.
Source: Hopper, Landscape Architectural Graphic Standards. Copyright 2007, John Wiley & Sons, Inc.

In the board and batten, 1 x 2 pieces are placed on the vertical joints between the boards. Board and batten fence adds more interest than solid board while still maintaining privacy.

A solid and semitransparent approach can be combined in the same design with different infills above and below midrail. Overhead trellising cantilevering from the posts can also be incorporated in fence design.

Gates

The gate is the focal point within a fence and can occasionally be found as a stand-alone element in the landscape. When used with a fence, it can be designed as either a complementing or contrasting element. Because the gate is a moveable structural component, it is critical that it be designed to counter the forces it is subjected to. Gate posts are typically oversized to bear the stresses caused by the weight and the motion of the gate. Depending on the dimensions of the gate, 6-in. by 6-in. solid wood post members or steel I-beams with a wood box post surround are often used. The post should be deeply embedded or mounted on an oversized footing to withstand the pull of the gate. A 3-ft depth for a small gate and at least 4 ft deep for a tall or wide gate are recommended, regardless of frost depth. For large gates at entry drives or very wide pedestrian paths, a structural engineer should be consulted to size the bearing posts and attachment mechanisms.

Figure 13.11   The boards are offset front and back between the rails, allowing a slight visual penetration and air circulation between the boards.

Figure 13.12   Basketweave type fence offers interest of texture and shadow while maintaining privacy.

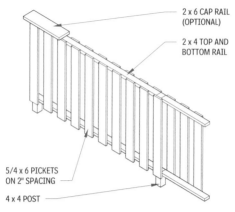

2 x 6 CAP RAIL
(OPTIONAL)

2 x 4 TOP AND
BOTTOM RAIL

5/4 x 6 PICKETS
ON 2" SPACING

4 x 4 POST

BOARD ON BOARD

Figure 13.13a

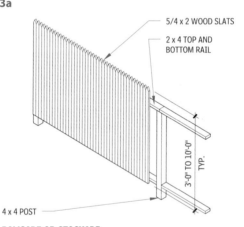

5/4 x 2 WOOD SLATS

2 x 4 TOP AND
BOTTOM RAIL

3'-0" TO 10'-0"
TYP.

4 x 4 POST

PALISADE OR STOCKADE

Figure 13.13b

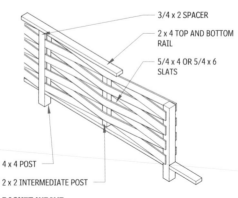

3/4 x 2 SPACER

2 x 4 TOP AND BOTTOM
RAIL

5/4 x 4 OR 5/4 x 6
SLATS

4 x 4 POST

2 x 2 INTERMEDIATE POST

BASKET WEAVE

Figure 13.13c

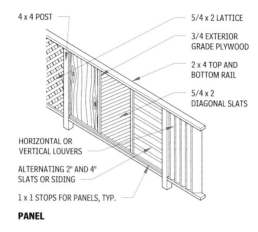

4 x 4 POST

5/4 x 2 LATTICE

3/4 EXTERIOR GRADE PLYWOOD

2 x 4 TOP AND BOTTOM RAIL

5/4 x 2 DIAGONAL SLATS

HORIZONTAL OR VERTICAL LOUVERS

ALTERNATING 2" AND 4" SLATS OR SIDING

1 x 1 STOPS FOR PANELS, TYP.

PANEL

Figure 13.13d

There are two basic gate frames: the Z-frame and the box frame. The Z-frame is simpler and is best used for gates 3 ft or less in width. It tends to be less formal than the box frame, and the rails and brace can be set flat, creating a thinner profile, while in the box style the frame must be set on edge.

The Z-frame is composed of a top and bottom rail joined by a diagonal brace crossing from the hinge-side bottom to the latch-side top. The hinges are attached to the top and bottom rails, and because the Z-frame has no vertical side members (stiles), the use of a middle hinge is not possible.

The gate connection from the swing-side stile to the post where the hinge is mounted is a critical one, and the hardware designed for hanging includes butt, "T" strap, and strap hinge/bolt systems.

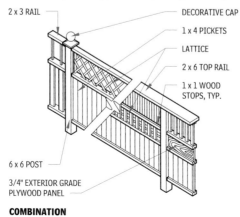

2 x 3 RAIL

DECORATIVE CAP

1 x 4 PICKETS

LATTICE

2 x 6 TOP RAIL

1 x 1 WOOD STOPS, TYP.

6 x 6 POST

3/4" EXTERIOR GRADE PLYWOOD PANEL

COMBINATION

Figure 13.13e

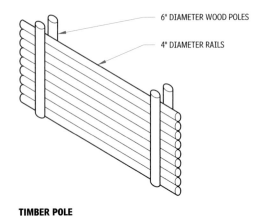

TIMBER POLE

Figure 13.13f   Wood privacy fences.
Source: Hopper, Landscape Architectural Graphic Standards. Copyright 2007,
John Wiley & Sons, Inc.

The second piece of hardware used in gate fabrication is a locking mechanism. Options range from the simplest hook and eye to spring-activated bolts. Other mechanisms include sliding bolts, hasp and locking shackle, and thumb hatches.

All the hardware required to hang and operate the gate should be considered for structural stability, aesthetics, and corrosion resistance, and should be galvanized or stainless steel.

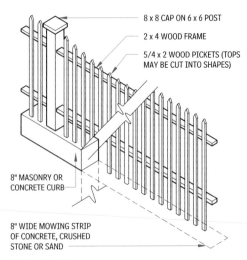

PICKET OR SLAT

Figure 13.14a

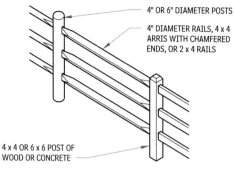

4" OR 6" DIAMETER POSTS

4" DIAMETER RAILS, 4 x 4
ARRIS WITH CHAMFERED
ENDS, OR 2 x 4 RAILS

4 x 4 OR 6 x 6 POST OF
WOOD OR CONCRETE

POST AND RAIL

Figure 13.14b

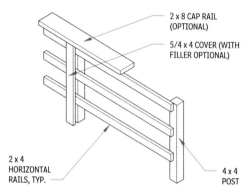

2 x 8 CAP RAIL
(OPTIONAL)

5/4 x 4 COVER (WITH
FILLER OPTIONAL)

2 x 4
HORIZONTAL
RAILS, TYP.

4 x 4
POST

POST AND BOARD (CORRAL)

Figure 13.14c

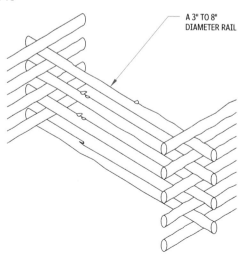

A 3" TO 8"
DIAMETER RAIL

ZIGZAG OR VIRGINIA

Figure 13.14d

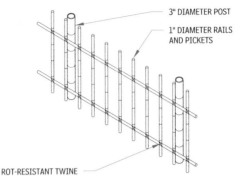

BAMBOO

Figure 13.14e

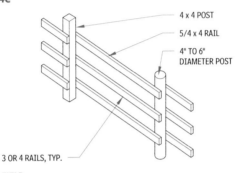

FIELD

Figure 13.14f   Wood boundary fences.
Source: Hopper, Landscape Architectural Graphic Standards. Copyright 2007,
John Wiley & Sons, Inc.

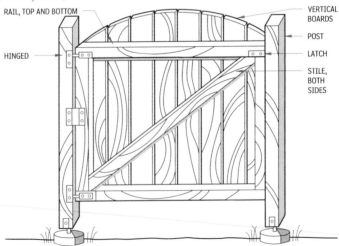

Figure 13.15   Typical Z-frame gate.
Source: Hopper, Landscape Architectural Graphic Standards. Copyright 2007,
John Wiley & Sons, Inc.

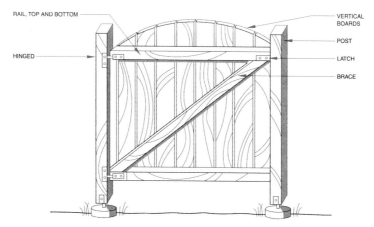

Figure 13.16 Typical box frame gate.
Source: Hopper. Landscape Architectural Graphic Standards, First Edition, Hoboken, NJ: John Wiley & Sons, 2007.

Practices to Avoid

Avoid premature deterioration of a wood fence by creating designs that:

- Protect end grains of wood members from water damage;
- Do not allow water to become trapped on horizontal members;
- Utilize post anchors that keep the end grain of wood posts elevated;
- Protect end grain at the top of posts with caps or finials.

Chain-Link Fence

Description

One of the most common types of metal fencing is the chain-link fence, which consists of posts, rails, fittings, and related hardware creating a framework that in turn supports a chain-link mesh that is stretched and attached to it. Each of the elements comes in a range of weights, thicknesses, and coatings that can address a variety of specific purposes.

Assessing Site Conditions

The lightest of chain-link fence systems does not hold up well to everyday use, as the mesh can be bent and distorted with ordinary impacts and the pipe framework is susceptible to bending. It is, therefore, important to match the appropriate strength and finish of the materials with the level of service and maintenance required for a specific application.

The strength of the chain-link fence framework is dependent on the thickness and the diameter of the pipe specified. The type of protective coating specified will affect the framework's longevity and level of maintenance. Pipe gauges in residential chain-link fence applications range from 20 (the lightest) to 15 (heavier). Commercial and heavy-duty applications often call for a Schedule 40 (Sch 40) pipe. In addition to thickness, the pipe should be made with a tensile strength of the steel that must have a minimum yield strength of 45,000 pounds per square in. The other factor affecting strength is the diameter of the pipe: the greater the diameter, the more steel, making for a stronger pipe and resulting in a stronger chain-link fence framework.

A galvanized zinc coating is the most common protective finish for the chain-link fence framework. The pipe is galvanized using one of three processes:

- An inline flow-coat process, which has the steel passing through molten zinc as it is formed into pipe;
- Pregalvanized pipe, whereby the metal is galvanized prior to being formed into pipe;
- Hot-dipped galvanized pipe, which is made by taking the formed pipe and completely immersing it in a tank of molten zinc.

The framework can be specified with a color coating on top of the galvanized pipe by calling either for a polyvinyl coating (10 to 14 mil) or a polyester powder coating (3 mil). Powder coating over galvanized metal requires careful preparation of the galvanized metal prior to the electrostatic application of the polyester powdered resins. Both coatings, when properly applied, result in good color and an additional layer of protection for the pipe.

Chain-link fence pipe framework can be conventionally painted using the proper primer and finish coat for galvanized metals. As with all outdoor painted surfaces, this method will require regular maintenance to be effective and remain aesthetically pleasing in appearance over time.

Acceptable Practices

Chain-Link Fence Framework

- Gateposts, end posts, and corner posts are generally larger than the typical line post.

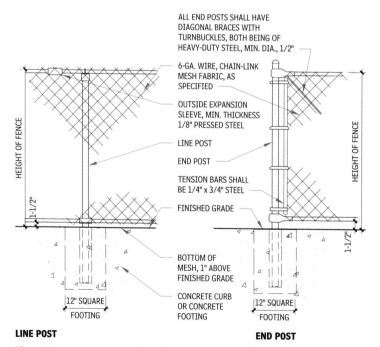

Figure 13.17 Typical chain-link fence line and end post detail.
Source: Hopper. Landscape Architectural Graphic Standards, First Edition, Hoboken, NJ: John Wiley & Sons, 2007.

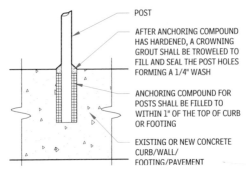

Figure 13.18 Typical post grouting detail.
Source: Hopper. Landscape Architectural Graphic Standards, First Edition, Hoboken, NJ: John
Wiley & Sons, 2007.

- Posts can be set into concrete curb or footings or secured with anchor bolts.
- Horizontal rails are generally used along the top and bottom of the fence, although in some cases, a tension wire can replace these rails.
- On taller fences, one or more intermediate horizontal rails may be required.
- An internal or external pipe sleeve is used to connect the lengths of pipe used for the rails to create a strong connection, as well as allow for expansion and contraction where necessary.
- A tension or stretcher bar is woven through the mesh at corner and end posts. This bar is attached to the post by clamps and is used in conjunction with a turnbuckle to ensure the mesh is stretched taut between end or corner posts.
- The mesh is then attached using galvanized metal or PVC-coated wire ties to the horizontal rails and line posts.

Mesh Fabric

The chain-link mesh fabric comes in a variety of thicknesses, mesh sizes, heights, and protective coverings.

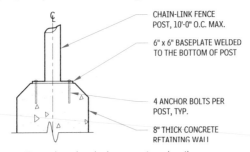

Figure 13.19 Typical anchor bolt mounting detail.
Source: Hopper. Landscape Architectural Graphic Standards, First Edition, Hoboken, NJ: John
Wiley & Sons, 2007.

Figure 13.20 Chain-link fence post with plate welded to pipe and anchored to curb with bolts. Note bottom tension wire in place of a bottom horizontal rail.

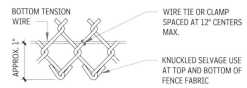

Figure 13.21 Typical detail of a bottom tension wire.
Source: Hopper. Landscape Architectural Graphic Standards, First Edition, Hoboken, NJ: John Wiley & Sons, 2007.

Figure 13.22 A tension wire replacing a top and bottom rail is not as strong an installation.

Figure 13.23 Small rings attach the tension wire to the chain-link mesh.

The gauge of the mesh is the diameter of the wire used to create the mesh fabric: The lightest is 13-gauge and the heaviest is 6-gauge, which is the most commonly available. The lighter gauges of chain-link mesh fabric are only suitable for temporary-type fencing. Generally, an

Figure 13.24 The taller the fence, the more intermediate rails may be required.

Figure 13.25 Fittings are used at each post to hold the intermediate horizontal rails in place. There is always some tolerance between the rail and the post. That is why the distance between posts is not as critical as with post and panel type fences.

Figure 13.26 The tension bar is woven through the mesh, pulled taut and is attached to the post with these clamps and bolts generally spaced 12 in. apart.

Figure 13.27 A turnbuckle is used to provide extra strength to end, corner and gate posts that are under greater stress from the attachment of the tension bar or the swinging of the gate.

Figure 13.28 The mesh is attached to the horizontal line posts with wire ties every 18 in. and to the posts every 12 in. after the mesh is stretched and the tension bars attached to the posts.

11-gauge mesh (.120 in.) would be suitable for light-duty residential uses; 9-gauge mesh (.148 in.) would be a good all-around choice; and 6-gauge (.192 in.) is a commonly specified thicker mesh used for installations where a heavier-duty fence is required.

The mesh size is the distance between the parallel wires of the mesh. Chain-link mesh comes in sizes ranging from $^3/_8$ to $2^3/_8$ in. Most commonly used for general applications is a 2-in. mesh. For some sport court applications, a smaller mesh of 1 or $1^1/_4$ in. may be a more appropriate functional choice, to contain the ball within the enclosure. From a design perspective, the smaller mesh can be used to create a greater visual impact and a feeling of a more screened appearance and sense of enclosure. For security applications, $^5/_8$-, $^1/_2$-, or $^3/_8$-, in. mesh can be used. These "mini" meshes are more difficult to climb, and because they contain more steel, are more difficult to cut through. For added security, the bottom of the mesh can be buried a minimum of 12 in. below grade, making unauthorized entry by cutting the ties and forcing the mesh up more difficult.

Mesh Fabric Details

Chain-link mesh fabric typically comes in the following heights: 36, 42, 48, 60, 72, 84, 96, 120, and 144 in. The tops and bottoms of chain-link mesh fabric are typically finished differently depending on the height (referred to as "selvage"). Chain-link mesh fabric less than 72 in. in height must be knuckled on both the top and bottom of the mesh, creating a smoother finished edge. Chain-link mesh fabric more than 72 in. in height is generally knuckled on one end (used for the top of the fence) and left twisted at the other, creating a barbed edge. When used for security purposes, the chain-link mesh can be specified with both ends twisted, creating a barbed effect on both the top and bottom.

The most common protective covering for chain-link mesh fabric is galvanized zinc. It can be applied in two ways. One way is *galvanized after weaving* (GAW). This refers to the process of taking the specified gauge of wire, weaving it into the chain-link mesh fabric and then

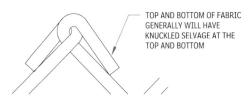

TOP AND BOTTOM OF FABRIC
GENERALLY WILL HAVE
KNUCKLED SELVAGE AT THE
TOP AND BOTTOM

Figure 13.29 Typical detail of knuckled selvage.
Source: Hopper. Landscape Architectural Graphic Standards, First Edition, Hoboken, NJ: John Wiley & Sons, 2007.

Figure 13.30 Vinyl clad chain-link fence mesh with knuckled selvage.

drawing the fabric through a pot of molten zinc. The other approach is *galvanized before weaving* (GBW). This refers to the process of taking the specified gauge of wire rod, pulling the wire through a pot of molten zinc, and then weaving the wire into the chain-link mesh fabric. Although both methods are acceptable, the GAW approach does have some advantages. One is that galvanizing after the fabrication of the mesh ensures that all cut ends made while forming the mesh fabric are galvanized. Second, a thicker coating of zinc is applied, and because zinc protects the steel underneath by slowly dissipating itself over time, the thicker the coating, the longer the steel is protected.

Chain-link mesh fabric is also available with polyvinyl coatings in a number of different colors. This coating is applied over the galvanized steel core wire, providing another layer of protective coating. The polyvinyl coating can be applied in three different ways: *extruded,* where the polyvinyl encompasses the steel wire of the mesh; *extruded bonded,* where an adhesive bonds the vinyl coating to the steel wire of the mesh; and *thermally fused,* a process that fuses the polyvinyl coating to the steel wire of the mesh. It is important to note that for polyvinyl-coated chain-link mesh fabric the gauge specified is the gauge of the coated fabric, not of the wire mesh. Therefore, the gauge of the wire core must be considered in determining the strength of the fence, not the gauge of the wire after it has received the polyvinyl coating.

Another commercially available process to add color to the mesh is polyester powder coating. In this process, the polyester powdered resins are electrostatically applied to the galvanized chain-link mesh and then fully cured at high heat in an oven for 15 to 20 minutes. The approximately 3-mil coating provides an even and durable finish.

Opening Access

A number of different gate styles are available to control access at openings, the most common being the swing gate. A single swing gate is almost always used for controlling pedestrian access. For vehicular access, there are a wider range of gate choices. A double swing gate is most common but is limited in how wide the opening can be because of the weight of the gate and the stresses put on the hinges and gateposts. In circumstances that call for wider openings, an overhead sliding gate, cantilever gate, or vertical lifting gate are all options. Gates can be opened and closed manually or they can be operated electrically. Electric-operated gates can be controlled by an attendant, telephone system, card reader system, wireless radio frequency device, or digital keypad system.

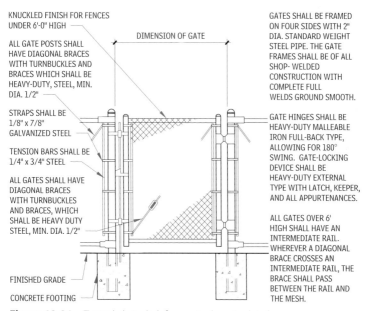

KNUCKLED FINISH FOR FENCES UNDER 6'-0" HIGH

DIMENSION OF GATE

ALL GATE POSTS SHALL HAVE DIAGONAL BRACES WITH TURNBUCKLES AND BRACES WHICH SHALL BE HEAVY-DUTY, STEEL, MIN. DIA. 1/2"

STRAPS SHALL BE 1/8" x 7/8" GALVANIZED STEEL

TENSION BARS SHALL BE 1/4" x 3/4" STEEL

ALL GATES SHALL HAVE DIAGONAL BRACES WITH TURNBUCKLES AND BRACES, WHICH SHALL BE HEAVY DUTY STEEL, MIN. DIA. 1/2"

FINISHED GRADE

CONCRETE FOOTING

GATES SHALL BE FRAMED ON FOUR SIDES WITH 2" DIA. STANDARD WEIGHT STEEL PIPE. THE GATE FRAMES SHALL BE OF ALL SHOP- WELDED CONSTRUCTION WITH COMPLETE FULL WELDS GROUND SMOOTH.

GATE HINGES SHALL BE HEAVY-DUTY MALLEABLE IRON FULL-BACK TYPE, ALLOWING FOR 180° SWING. GATE-LOCKING DEVICE SHALL BE HEAVY-DUTY EXTERNAL TYPE WITH LATCH, KEEPER, AND ALL APPURTENANCES.

ALL GATES OVER 6' HIGH SHALL HAVE AN INTERMEDIATE RAIL. WHEREVER A DIAGONAL BRACE CROSSES AN INTERMEDIATE RAIL, THE BRACE SHALL PASS BETWEEN THE RAIL AND THE MESH.

Figure 13.31   Typical chain-link fence single gate detail.
Source: Hopper. Landscape Architectural Graphic Standards, First Edition, Hoboken, NJ: John Wiley & Sons, 2007.

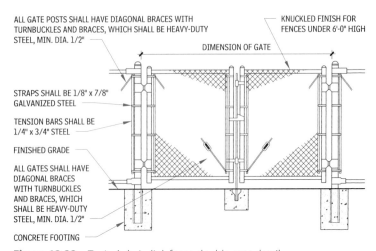

ALL GATE POSTS SHALL HAVE DIAGONAL BRACES WITH
TURNBUCKLES AND BRACES, WHICH SHALL BE HEAVY-DUTY
STEEL, MIN. DIA. 1/2"

KNUCKLED FINISH FOR
FENCES UNDER 6'-0" HIGH

DIMENSION OF GATE

STRAPS SHALL BE 1/8" x 7/8"
GALVANIZED STEEL

TENSION BARS SHALL BE
1/4" x 3/4" STEEL

FINISHED GRADE

ALL GATES SHALL HAVE
DIAGONAL BRACES
WITH TURNBUCKLES
AND BRACES, WHICH
SHALL BE HEAVY-DUTY
STEEL, MIN. DIA. 1/2"

CONCRETE FOOTING

Figure 13.32 Typical chain-link fence double gate detail.
Source: Hopper. Landscape Architectural Graphic Standards, First Edition, Hoboken, NJ: John
Wiley & Sons, 2007.

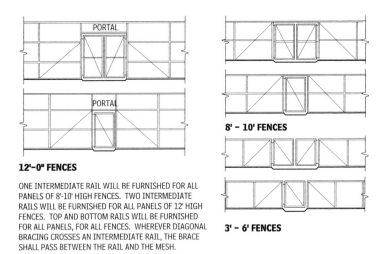

PORTAL

PORTAL

12'-0" FENCES

ONE INTERMEDIATE RAIL WILL BE FURNISHED FOR ALL
PANELS OF 8'-10' HIGH FENCES. TWO INTERMEDIATE
RAILS WILL BE FURNISHED FOR ALL PANELS OF 12' HIGH
FENCES. TOP AND BOTTOM RAILS WILL BE FURNISHED
FOR ALL PANELS, FOR ALL FENCES. WHEREVER DIAGONAL
BRACING CROSSES AN INTERMEDIATE RAIL, THE BRACE
SHALL PASS BETWEEN THE RAIL AND THE MESH.

8' – 10' FENCES

3' – 6' FENCES

Figure 13.33 Typical diagonal bracing for chain-link fence gates.
Source: Hopper. Landscape Architectural Graphic Standards, First Edition, Hoboken, NJ: John
Wiley & Sons, 2007.

Figure 13.34 Typical chain-link fence single gate with portal above.

Figure 13.35 Typical chain-link fence double gate with portal above.

Figure 13.36 Turnbuckle is attached to triangular plate welded to the gate panel frame to keep the gate from sagging.

Figure 13.37 Heavy-duty hinge is clamped to the post for chain-link fence gate.

Figure 13.38 Single gate panel locks into a keeper set into the concrete curb that allows the gate to close securely.

Figure 13.39 Double gate panels lock into a keeper set into the concrete curb that allows the gate to close securely.

Figure 13.40 Double gate panels lock into the horizontal portal bar at the top of the gate panels.

Practices to Avoid

- Where chain-link fence steps down in curbs or walls, the location of the posts should be coordinated with the steps in order to avoid awkward situations.

Figure 13.41 Chain-link fence has post locations coordinated with wall steps, allowing the horizontal rails from both levels of fence to share the same post.

Figure 13.42   Where chain-link fence post locations are not coordinated, this type of makeshift post detail is created.

- Playgrounds and recreation fields are notorious for having kids lean on the mesh, stretching and bowing it out and snapping through the wire ties holding the mesh to rails and posts. The installation of an intermediate rail for them to lean against can avoid maintenance problems and premature replacement of the mesh.

Figure 13.43   This mesh has been stretched and bowed out with the mesh now separating from the bottom rail and posts.

Figure 13.44 An additional horizontal rail between the bottom and required midrail, will give users of the recreation area something to lean on and protect the mesh from being stretched and bowed.

- Avoid chipping and peeling of paint by proper preparation of the galvanized chain-link fence framework and painting with a compatible primer and finish coat of paint.

Metal Fences

Description

Tubular Steel Fence

Typically, the fence posts and rails of a tubular steel fence are constructed of hollow tubular steel. However, there are many variations of a largely tubular steel fence where combinations of the posts, rails, or pickets can be made from solid steel and integrated with the hollow tube elements to increase the strength of the fence.

Tubular steel fences always have a top and bottom rail, but there are many variations that use three or more rails at a variety of elevations in the panel. Although tubular rails are often welded directly to the posts, a mechanical connection that allows for some contraction/expansion of the steel elements is more advisable. Pickets can be welded to the rails but are often connected using mechanical connectors such as screws or rivets.

Solid-Steel Fence

Solid-steel (sometimes mistakenly referred to as "wrought iron") fences offer a maximum of strength and durability. Flat steel bars used for the rails will emphasize the vertical qualities of the fence. If channels or angles are used, their thicker appearance will give the fence a more horizontal emphasis.

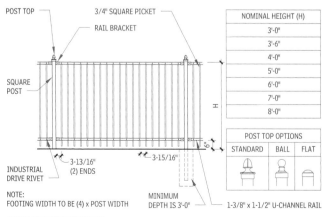

FENCE SECTION ELEVATION

Figure 13.45   Typical tubular steel fence panel.
Source: Hopper. Landscape Architectural Graphic Standards, First Edition, Hoboken, NJ: John Wiley & Sons, 2007.

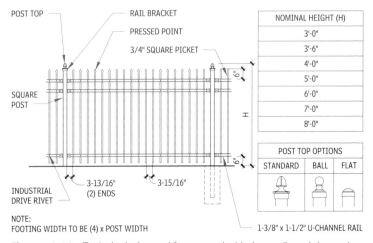

Figure 13.46 Typical tubular steel fence panel with three rails and decorative picket.
Source: Hopper. Landscape Architectural Graphic Standards, First Edition, Hoboken, NJ: John Wiley & Sons, 2007.

Steel Wire Mesh Fences

Fences can also be constructed of a variety of wire mesh products that are stretched and attached to a number of combinations of rails and posts. While these can be very simple, light-gauge steel meshes are used for very utilitarian functions such as enclosing pets or animals or for agricultural uses. Wire mesh panels can also be made of more sturdy wire gauges to form very decorative screens and barriers.

Figure 13.47 Typical run of tubular steel fence installed in footings adjacent to the sidewalk.

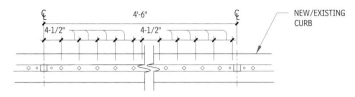

PLAN

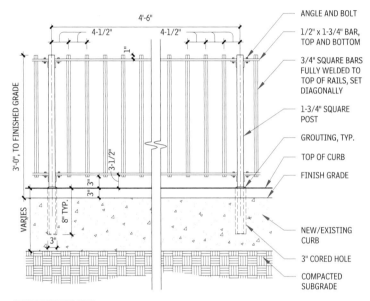

ELEVATION/SECTION

Figure 13.48 Typical detail for a 3-ft-high steel bar fence in a concrete curb.
Source: Hopper. Landscape Architectural Graphic Standards, First Edition, Hoboken, NJ: John Wiley & Sons, 2007.

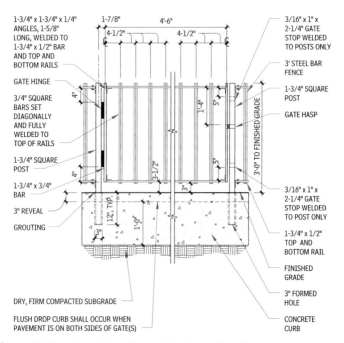

Figure 13.49 Typical detail for a 3-ft-high steel bar fence single gate in a concrete curb.
Source: Hopper. Landscape Architectural Graphic Standards, First Edition, Hoboken, NJ: John Wiley & Sons, 2007.

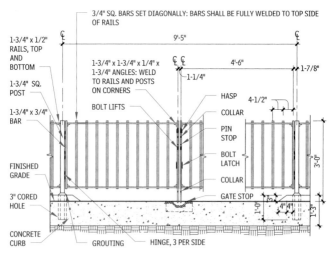

Figure 13.50 Typical detail for a 3-ft-high steel bar fence double gate in a concrete curb.
Source: Hopper. Landscape Architectural Graphic Standards, First Edition, Hoboken, NJ: John Wiley & Sons, 2007.

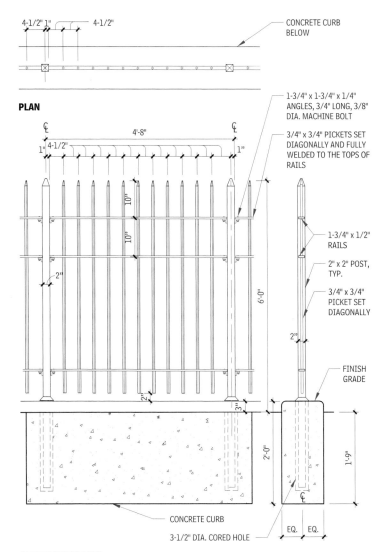

PLAN

SECTION/ELEVATION

Figure 13.51 Typical detail for a 6-ft-high steel bar fence in a concrete curb.
Source: Hopper. Landscape Architectural Graphic Standards, First Edition, Hoboken, NJ: John Wiley & Sons, 2007.

Figure 13.52 Typical run of a 6-ft-high steel bar fence in a concrete curb.

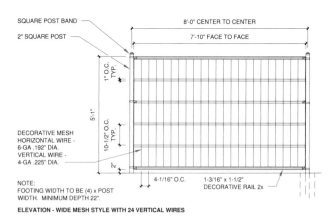

Figure 13.53 Typical mesh fence details.
Source: Hopper. Landscape Architectural Graphic Standards, First Edition, Hoboken, NJ: John Wiley & Sons, 2007.

Figure 13.54 Typical run of a wire mesh fence installed in a wall.

Steel Wire Cable Fences

A very transparent barrier can be created using a steel-wire cable fence. In this type of fence a stainless-steel wire cable is used to create the horizontal members of the fence. The thickness of the cable ($\frac{1}{8}$ in.

Figure 13.55 Thicker wire gauge is welded together to form a sturdy decorative barrier.

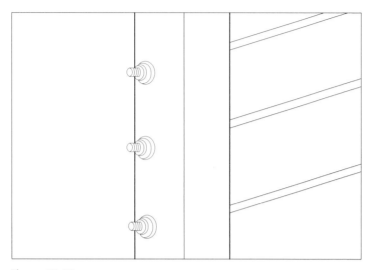

Figure 13.56a

or greater) is very unobtrusive and allows good views to be enjoyed with little visual impact from the fence itself.

Figure 13.56b Steel cable fence in conjunction with a wood railing barrier provides the required security and at the same time allows visibility through that a wood barrier would have obstructed. Photo courtesy of Mark K. Morrison, FASLA, RLA.

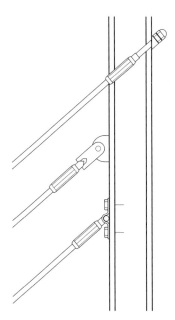

CABLE RAIL CONNECTIONS ALL HAVE A TIGHTENING DEVICE
THAT KEEPS THE CABLE RIGID

Figure 13.57   Typical cable rail connections.

Assessing Site Conditions

There are a few general recommendations for the design and installation of the ornamental fence such as the types previously described:

- Fence installed in concrete curbs or walls require less maintenance than fence in footings, where the fence panels span over planted areas (unable to be mowed) that require constant maintenance to keep grass or weeds from growing up beneath the fence panels.
- For installation on gentle sloped sites, the fence looks best when the rails follow the slope of the finished grade and the pickets are truly vertical.
- For installation on steeply sloped sites, the fence looks best when the fence panels and wall step along the slope.

Acceptable Practices

Tubular Steel Fence

The use of tubular steel rails, given the larger overall dimensions, usually gives the fence a stronger horizontal emphasis. The tubular steel elements often are sealed with welded caps to prevent the entry of

Figure 13.58 Lawn growing underneath this fence installed in footing will require a high level of maintenance to keep the lawn cut under the fence panels where the mower can't reach.

Figure 13.59 A continuous concrete curb will not allow anything to grow under the fence panels, requiring less intensive maintenance over time.
Source: Photo courtesy of Mark K. Morrison, FASLA, RLA, GRP

Figure 13.60 The steel wire mesh fence on this sloping site steps down the slope, with the top of the wall level and steel mesh panels horizontal. Note the careful planning that coordinates the location of the fence posts with the steps in the wall.

Figure 13.61 Tubular steel fence with decorative rings and caps screwed onto the posts and pickets to keep water out of the tubes.

Figure 13.62 Pickets are not fully welded to the tops of the rails on all sides so water can get between the picket and rail tube, become trapped in the horizontal tube, that could lead to early deterioration of the fence.

Figure 13.63 Tubular picket to rail and rail to post connection allow water penetration that can lead to early deterioration of the fence.

Figure 13.64 The rail connects to the post bracket with a screw that fits into a slot in both the rail and bracket. This allows for some necessary tolerance when fitting the panels between the posts as well as allowing for expansion and contraction of the fence. The rail does not penetrate the post.

moisture into the tube. Tubular steel fencing is not as strong as a fence made from solid steel components; however, it is lighter in weight, and a wide range of different styles, shapes, and sizes are available for each of the elements that make up the fence, making it very versatile and easily adaptive to almost any design situation. Design elements can be added to a tubular steel fence and steel cables or crash plates can be integrated into the tubular steel fence, increasing its capability to withstand vehicular impact, thus its value as a security design feature.

In terms of finishes, tubular steel fence can be galvanized and painted with a compatible primer and finish paint. But as with all outdoor painted surfaces, these fences will need regular maintenance and repainting to maintain their appearance. A galvanized fence that receives an electro-statically applied powder coating has a much more durable finish. Although a powder coating can be applied over bare steel, this offers less protection against rust if the powder coating should become chipped and allow the bare steel to be exposed to the elements.

Solid-Steel Fence Construction

The panels that form the most visible part of the fence can be varied in an almost unlimited number of ways. Outside of the basic concerns of head entrapment (unless otherwise governed by local codes, openings should be less than 4 in. or greater than 9 in.), and whether horizontal elements can be used to climb up and over the fence itself, there are few constraints on the design of an ornamental panel.

Square pickets that are set diagonally give the panels an added interest compared to pickets that are set parallel to the line of the fence. Pickets that alternate in height can be more interesting than a fence panel that has a constant height. A variety of different ornamentations can be welded and integrated into a standard fence panel. In considering one of these manufactured pieces, check their dimensions first, as this will affect the picket or rail spacing to which these pieces will be welded. Louvered-type fencing panels can create a screening effect where desirable. Panels welded to the pickets can be used to create a solid, totally opaque screening barrier.

Because of the difficulty of drilling through thick, solid-steel members, many of the connections in this type of fence are often welded. For solid-steel rails, the holes for the pickets are generally punched through the rail; the picket is inserted and then fully welded to the tops of the rails (to prevent water from accumulating at the joint). This type of construction creates a very strong joint, and having the pickets passing through the rails allows a greater tolerance for fabrication differences in the length of pickets.

Figure 13.65 Square pickets set diagonally add interest to the fence panel. Note that the pickets are fully welded on the top to prevent water from sitting between the picket and rail.

Figure 13.66 Louvered steel panels allow limited visual penetration.

Figure 13.67 The "Z" shaped vertical steel members are welded to the solid horizontal rails and attached to the post with a standard angle and bolt detail which allows for expansion and contraction.

The attachment of the rails to the posts should be accomplished with a mechanical connection that allows for construction tolerances to fit the panels to the fence posts and, at the same time, allows for differential expansion and contraction of the fence from the curb or wall in which it is anchored. The horizontal rails can be attached to a building using a masonry connection to minimize the gap between building and fence. In other cases, a filler panel can be used to close the gap.

At the end of a run of fence where any gap between the fence and adjacent fence or structure must be kept at a minimum, it is advisable to install a filler panel, as opposed to trying to have a fence post installed too close to the end of the anchoring curb or wall. Fence posts that are too close to an edge of concrete run the risk of breaking through the edge and becoming unstable. A filler panel allows the fence post to be set back, allowing for adequate concrete cover on all sides of the end post. In a similar manner, end posts that are adjacent to structures can be attached to the structure, giving the end post added stability and strength.

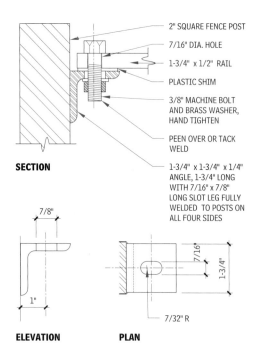

Figure 13.68 Angle and bolt detail connecting the fence panel to the post.
Source: Hopper. Landscape Architectural Graphic Standards, First Edition, Hoboken, NJ: John Wiley & Sons, 2007.

Figure 13.69 Rails are attached to the post with an angle and bolt connection. The angle has a slot cut in it that allows the fence panels to expand and contract between posts, independently of the concrete curb.

Figure 13.70 Typical masonry connection attaching post to building.

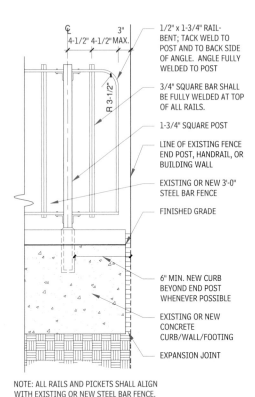

3" 4-1/2" 4-1/2" MAX.

R 3-1/2"

1/2" x 1-3/4" RAIL-BENT; TACK WELD TO POST AND TO BACK SIDE OF ANGLE. ANGLE FULLY WELDED TO POST

3/4" SQUARE BAR SHALL BE FULLY WELDED AT TOP OF ALL RAILS.

1-3/4" SQUARE POST

LINE OF EXISTING FENCE END POST, HANDRAIL, OR BUILDING WALL

EXISTING OR NEW 3'-0" STEEL BAR FENCE

FINISHED GRADE

6" MIN. NEW CURB BEYOND END POST WHENEVER POSSIBLE

EXISTING OR NEW CONCRETE CURB/WALL/FOOTING

EXPANSION JOINT

NOTE: ALL RAILS AND PICKETS SHALL ALIGN WITH EXISTING OR NEW STEEL BAR FENCE.

Figure 13.71 Typical filler panel detail for a steel bar fence.
Source: Hopper. Landscape Architectural Graphic Standards, First Edition, Hoboken, NJ: John Wiley & Sons, 2007.

Steel Wire Mesh Fence

The thicker-gauge wires are welded together to form a relatively rigid mesh panel that is then attached to a top and bottom rail. The horizontal wires can also be attached to a vertical rail at each end, giving the panel additional rigidity and strength. The wire mesh panels are then attached to the posts with a mechanical connection such as a clamp or angle and bolt. The horizontal and vertical wires can be the same gauge or can differ. They can be welded together in a wide range of different dimensions to create a variety of looks, from a very open barrier to one that is denser and offers a greater sense of privacy and visual impact. These decorative fences can be electrostatically powder-coated with polyester resins to create a durable and attractive finish.

Figure 13.72 Steel bar fence filler panel.

Figure 13.73 Steel wire mesh fence panel attached to the post with an angle and bolt.

Steel Wire Cable Fence

The fence is constructed of multiple horizontal cables that run through holes in intermediate posts and are attached at end or corner posts. The cable is tensioned at the attachments to these corner or end posts, creating a rigid horizontal cable for the length of the fence. For long straight runs of fence, tightening devices approximately every 50 ft will aid in keeping the cable taut.

Fence Installation Considerations

It is advisable to install the fence post in holes that are cored into the curb or wall to which the fence is to be anchored. Post holes that are formed during the construction of the curb or wall tend to vary and shift, thereby creating variances in the distance between fence posts, and these differences tend to be compounded over the length of the fence run, making the fitting of standard fence panels between posts virtually impossible. This can lead to the eventual coring of new holes, almost immediately adjacent to the formed holes, to install fence posts at the proper distance to accommodate the standard fence

Figure 13.74 A water lubricated diamond core drill coring a hole for a steel bar fence post to be installed in the concrete curb.

Figure 13.75 The cored concrete is hit at an angle between the core and curb with a hammer and chisel breaking it at the base.

panels. A cored hole can be executed with a great deal of accuracy after the curb or wall is constructed; this is usually done by the same contractor that is fabricating the fence, which can lead to less finger-pointing when things don't fit the way they should.

Figure 13.76 The concrete cored cylinder can then be lifted out leaving a perfect hole for the fence post.

During fence installation, the fence is usually loosely connected together, chocked plumb and true to line in the cored holes, and then anchored with a quick-setting grout. After the grout has hardened, a sealer is placed in the hole with a wash that directs water away from the post and post hole. This is a much better installation than trying to set the post directly into a wet concrete curb or wall.

Solid-steel fences are generally painted with a primer and two coats of finished paint applied in the shop (plus a touch-up coat in the field after installation to take care of little nicks and scrapes). Fabricators will sometimes dip the fabricated fence panels into large tanks of paint to ensure coverage of the entire panel.

Practices to Avoid

- Avoid designing fences that have welds that trap water, it leads to early deterioration of the fence;

Figure 13.77   Steel bar fence posts set loosely in holes, chocked until plumb and straightened so that panels are aligned before grout and sealer secure the post into place.

Figure 13.78 Steel bar fence post grouted in place with a sealer providing a wash to deflect water away from the post.

- Avoid rust forming on the bottom rail and staining the top of curb. Be sure that the bottom rail is painted underneath. Use a mirror to check as there isn't enough room between the underneath side of the bottom of the rail and the top of curb to check any other way.
- Avoid concrete curbs cracking at post holes due to the fence contracting and expanding at a different rate than the concrete. Panel to post connections should allow for this; fence panels that are continuously welded to posts do not.
- Avoid forming post holes in curbs only to have to go back later and core holes in the correct location because the formed holes have shifted during the concrete pour. Formed holes cannot be placed with the degree of accuracy that is required for a steel post and panel type fence. Any errors made in the formed holes compound themselves over the run of fence, making fitting the standard fence panels between the posts impossible.
- Avoid panels that look crooked. For fences that follow the slope be sure that the rails are parallel with the grade and the pickets are truly vertical. Even fences that are on slopes of 1% should be "racked" in this manner.
- Avoid weak points in the concrete curb at post holes by ensuring that the horizontal reinforcing bars are properly secured in place during the pouring of the concrete.

Figure 13.79 These concrete cores that were cut for the post holes all have steel reinforcing embedded in them. This indicates that the rebar was not secured and instead of running on each side of the post hole strengthening it, they've shifted to the middle of the curb and have been cut out with the core drill.

References

ALSO IN THIS BOOK:

- Concrete
- Concrete Curbs
- Concrete Steel Reinforcing
- Wood

OTHER RESOURCES:

- Daniel M. Winterbottom. Wood In The Landscape, Hoboken, NJ: John Wiley & Sons, 2000.
- Hopper. Landscape Architectural Graphic Standards, First Edition, Hoboken, NJ: John Wiley & Sons, 2007.

Chapter 14

Walls

Concrete Walls

Description

The use of poured-in-place concrete is commonly used for freestanding or retaining gravity walls, cantilever walls or counterfort walls. The finish of concrete walls can be enhanced using the following techniques:

- Bush hammering
- Sandblasting
- Creating various reliefs from the outlines left by the rough-cut or sandblasted plywood formboards used to cast the wall
- Inserting rubber mats or wood strips inside the form
- Applying an exposed aggregate finish

Concrete walls are generally a minimum of 12 in. wide, which allows for the proper clear distance of steel reinforcing from the edges of the wall. The depth of a concrete wall varies, however, wherever it is a factor, the base of the wall should be set below the frost line.

Assessing Site Conditions

Existing soil conditions (weight, bearing capacity, angle of repose, texture, etc.) need to be investigated to determine the design and dimensions of the type of concrete wall that will be constructed.

Figure 14.1   Example of a horizontal shadow line and textured finish imparted to the face of the concrete wall using a formliner.

Figure 14.2 The plastic formliner attached to the inside of the formwork will impart this pattern into the surface of the concrete wall.
Source: Photo courtesy of the Portland Cement Association.

Concrete walls require formwork for the full depth of the wall to be built that will contain the concrete when it is poured. This formwork requires that the area be excavated deep and wide enough to allow crews room to work and brace the forms to prevent the forms from shifting during the concrete pour. This will require that an area wider than the wall itself will be disturbed during construction. Any existing structures, site amenities or planting need to be considered when planning to design and construction of a concrete wall. Anything within the area of construction will need to be removed and replaced, anything outside the area of construction should be specified to be protected.

Acceptable Practices

The area where the concrete wall is to be constructed should be excavated to the required depth specified in the contract documents and to a sufficient width to allow crew access to work safely. It is important that the excavation does not go deeper than required for the bottom of the wall. Backfilling with loose soil risks initial settling of the wall. If the excavation is too deep, compact the soil at the bottom of the excavation and backfill with 1 in. or larger gravel and compact to provide a firm base.

As the machine excavates for the wall, the teeth on the bucket will loosen the soil a few inches below the bottom of the trench for the wall. In addition, some loose soil from the side of the excavation inevitably falls to the bottom of the trench during excavation. It is important that the subgrade under the wall be compacted using a rammer or plate vibrator to avoid any settling.

Concrete forms should ideally be set with the top of the forms at the top of wall elevation or have a chamfer strip secured to the inside of the form to indicate the top of wall. In addition to making the tops of walls easier to finish, it is much easier to see whether the wall is being constructed at the correct height than when the top of wall is marked with a chalk line somewhere down from the top of the form.

Formwork is typically constructed with exterior plywood (generally ¾ in. thick) or re-usable steel forms. The joints between the formwork need to fit together tightly to avoid any concrete leakage between sections. The formwork must be strong enough, anchored and braced sufficiently to prevent shifting, bowing, distortion or complete failure (blow-out) during the concrete pour.

If the wall is a cantilever wall, the spread footing is constructed first as a separate pour, with a mechanical key and reinforcing bars extending up, to lock the footing to the stem of the wall. A 2 x 4 plate is anchored to the spread footing to hold the vertical form boards in place and prevent them from shifting upwards which would allow concrete to flow under them when the stem is poured.

Figure 14.3 Spread footing poured with vertical steel reinforcing bars that will tie the footing to the stem of the wall. The mechanical key formed with a 2" x 4" runs down the center of the footing.
Source: Photo courtesy of Mark K. Morrison, FASLA, RLA, GRP.

For a typical wall, one side of the formwork is constructed and the reinforcing bars, dowels, weep holes, chamfer strips, and formliner (if used) are all installed while the construction workers have easy access to what will become the inside of the wall. After the internal framework is constructed and anchored in place, the opposite form is constructed and secured in place, in effect forming a mold for the concrete to be poured. Often contractors will pre-drill holes for ties and brackets through several sheets of plywood at the same time, which allows the opposite form to align with the initial form and ties more easily.

The forms are held together by spacers, wire ties, walers, and strongbacks, in addition to being braced from the outside, to prevent any shifting or bowing from the pressure of the concrete when it is placed into the forms. The commercially available steel forms have compatible ties, braces and waler brackets that make securing the formwork a very methodical process. Walers are 2 x 4's that provide horizontal support to the forms. Strongbacks provide vertical support to the forms and help hold panels together at the joints.

▶ **The forms should be treated with a form release agent prior to pouring the concrete to prevent concrete from sticking to the form when it is stripped and damaging the face of the wall. Oil should never be used as a form release agent.**

Steel reinforcing should be cleaned of dirt and loose rust before installing. They should be tied and secured in place to prevent shifting

Figure 14.4   The steel forms are erected on one side of the wall first allowing workers to secure the steel reinforcing and PVC pipe weep holes in place. The steel reinforcing for the spread footing is incorporated into the steel reinforcing for the wall stem.
Source: Photo courtesy of Mark K. Morrison, FASLA, RLA, GRP.

Figure 14.5 In progress photo of concrete formwork. Expansion joint material with chamfer strip will be backed with plywood and bracing for the first pour of the wall to the left of the joint. The smooth steel will be set into the concrete on the left side, on the right side the PVC sleeve will allow the wall to expand and contract while staying aligned with the dowels.

during the concrete pour. The reinforcing bars should be continuous at intersections and corners and be overlapped at the joints between bars. The concrete should be worked and compacted around the bars to provide complete coverage.

The concrete should be placed into the forms as close as possible to the top of the forms, starting at one end of the wall and working toward the opposite end of the wall or expansion joint break. The concrete should be placed in approximately 18-in. layers and tamped into place using a puddle stick or square pouring shovel (although many contractors will use a 2 x 4). This removes any air pockets within the concrete, helps mesh the layers together, consolidates the concrete around the steel reinforcing bars and up against the surface of the forms for a good finish. As the concrete is being poured, any spacers in the formwork should be removed. When the concrete level is close enough to the top of the form, an internal vibrator should be inserted to consolidate the concrete.

Formwork should be kept in place for a minimum of 3 days after the concrete pour, however, if kept in place longer (7 days), it helps keep moisture in the concrete aiding the curing process. Covering the top of the wall with a plastic sheet or other means to keep the moisture in

Figure 14.6 Form ties hold the forms together resisting the outward force of the concrete as it is placed into the form. The plastic cones keep the forms from sliding along the ties.
Source: Iano, Fundamentals of Building Construction. Copyright 2008, John Wiley & Sons, Inc.

Figure 14.7 This cutaway view shows the relationship of the form tie to the inside of the form boards, through the form boards and anchored behind the walers.
Source: Iano, Fundamentals of Building Construction. Copyright 2008, John Wiley & Sons, Inc.

Figure 14.8 After the forms are stripped the metal end of the form tie is snapped off, leaving a conical dimple in the wall face that can be filled with mortar.
Source: Iano, Fundamentals of Building Construction. Copyright 2008, John Wiley & Sons, Inc.

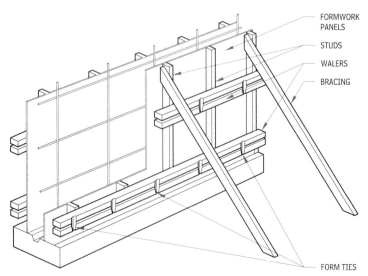

FORMWORK PANELS

STUDS

WALERS

BRACING

FORM TIES

Figure 14.9 The various elements of the form framework for a concrete wall.
Source: Iano, Fundamentals of Building Construction. Copyright 2008, John Wiley & Sons, Inc.

the concrete allows the process of hydration to continue, helping the concrete reach its specified strength. Concrete forms should be removed carefully, particularly at corners or if a formliner is being used, to prevent damage to the wall's finished surface.

After the forms are removed some touch-up may be necessary. Any ridges created by some concrete leakage at the form joints should be carefully chipped off. With the surface wet, rough spots can be smoothed by rubbing with a carborundum stone. The sooner the concrete is rubbed after the forms are removed, the better the results.

Practices to Avoid

- Avoid non-bonded layers of concrete in the wall by pouring each layer as soon as possible after the previous layer.
- Do not use steel reinforcing that is covered with dust or dirt without cleaning first.
- Plastering the wall with a thin coat of cement and water mixed together (sometimes called a cement wash) is not advisable although it will look good initially, it tends to develop hairline cracks and scales off in a short period of time.

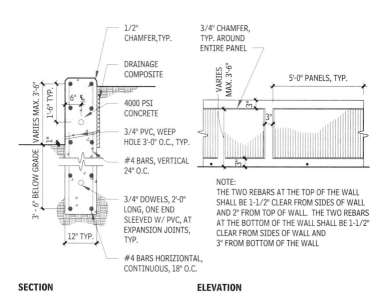

SECTION

ELEVATION

Figure 14.10 Typical detail showing a concrete retaining wall with form liner and shadow lines.

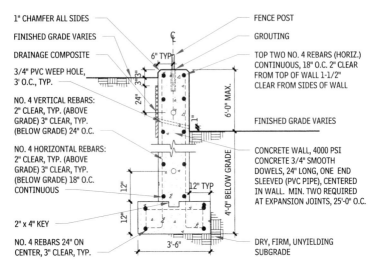

1" CHAMFER ALL SIDES

FINISHED GRADE VARIES

DRAINAGE COMPOSITE

3/4" PVC WEEP HOLE, 3' O.C., TYP.

NO. 4 VERTICAL REBARS: 2" CLEAR, TYP. (ABOVE GRADE) 3" CLEAR, TYP. (BELOW GRADE) 24" O.C.

NO. 4 HORIZONTAL REBARS: 2" CLEAR, TYP. (ABOVE GRADE) 3" CLEAR, TYP. (BELOW GRADE) 18" O.C. CONTINUOUS

2" x 4" KEY

NO. 4 REBARS 24" ON CENTER, 3" CLEAR, TYP.

FENCE POST

GROUTING

TOP TWO NO. 4 REBARS (HORIZ.) CONTINUOUS, 18" O.C. 2" CLEAR FROM TOP OF WALL 1-1/2" CLEAR FROM SIDES OF WALL

FINISHED GRADE VARIES

CONCRETE WALL, 4000 PSI CONCRETE 3/4" SMOOTH DOWELS, 24" LONG, ONE END SLEEVED (PVC PIPE), CENTERED IN WALL. MIN. TWO REQUIRED AT EXPANSION JOINTS, 25'-0" O.C.

DRY, FIRM, UNYIELDING SUBGRADE

6" TYP

24"

3" 3"

6'-0" MAX.

1"

4'-0" BELOW GRADE

12"

12"

12" TYP

3'-6"

SECTION

Figure 14.11 Typical detail of a concrete retaining wall with spread footing.
Source: Hopper, Landscape Architectural Graphic Standards. Copyright © 2007 by John Wiley & Sons, Inc. Reprinted by permission of John Wiley & Sons, Inc.

Modular Gravity Wall Systems

Description

Modular gravity wall systems (sometimes referred to as segmental block systems) are an increasingly popular and economical alternative to conventional gravity and cantilevered retaining wall systems, especially for walls on a residential scale. Modular concrete walls are very similar in concept to dry-laid gravity masonry retaining walls. The weight of the wall creates sufficient stability against the lateral pressure of retained earth, yet the entire system remains flexible to the differential movement and settlement of the foundation soil and the wall mass. They are available in a wide variety of different shapes, sizes, colors, textures and styles.

Modular gravity wall systems are of two general types, interlocking and connecting pin:

- The interlocking system involves mortarless, stack, concrete units with or without a bin for soil interfill. The weight of the wall and soil interfill create shear resistance between units, which provides overall stability. The units are allowed to move, to absorb the action of soil expansion, contraction, and settlement. As a result, considerable heights can be achieved at a relatively low cost. The front lips of the stackable units are designed to create the wall batter and lock the units together up from a concrete course. Batters vary from 25 to 70 degrees for interconnecting plantable walls and from 12 degrees to $1/4$ in. per course for connecting pin non-plantable systems. The units can be set at staggered widths to conform to a great variety of convex and concave radii.
- Connecting pin wall systems join concrete units together with metal or fiberglass pins to achieve stability from one course to the next. The pins can be adjusted to a number of positions, which allows for great flexibility in the degree of curvature of the wall. High-strength fiberglass pins are preferable to metal pins because they do not rust and create unsightly stains on the units after construction.

There are many different systems available that create a strong mechanical connection between the courses of block. Some are hollow and filled with stone for greater stability. Some have an interlocking system of cast concrete tiebacks similar to a deadman in a wood retaining wall. Others utilize a geogrid between the courses that is tied back into the retained soil behind.

Certain types of interlocking wall systems can be inter-planted with vegetation. The troughs or bins of the units retain sufficient moisture to create suitable environments for decorative groundcover or bedding plants. Such "green walls" reduce the potentially negative visual impact of massive concrete retaining walls.

Assessing Site Conditions

As with building any wall, the condition of the subgrade must be even bearing and free from loose or spongy material, in order to support the wall. Identify the location of any utility lines before digging. If the wall is to be constructed along the property line, be sure that this line is properly identified and if necessary, staked by a licensed surveyor.

For proposed modular block retaining walls the existing slopes, cut and fill requirements and area necessary for installation of required geogrids need to be taken into account before construction begins. In addition, grading to direct surface runoff away from the wall should be considered wherever possible.

The number of courses required to be buried below grade depends on the soil conditions and the height of the wall. Generally, one course is required for walls under 4 ft in height, and the number increases to two courses for walls from 4 to 10 ft high on a 95 % compacted granular fill base. If soil conditions are poor, including low bearing

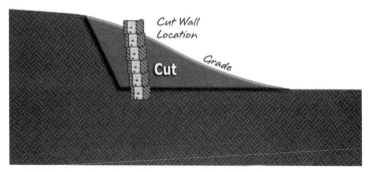

Figure 14.12 If the wall is to be built into the slope, soil will have to be removed.
Source: Image courtesy of Allan Block.

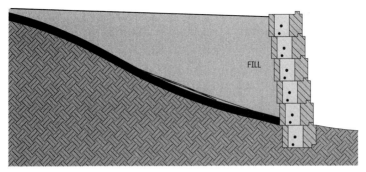

Figure 14.13   If the area behind the wall will be filled, additional backfill will need to be brought to the site.
Source: Image courtesy of Allan Block.

capacity and permeability (soft clay, organic silts, and silt clays), additional courses, pilasters, and concrete beam foundations may be required for strength and leveling.

The placement of a tensar geogrid system, a high-density non-deteriorating polyethylene or polyester fiber, as a soil reinforcement material between courses is recommended for taller retaining walls. It is also recommended that the design of the wall be made using the grid manufacturer's design criteria for the specific grid type.

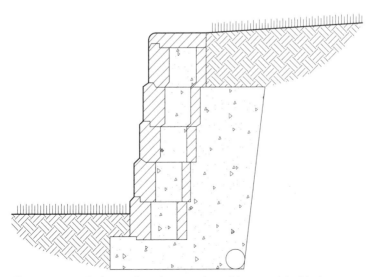

Figure 14.14   For low walls under normal conditions, modular block systems are able to stabilize a slope based on their own weight and interlocking design.
Source: Image courtesy of Allan Block.

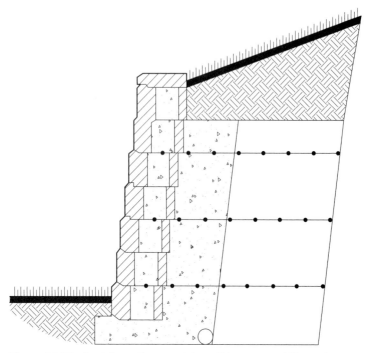

Figure 14.15 For taller walls or special conditions, a geogrid is used to reinforce the wall by tying the modular block back into the retained soil.
Source: Image courtesy of Allan Block.

Drainage of modular wall systems is inherent to the design of modular systems; water table and surface runoff are filtered through the spaces between the units. Such a built-in drainage system reduces the threat of wall failure due to water pressure. In certain conditions, however, drainage tile or weep holes may still be necessary.

Acceptable Practices

Low Modular Block Walls

The different modular wall systems for walls have varying installation techniques and instructions that need to be followed. However, there are the following are basic steps that they have in common:

- The first step is to lay out where the wall will be constructed and mark the line of the wall with stakes and string.
- The soil should be excavated to form a level trench of the width and depth recommended by the manufacturer. Although this will vary by manufacturer, the trench always needs to be wider than the block being used and generally requires that all or a significant portion of

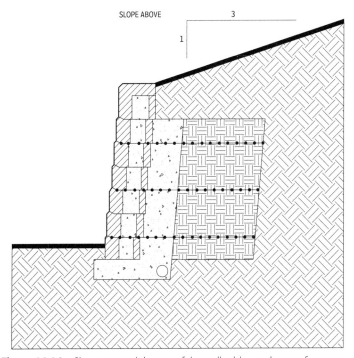

Figure 14.16 Slopes toward the top of the wall add a surcharge of pressure and weight that may require additional reinforcement.
Source: Image courtesy of Allan Block.

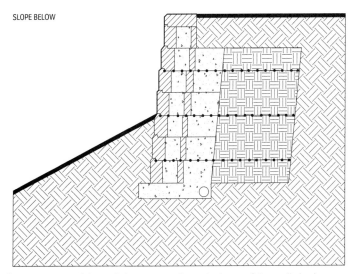

Figure 14.17 If the soil slopes away from the base of the wall, the base may need to be set deeper to mitigate erosion or sliding concerns.
Source: Image courtesy of Allan Block.

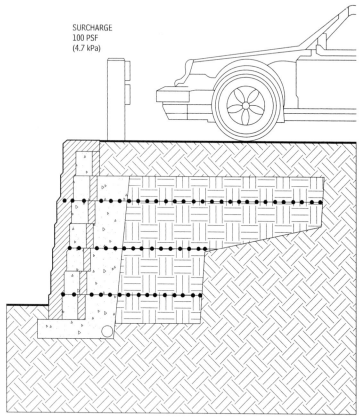

SURCHARGE
100 PSF
(4.7 kPa)

Figure 14.18 Uses above a wall that can exert additional pressure and weight on the wall, such as a driveway or parking area, may need to be compensated by using additional reinforcement and support.
Source: Image courtesy of Allan Block.

the first block be buried below grade. If the wall will be constructed using a geogrid, the slope behind the wall will need to be excavated far enough back to allow the geogrid to be laid flat when installed.

- With the trench excavated and leveled, the base should be compacted. This can effectively be done with a rammer, plate vibrator or hand tamper. A base layer of gravel or crushed rock (size may vary from a ¼-¾ in.) typically between 6 to 12 in. deep should be placed in the trench, leveled and the compaction process repeated. If a backdrain is required, the perforated pipe should be installed and sloped toward the outlet.

▶ For sites that slope parallel to the face of the wall, the trench may be stepped the height of a base block, but always keep the required depth below grade for the first layer of block.

SETBACK

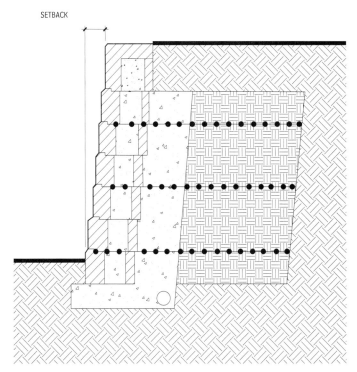

Figure 14.19 Most modular block systems incorporate a setback feature into their design that inherently provides additional support.
Source: Image courtesy of Allan Block.

Figure 14.20 Stakes should be laid out to mark the front line of the wall.
Source: Image courtesy of Allan Block.

Figure 14.21   Excess slope soil along the line of proposed wall should be removed.
Source: Image courtesy of Allan Block.

Figure 14.22   The trench should be excavated slightly wider than the block to be installed and deep enough to bury the first block at the desired depth below grade on top of the recommended depth of stone base.
Source: Image courtesy of Allan Block.

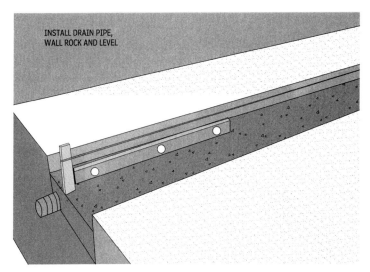

Figure 14.23 Install a perforated backdrain if required, backfill with the required depth of stone base.
Source: Image courtesy of Allan Block.

- The laying of the first course of block is critical. The entire rest of the wall builds upon it. Typically, the laying of the first course of block starts at one end or a corner, and is laid across from that point. As the blocks are laid in place, each should be checked for proper level and alignment in all directions. A string line set true to line and grade on the backside of the block can help with this step, along with a small hand or torpedo level.

▶ Adjustments to the positioning of the blocks should be made with a rubber mallet or hammer and wood block. Directly using a hammer to level the block can cause damage to the block.

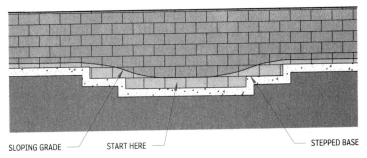

SLOPING GRADE   START HERE   STEPPED BASE

Figure 14.24 For sites that slope along the wall, set the first course of block at the lowest point and step up the base as the grade rises, always keeping the lowest course of block at the required depth below grade.
Source: Keystone Retaining Wall Systems, Inc.

Figure 14.25 The first course of block needs to be checked very carefully to be sure it is set level in every direction.
Source: Keystone Retaining Wall Systems, Inc.

▶ Some segmental block systems are designed to allow for gentle curves without cutting. Curved walls with small radii may require cutting of the blocks at the required angle with a masonry saw.

- After the first course is in place, the rest of the wall can be built up one course at a time. Different systems provide for the second

Figure 14.26 In this modular block system, pins are set in place that will interlock with the next course of block providing the setback and staggering of vertical joints required.
Source: Keystone Retaining Wall Systems, Inc.

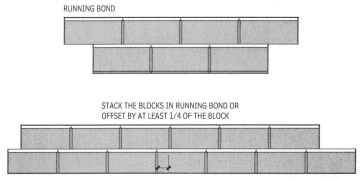

RUNNING BOND

STACK THE BLOCKS IN RUNNING BOND OR
OFFSET BY AT LEAST 1/4 OF THE BLOCK

Figure 14.27 Vertical joints should always be staggered. The different block systems have shapes or pins that will interlock the courses to provide the required overlap.
Source: Keystone Retaining Wall Systems, Inc.

course to interlock with the first course with the joints in the blocks offset so they do not line up vertically. In some systems this may require cutting the block with a masonry saw.

- Drainage stone, if required, should be backfilled and compacted as the wall is being constructed.
- As additional courses of block are installed, the area in front of the wall and the area behind the wall should be backfilled with soil and compacted. This should typically be done in 6 to 12 in. lifts.

Figure 14.28 In this modular block system, the hollows and area behind the block are filled with stone. The stone backfill should be compacted with a plate vibrator.
Source: Keystone Retaining Wall Systems, Inc.

Figure 14.29 Area in front of and behind the wall should be backfilled and compacted as the wall is built.
Source: Keystone Retaining Wall Systems, Inc.

- ▸ ▪ If a roller is used to compact the backfill, it they should be kept away from the edge of the wall to prevent the pressure and weight from shifting the blocks. The area immediately adjacent to the wall should be compacted with a plate vibrator.
- ▪ For taller walls, a geogrid may need to be installed between courses. It is rolled out on the finished course of block and extending onto the compacted backfill behind the wall. The subsequent course of block locks the wall and geogrid in place and after being pulled as taut as possible, the geogrid is staked into the compacted backfill to secure the wall into the retained soil providing the wall with added stability.
- ▪ For corners and curves the geogrid must be overlapped to provide required coverage and support. The front edge of the geogrid should be trimmed to follow the curve of the wall. (See figures 14.32, 14.33, 14.34, and 14.35)

- ▸ Geogrids should not be overlapped in direct contact with each other but always separated by a layer of soil or by an entire course of block.

Figure 14.30   In this modular block system, the geogrid locks into the pins and is held in place by the next course of block.
Source: Keystone Retaining Wall Systems, Inc.

- The process is repeated until the wall reaches its desired height. A capstone is generally installed, providing a bit of an overlap with the face of the wall and giving it a finished appearance. The capstone is often held in place by a construction adhesive.

Figure 14.31   The geogrid is pulled tight and staked into the compacted backfill. The geogrid should not be directly compacted with roller or plate vibrator but only after the next lift of backfill is placed over it.
Source: Keystone Retaining Wall Systems, Inc.

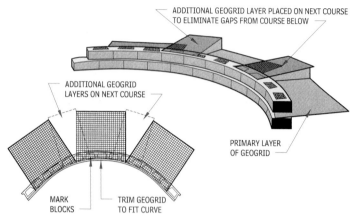

TOP VIEW

Figure 14.32 For inside curves, the geogrid should be placed on the next course of block overlapping with the geogrid below.
Source: www.allanblock.com.

Tall Modular Block Walls

Modular block wall systems can be used to construct walls 40 ft in height or greater with the appropriate system, design and installation. Some modular block wall systems for these taller walls utilize larger blocks, some using unique stabilizing systems in addition to their sheer mass and size. Walls of this type require the use of mechanized equipment to install. They are available in a variety of shapes, sizes, textures, colors and styles.

These taller modular block wall systems, like their lower wall counterparts, depend on proper installation of the first course of stone. This requires excavation of the proper width and depth, compacting the

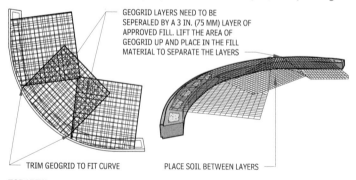

TOP VIEW

Figure 14.33 For outside curves, the geogrids should be separated by a layer of soil so that the overlaps are not in direct contact with each other.
Source: www.allanblock.com.

GEOGRID WITH INSIDE 90° CORNERS

LOCATION OF 1ST REQUIRED
LAYER OF GEOGRID

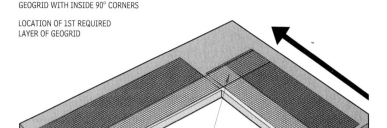

THE LENGTH OF GEOGRID THAT EXTENDS PAST
THE WALL, 25% OF THE ENTIRE WALL HEIGHT.

LOCATION OF 2nd REQUIRED
LAYER OF REORAID.

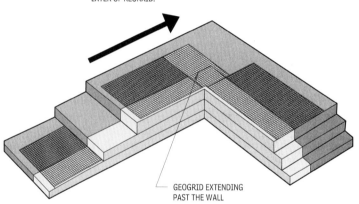

GEOGRID EXTENDING
PAST THE WALL

Figure 14.34　For inside corners, the geogrid should overlap on each alternate course of block. In this block system, the recommended overlap extends past the wall a distance of 25% of the wall height.
Source: www.allanblock.com.

subgrade, placing and compacting the required layer of stone, installation of the specified system for drainage, and the critical laying, aligning and leveling of the first course of block.

Some modular wall systems use hollow core block filled with stone, coupled with a geogrid, these relatively easy to handle concrete blocks can be used for building tall retaining walls. As these walls are built up the voids in the block are filled with stone.

Some "big block" systems use large interlocking blocks of precast concrete (some where each block literally weighs a ton or more) that depend on their own mass for stability. Because of their size and weight, geogrids are only required in the higher walls.

GEOGRID WITH OUTSIDE 90° CORNERS

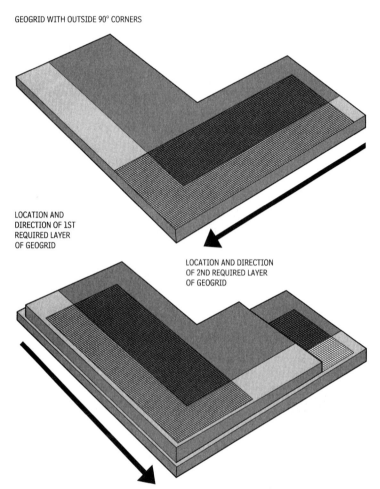

LOCATION AND
DIRECTION OF 1ST
REQUIRED LAYER
OF GEOGRID

LOCATION AND DIRECTION
OF 2ND REQUIRED LAYER
OF GEOGRID

Figure 14.35 For outside corners, the geogrid should overlap on each alternate course of block.
Source: www.allanblock.com.

Some systems provide a panel and tieback system for stability. These systems rely on the equivalent of a deadman or counterfort to resist the lateral pressures of the earth behind.

Battering is a traditional approach to strengthening a wall and providing additional resistance to the lateral pressure of the retaining soil behind it. In some segmental block wall systems, this is incorporated into the interlocking design of the block that offsets each course of block slightly back toward the high side of the retaining wall. For taller segmental block walls this is generally accomplished by tilting the wall back slightly toward the high side of the retained soil.

Figure 14.36 This "big block" system incorporated with a geogrid can build walls up to 40 ft high. It relies on large blocks weighing over a ton and its interlocking shapes for stability.
Source: Redi-Rock International

Figure 14.37 In this system the base is excavated and compacted and the base counterforts are interlocked with the wall panels and set level.
Source: Lock + Load Retaining Walls Ltd.

Figure 14.38 Stone is backfilled and compacted over counterfort supports.
Source: Lock + Load Retaining Walls Ltd.

▶ Battering may be used in conjunction with geogrids, anchors or steel reinforcement.

Geogrids

In taller walls where additional resistance to lateral soil pressure is required, the installation of horizontal layers of geotextiles are locked into the segmental wall and pinned back into the retained soil layer. The additional stability provided by the use of these geogrids allow segmental walls to be built higher than if they had to depend on their own mass for stability.

Some geogrids are manufactured where their tensile strength is directional and must be installed as recommended in order for them to function properly. This is often in the direction of the machine roll, therefore requiring that the geogrids be cut to the length specified to extend into the retained soil area. The geogrid should be slightly overlapped where they join together.

Practices to Avoid

- Avoid problems with the level of the wall as it is built. The laying of the first course of block is critical. The entire rest of the wall builds upon it. The level of each block in this first row should be checked in every direction.

- Avoid installing a geogrid in the wrong direction, some geogrids are manufactured where their tensile strength is directional and this often in the direction of the machine roll. This means that the lengths need to be cut from the roll and placed perpendicular to the wall face, not rolled out behind the wall in one long parallel piece.
- Avoid any drainage problems, whenever possible direct surface runoff away from the wall.
- Avoid problems during construction, the manufacturers of these modular block systems will often provide professional guidance and instructions for building walls in more difficult situations. Their information and expertise can be very helpful during the design phase and initial construction meetings.

Masonry Walls

Description

The traditional bonding method for solid walls has been the transverse overlapping of adjacent wythes of continuous courses of masonry headers. Most codes require that masonry headers compose a minimum of 4 % of the wall face and that the maximum vertical and horizontal spacing be 24 to 36 in. Another accepted guideline calls for one header course for every seven courses of masonry. For sufficient bonding to take place between wythes, each header must extend 3 to 4 in. into the next wythe.

At present, masonry bonding is used less due to the increased popularity of horizontal steel reinforcement and cost. The National Concrete Masonry Association (NCMA) recommends the use of continuous horizontal steel reinforcement and unit ties because of the superior moisture protection provided and greater flexibility against differential movement between wall wythes. Evidence exists, however, of deterioration of metal unit ties over time in hurricane-prone and humid environments due to rust and corrosion.

Assessing Site Conditions

A subgrade that is firm and well draining is critical to the long-term success of a masonry wall. Assess the characteristics of the existing subgrade in order to properly construct the base of the masonry wall.

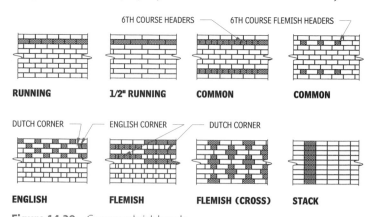

Figure 14.39 Common brick bonds.
Source: Hopper, Landscape Architectural Graphic Standards. Copyright 2007, John Wiley & Sons, Inc.

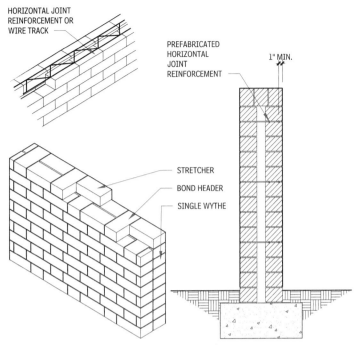

Figure 14.40 Masonry bonding and steel reinforcement in a solid wall.
Source: Hopper, Landscape Architectural Graphic Standards. Copyright 2007,
John Wiley & Sons, Inc.

Masonry plays both an aesthetic and structural role in wall design. Available in a rich palette of colors, textures, and dimensions, masonry can provide a broad spectrum of characteristics that should be considered in the overall context of the project, as the choice of specific materials are made.

Acceptable Practices

Materials

Brick

Bricks designated as "solid" are permitted to have holes or voids not to exceed 25% of their bearing or cross sectional area. Bricks designated as hollow have void space greater than 25% but do not exceeding 40% of their cross-sectional area. The strength of bricks used for constructing walls typically range between 10,000 to 14,000 psi.

Bricks are classified by their intended use and ability to withstand weather conditions as follows:

- SW bricks are manufactured to resist frequent exposure to water and freeze-thaw cycles making it the best choice for below grade applications or when exposed in areas that are subjected to severe weather;

- MW bricks have less resistance to severe weather conditions and are chosen for above ground applications in areas that are likely to experience moderate weather conditions;
- NW brick has very little resistance to weather conditions (negligible weathering) and is not recommended for landscape applications.

▶ Because the cost of SW brick vs. MW brick is not very significant, SW brick is almost always specified for landscape applications in any area.

Facing brick (brick manufactured to have at least one face visible after installation) is the most common type of brick used for freestanding and retaining wall applications. Facing brick can be specified in specific finishes, textures and colors. Facing brick has three designations:

- FBS—facing brick standard, for general masonry use;
- FBX—facing brick select, where a higher level of overall size and dimension precision is required;
- FBA—facing brick architectural, is used for non-uniform size, color, or texture in special architectural applications.

Bricks have an initial rate of absorption or suction that can affect the curing and bond strength of the mortar. The initial rate of absorption is a measure of how much water a brick absorbs during the first minute after contact with water. Bricks with high initial rates of absorption (bricks capable of absorbing over 30 grams of water in a minute/30 square in.) should be thoroughly wetted for 3–24 hours before laying.

Bricks can be laid in several positions in a wall, depending on their structural role. A brick's position designation relates to the orientation of its exposed face within a wall. There are six possible brick positions: stretcher, header, rowlock stretcher, soldier, sailor, and rowlock. A brick in the rowlock stretcher position is sometimes called a "shiner." The stretcher is the most common position in brick masonry. Headers are frequently used to provide bonding between wythes. Rowlock, soldier, and sailor courses are commonly used to create interest and detail in brick walls.

Concrete Masonry

Concrete masonry units are available in a variety of colors, sizes, shapes, textures, configurations, and weights to accommodate design, detailing, and construction. Reused and recycled masonry units, both concrete and brick, are available and provide an environmentally responsible alternative to new material.

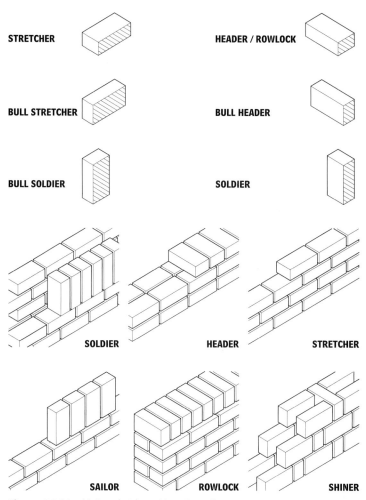

Figure 14.41 Various brick positions in wall
Source: Hopper, Landscape Architectural Graphic Standards. Copyright 2007, John Wiley & Sons, Inc.

Concrete masonry units are specified as width by height by length. The nominal dimensions are usually $\frac{3}{8}$ in. larger than the actual unit dimensions. The most common nominal widths of concrete masonry units are 4, 6, 8, 10, and 12 in. The nominal heights are mostly 8 and 4 in., except concrete bricks are typically $2\frac{2}{3}$ in. high. The nominal lengths are usually 16 or 18 in. Concrete brick length is usually 8 in. but is often 12 in. Lengths may be 18 or 24 in. in some regions. These longer lengths are usually more economical for placement.

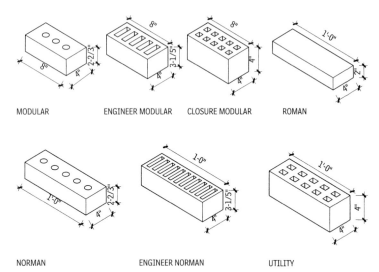

MODULAR   ENGINEER MODULAR   CLOSURE MODULAR   ROMAN

NORMAN   ENGINEER NORMAN   UTILITY

Figure 14.42 Nominal sizes of modular building brick
Source: Hopper, Landscape Architectural Graphic Standards. Copyright 2007, John Wiley & Sons, Inc.

The weight of the units also varies. The lighter units tend to provide more fire resistance and have an improved noise reduction coefficient, and they often are more economical to place in the wall. Heavier units tend to provide increased compressive strength, better resistance to sound penetration, higher water penetration resistance, and greater thermal storage capabilities.

Stucco

Stucco provides a great deal of textural and color variety in wall design. Since stucco sets slowly, a great variety of textures and patterns can be created on the surface coat with any number of tools, including gloves, combing tools, rubber sponges, a cork float, or a wire brush.

Stucco, otherwise known as *Portland cement plaster*, is a mixture of Portland cement, hydrated lime, aggregate, and water. Stucco is typically used as a veneer material in moderate to warm climates due to susceptibility to temperature extremes, including freezing, excessive heat, and direct sun exposure. Recent formulations have increased resistance to rapid freeze-thaw cycles and expanded the zone of use of this material. Stucco can be applied either as an integral part of the wall or onto a wall-backing material, such as metal reinforcement or stucco mesh.

Poured-in-place concrete and concrete masonry walls serve as good bases for the direct application of stucco if the surfaces are sufficiently rough and clean to serve as a good mechanical key and create a strong chemical bond.

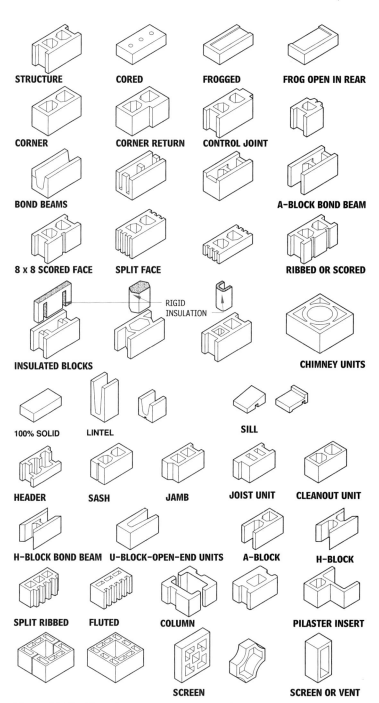

Figure 14.43 Typical concrete masonry unit shapes
Source: Hopper, Landscape Architectural Graphic Standards.Copyright 2007, John Wiley & Sons, Inc.

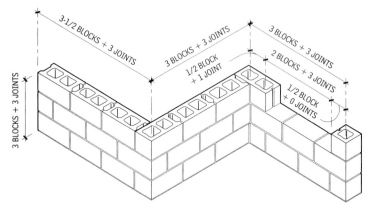

Figure 14.44 Concrete block wall dimensions should work with the module of the block to minimize the need to cut the block or work with small pieces. *Source:* Iano, Fundamentals of Building Construction. Copyright 2008, John Wiley & Sons, Inc.

The application of stucco onto surfaces that are not suitable bases or onto a wood or steel frame requires a continuous sheet of metal reinforcement or stucco mesh of a minimum weight of 1.8 pounds/square yard. Stucco mesh should have openings of ¾ in. by 3 in. to allow the stucco to be forced all the way through to the backing wall. Complete embedment of the mesh is essential to ensure a strong bond and protect the mesh from exposure to moisture. Corroded mesh can weaken the bond and stain the wall face.

Construction

Brick

The first step in constructing a brick wall is to pour a concrete footing on a well compacted subgrade set below the frost line. The dimensions of the concrete footing and any reinforcing that may be required will be based on a number of factors including the weight of the wall, if soil is being retained on one side and the bearing capacity of the soil. The concrete footing must be allowed to dry before laying the brick; this may take from 3 to 4 days.

After the concrete is dried, the footing should be chalked with the layout of where the brick wall is to be constructed. Stacks of brick should be laid out along the wall instead of one place, to save time during the laying of the brick. Prior to laying the brick, they should be moistened to prevent them from drawing too much moisture away from the mortar.

Dry lay the first course of bricks in along the footing, leaving a ½ in. between them to allow for the mortar joint. It should be possible to adjust the joint widths so that no bricks need be cut.

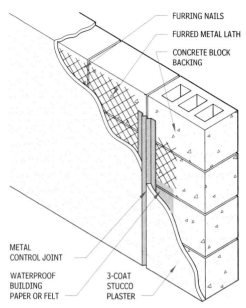

FURRING NAILS

FURRED METAL LATH

CONCRETE BLOCK
BACKING

METAL
CONTROL JOINT

WATERPROOF
BUILDING
PAPER OR FELT

3-COAT
STUCCO
PLASTER

Figure 14.45 Stucco wall
Source: Hopper, Landscape Architectural Graphic Standards.Copyright 2007,
John Wiley & Sons, Inc.

After mixing the mortar, the wall should be started from one end by removing the dry laid bricks from the concrete footing, and throwing a mortar line down about 1 in. thick by the width of the brick for about 3 to 4 bricks long. The center of the mortar line should be furrowed using the point of the trowel. The first course of bricks should be laid with mortar being applied to the end of each brick and then pressed firmly into the mortar line. The first course of brick should be checked to make sure it is level and plumb.

After the first course of bricks is laid, the wall should be built up 3 or 4 courses on each end and a level line stretched between to keep the courses level as the bricks are laid toward the middle of the wall. The corners should always be built up 3 or 4 courses higher before the wall is finished toward the middle. End bricks in the second course should be cut in half in order to stagger the vertical joints. Subsequent courses should have cut or header bricks installed in the desired pattern to stagger the vertical joints. If a brick needs to be adjusted, it should be adjusted by tapping with the handle of the trowel. Pulling a brick should be avoided, as this breaks the bond with the mortar. Excess mortar on the face of the wall should be trimmed off with the trowel.

As the mortar begins to harden, a jointing tool should be used to compress and finish the joints. Generally the vertical joints are tooled first and then the horizontal joints.

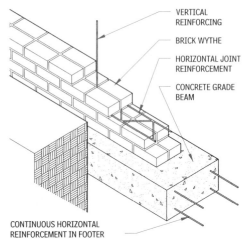

VERTICAL
REINFORCING

BRICK WYTHE

HORIZONTAL JOINT
REINFORCEMENT

CONCRETE GRADE
BEAM

CONTINUOUS HORIZONTAL
REINFORCEMENT IN FOOTER

Figure 14.46 Freestanding masonry wall detail with steel reinforcement.
Source: Hopper, Landscape Architectural Graphic Standards. Copyright 2007,
John Wiley & Sons, Inc.

Figure 14.47 A line of mortar thrown on the previous layer of brick and a
furrow made down the center with the point of the trowel.

Figure 14.48 The mason's line is set slightly off the face of the wall and the bricks with these special clamps that grip onto the end of the wall. The corners of the wall are built up first and the wall courses are filled in toward the middle.

Figure 14.49 The bricks have a generous amount of mortar troweled onto their ends before being pressed into the bed of mortar.

Figure 14.50 The bricks are pressed into the mortar bed and tapped into final alignment with the edge of the trowel.

Figure 14.51 Excess mortar being squeezed out from the setting bed is cleaned up with the trowel.

Figure 14.52 Horizontal reinforcing is placed between the two wythes of the wall on the course of brick. Next line of mortar is thrown onto brick over the horizontal reinforcing and the next course of brick is set. The next course of brick is set on the horizontal reinforcing and mortar bed.

Figure 14.53 As the mortar begins to set, a concave jointer is used to compress and smooth the mortar joints.

Concrete Masonry

Masonry walls are generally laid on a concrete footing that is wide enough to provide the wall with the required stability, generally at least twice the width of the block being used (an 8-in.-wide block would be set on a 16-in.-wide footing). The concrete footing should be set below the frost line. Expansion joints in the concrete should line up with expansion joints in the masonry wall. A chalk line is snapped on the surface of the concrete footing to indicate the desired alignment of the wall.

It is common practice to place and mark the first course of masonry units on the concrete footing including the space for the mortar joints dry (without mortar) to see how the masonry units layout and make any adjustments to avoid or minimize any cutting.

The mortar should be mixed in a wheelbarrow or a piece of $3/4$-in. plywood to be used as a mortarboard. Only enough mortar should be mixed that can be used in less than 2 hours, keeping it covered in hot weather to keep it from dying out.

After the dry layout, the mortar mix is placed on the concrete footing for a length of 3–4 masonry units long by the width of the masonry unit and 1-in. thick. The mortar bed should be furrowed using the point of the trowel to divide it evenly. Furrowing the mortar bed helps to lay the bricks evenly and force any excess mortar out the sides.

If vertical steel reinforcing rods are extending up from the footing, the mortar bed does not have to be continuous around them. The mortar bed can be spaced around them so that the concrete block will be set into the mortar bed. As the rods will extend up through the cavities in the concrete blocks and then filled with grout, there's no need for the mortar bed to come right up and around the reinforcing bars.

The masonry units should be placed starting at the corners or ends and laid toward the middle. Be sure that a corner block is used where required. Use a steel square to make sure the corner block is set square. The corner block should be checked very carefully to ensure that it is leveled horizontally in both directions and plumb vertically as the alignment of all other blocks are dependent on this first block.

▶ **All blocks should be laid with the thicker end of the face shell up.**

The wall ends or corners are generally built up 2 or 3 courses before finishing a course through the middle. Mortar should be applied to the head joint of each unit with the trowel and then firmly put into place with the desired sized joint between them. If a masonry unit needs to be adjusted, it should be adjusted by tapping with the handle of the trowel. Pulling a masonry unit should be avoided, as this breaks the bond with the mortar. A masonry unit should not be adjusted once the mortar has begun to set. Excess mortar on the face of the wall should be trimmed off with the trowel.

As the wall is built up, mason's lines and levels are used to constantly monitor that the wall is vertical and the courses are level. An even amount of mortar should be placed between each of the courses, between ½ to 1 in. Cut the masonry units for the second course and higher as required for the staggering of the joints based on the pattern chosen. Steel reinforcement should be used as required.

As the mortar begins to harden, a jointing tool should be used to compress and finish the joints. Generally the vertical joints are tooled first and then the horizontal joints.

Stucco

Stucco is typically applied in three wet coats either by hand or with new formulations that can be sprayed on. Each coat must be allowed to dry before another can be added; this usually takes at least a day or two. The final coat should be kept moist for a few days to aid curing. If it dries too fast, it can weaken and crack.

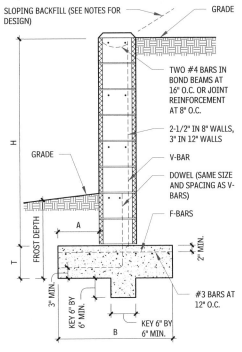

SECTION

Figure 14.54 Typical detail for a reinforced concrete masonry unit retaining wall.
Source: Hopper, Landscape Architectural Graphic Standards. Copyright 2007, John Wiley & Sons, Inc.

In using stucco, as with other types of wall material, consideration must be given to the potential for moisture penetration, corrosion of reinforcement, and stresses due to expansion and contraction. Stucco is especially susceptible to spalling and separation in regions where freezing and thawing take place. Cracks are controlled by the placement of metal control joints every 20 ft or where existing joints occur in the base. The stucco netting should be broken at the joints. It is especially important that the control joints in stucco walls be weatherproofed.

Stucco is porous allowing moisture to pass through. Painting can have a detrimental effect on porosity and only an acrylic latex paint designated specifically for use on stucco surfaces should be used.

Veneer Walls

Veneer anchor ties are typically $7/8$-in.-wide, 22-gauge corrugated galvanized steel strips. The wrinkles in the metal strip increase the

UNIT TIES, MASONRY

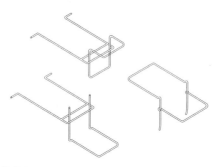

ADJUSTABLE UNIT TIES, MASONRY

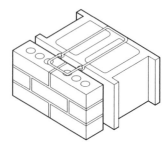

TIE DETAIL

Figure 14.55 Typical unit ties for masonry backup.
Source: Hopper, Landscape Architectural Graphic Standards. Copyright 2007, John Wiley & Sons, Inc.

Figure 14.56 Corrugated veneer anchor ties. Holes are provided if the anchor tie is to be nailed to the backup wall.

bonding between the mortar and the steel. The BIA recommends veneer anchor ties every 2 and ⅔ square ft of wall area, or one tie for every third wall course. The nail holding the tie to the wall should be within ½ in. of the 90 degree bend in the tie.

Most codes require a spacing of 16 in. vertically and 32 in. horizontally. A minimum 2-in. embedment of the tie into the joints of the veneer and the backup is required to maintain a strong anchor. Care should be taken during installation to ensure that all ties receive a minimum 1-in. mortar cover to prevent deterioration.

Wall Joints, Grout and Reinforcement

Mortar, grout, control, and expansion joints are essential to the maintenance of the structural integrity of freestanding walls. Each plays an important role in the bonding of units and the control of movement within the unit system.

Mortar and Grout

Mortar and grout are the cementitious bonding agents that integrate masonry units into masonry assemblages. Because concrete, masonry mortar, and grout contain the same principal ingredients, some designers assume what is good practice for one will also be good practice for another. In reality, the three materials differ in proportions, working consistencies, methods of placement, and structural performance.

Figure 14.57   Corrugated veneer anchor ties embedded in the concrete block wall will tie brick veneer to the backup wall.

Mortar and grout structurally bind masonry units together, whereas concrete is usually itself a structural material. One of the most important functions of concrete elements is to carry load, whereas the principal function of mortar and grout is to develop a complete, strong, and durable bond with masonry units. It is important to distinguish between the requirements for concrete, masonry mortar, and grout.

▶ When mortar or grout is placed with masonry units, the water/cement ratio rapidly decreases because of the bricks' absorbency.

Mortar Joints
Mortar joints serve the following functions:

- Joins and seals masonry, allowing for dimensional variations in masonry units;
- Affects overall appearance of wall color, texture, and patterns;
- Bonds reinforcing steel to masonry, creating composite assembly.

Mortar joint finishing methods:

- Troweled: Excess mortar is struck off. The trowel is the only tool used for shaping and finishing;
- Tooled: A special tool is used to compress and shape mortar in the joint.

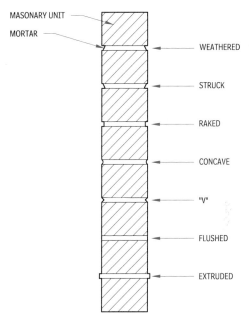

Figure 14.58 Mortar joint types.
Source: Hopper, Landscape Architectural Graphic Standards.Copyright 2007, John Wiley & Sons, Inc.

No single type of mortar is best suited for all purposes, but there are several rules for selecting mortar type. Following are the recommended uses for different types of mortar:

- Type N mortar: A medium strength mortar suitable for general use in exposed masonry above grade and recommended specifically where high compressive or transverse masonry strengths are not required;
- Type S mortar: A high strength mortar suitable for general use and specifically for circumstances where high transverse strength of masonry is desired; for reinforced masonry, where mortar bonds the facing and backing; and for areas subject to winds greater than 80 mph (130 kph);
- Type M mortar: A high strength mortar suitable for general use and recommended specifically for masonry below grade or in contact with earth, such as foundations, retaining walls, or paving;
- Type O mortar: A low strength mortar suitable for use in non-load-bearing applications in walls of low axial compressive strength and where masonry is not subject to severe weathering.

Troweled joints, which include flush, struck, and weathered, are formed by striking the mortar with a trowel. The weathered joint is recommended over the struck joint for cold regions because it drains better, which helps to prevent crumbling mortar due to freeze-thaw action.

Table 14.1 Figure Recommended Mortar Joint Sizes

Wall Type	Joint Width Size (In.)
Brick	$^3/_8$
Block and cut stone	$^1/_2$
Rubble or rough stone	$^3/_4$ or more

Source: Hopper, Landscape Architectural Graphic Standards. Copyright 2007, John Wiley & Sons, Inc.

Troweled joints can then be tooled to provide a decorative appearance and to provide protection from moisture. Tooled joints include V-shaped and concave joints, both of which are recommended for walls exposed to high winds and heavy rains. Tooling compresses the mortar tightly into the joint, which reduces the amount of airspace for moisture to penetrate.

Grout for Masonry

Grout consists of cementitious materials and aggregate thoroughly mixed with sufficient water to attain the desired consistency. Grout can be used to bond two wythes of masonry, to provide additional material to resist load, or to bond steel reinforcement to masonry so the two materials exert common action under load. Grout should be wet enough to pour without segregation of the constituents. Add enough water to achieve a slump of 8 to 11 in.

▶ Admixtures containing chlorides should never be used because they tend to corrode metal.

Control Joints

Walls are exposed to varying climates and weather conditions that can cause expansion and contraction of wall materials. Rigid restraint of wall movement can create stresses within the wall that can lead to cracking and, ultimately, wall failure. Control and expansion joints must be included as an integral part of wall design to control such movement and maintain the integrity of the wall.

Shrinkage of wall material is one of the major characteristics to be considered in walls constructed of concrete and concrete masonry units. Initial shrinkage can cause stress buildup that exceeds the tensile strength of the masonry units and the shearing strength of mortar joints, which will cause minute cracks to form in the areas of weakness and concentrated stress. Care must be taken to ensure the proper moisture content of concrete masonry units to avoid excessive shrinkage. The firing process of brick and other clay units during manufacturing, in contrast, minimizes moisture content in brick or other clay masonry products. Eventually, the units will expand as they take in water, which causes cracks to form. Masonry units will also expand and contract as the moisture content of the unit varies during weather changes.

Cracking can quickly disfigure a wall and is difficult and costly to repair. One method for controlling cracking is the use of control joints. Control joints are purposely weakened continuous vertical joints built into the wall with sufficient depth to control the location of cracks. Once cracked, the joint permits a slight amount of longitudinal wall movement to further reduce stress concentration. Wall bonds or steel reinforcements maintain the wall's configuration.

▶ Control joints are most commonly 1-in. wide tapered to a ½-in. depth. The BIA recommends that the spacing for control joints be between 20 ft (minimum) and 35 ft (maximum) on center.

Expansion Joints

Brick masonry, poured concrete, and concrete masonry walls expand and contract during temperature and moisture changes. According to the Brick Industry Association, concrete either expands or contracts 0.62 in. per 100 ft of wall length per 100 degrees Fahrenheit of temperature change. Concrete will also, in arid regions, shrink considerably over time due to initial drying. A brick wall of 100 ft in length expands or contracts approximately 0.43 in. per 100 degrees Fahrenheit of change in temperature. Fired brick will also expand initially upon contact with moisture. A maximum spacing of 25 to 30 ft is recommended because each expansion joint allows for only a maximum of ¼ in. of movement.

Expansion joints involve a complete vertical break through the wall with no bonding at the break. Joints should be, at their minimum, ½ in. wide and filled with a water-resistant material that is flexible and durable. The BIA recommends that filler materials include 20 ounce/ft squared copper; premolded compressible elastic fillers; preformed rubber or plastic sections; or a vinyl waterstop covered by an elastic joint sealer to maintain a weather seal. It is also recommended that for joints deeper than ¾ in. or wider than ⅜ in., a compressible backer rope material be used.

To maintain the horizontal alignment of the wall across the expansion joint, a tapered 2-by-4-in. vertical key is formed, or a horizontal plain steel dowel rod (minimum of 12 in. long and ½ to 1 in. in diameter) is installed at 12-in. intervals across the joint. A 16-gauge galvanized steel sleeve coated with a bond breaker or a PVC plastic pipe sleeve is slipped over one end of the rod to allow for movement of one side of the wall during expansion and contraction while maintaining the horizontal alignment. Good grades of weather-resistant polysulfide,

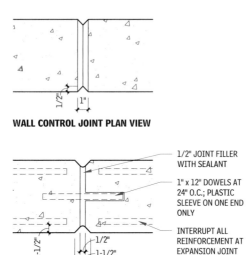

WALL CONTROL JOINT PLAN VIEW

1/2" JOINT FILLER
WITH SEALANT

1" x 12" DOWELS AT
24" O.C.; PLASTIC
SLEEVE ON ONE END
ONLY

INTERRUPT ALL
REINFORCEMENT AT
EXPANSION JOINT

WALL EXPANSION JOINT PLAN VIEW

Figure 14.59   Control and Expansion Joints.

polyurethane, butyl, or silicone rubber sealants are recommended as expansion joint sealers.

Wall Reinforcement

The placement of vertical and horizontal steel reinforcing bars or prefabricated horizontal joint reinforcement is required in a freestanding wall to provide lateral stability against wind pressure and to control the effects of masonry expansion and contraction. Steel reinforcement minimizes the width of cracks and encourages a more evenly distributed pattern of minute cracks.

Reinforcement also helps to prevent cracks in the wall panel and foundation due to settlement. The placement of prefabricated horizontal joint reinforcement is used in multi-wythe masonry walls to add transverse stability to the face and corners.

Wall reinforcement with steel reinforcement bars generally consists of bars being placed both horizontally and vertically to create a reinforcement grid. Generally, the estimated stress determines the size of the reinforcement, but typical building codes require a minimum bar diameter of ³⁄₈ in. (No. 3 bar) for both horizontal and vertical reinforcement. Vertical reinforcing bars are aligned with a clear distance from the surface of a poured-in-place concrete wall, through the grout-filled cores of a single-wythe masonry unit wall, or through the grout-filled space between wythes of multi-wythe solid, cavity, or veneer walls. The maximum spacing for vertical bar placement is 48 in. on center. All

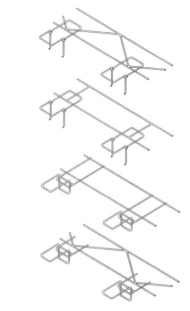

ADJUSTABLE JOINT REINFORCEMENT

TRUSS TYPE   LONGITUDINAL WIRE   LONGITUDINAL
              LADDER TYPE   TRUSS TYPE

Figure 14.60   Mortar joint steel reinforcement.
Source: Hopper, Landscape Architectural Graphic Standards. Copyright 2007, John Wiley & Sons, Inc.

horizontal wall reinforcement must be discontinued at expansion joints to allow for free movement.

In the construction of freestanding, non-load-bearing masonry walls, horizontal reinforcing bars are often replaced with prefabricated horizontal joint reinforcement or what is often called "wire track." In cavity and veneer walls, prefabricated horizontal joint reinforcement is placed to tie the two adjacent wall wythes together and provide additional lateral stability.

Prefabricated horizontal joint reinforcement generally consists of 9-gauge galvanized steel wire in either a truss or ladder configuration that is usually manufactured in 10- to 12-ft lengths. A minimum overlapping of 6 to 8 in. for consecutive wire sections is required to maintain continuous tensile strength along the joint. Placement of continuous prefabricated horizontal reinforcement wire within the course should ensure that one side of the wire sits in each wythe of the wall.

Figure 14.61 Vertical steel reinforcing bars aligned through the center of the concrete block cores and grouted in place.

Types M, S, and N mortar are recommended by the BIA for use with joint reinforcement. All wall reinforcement should be sufficiently covered with mortar or concrete to prevent exposure and deterioration of the reinforcement, resultant staining of the wall face, and crumbling of the mortar joint. The American Concrete Institute recommends a minimum bar cover of 2 in. for No. 6 to 8 rebars and a cover of 1 ½ in. for No. 5 or smaller bars. If sufficient coverage cannot be ensured during construction, corrosion-resistant bars should be used.

To prevent the wall stem and footer from separating, they should be tied together by extending the horizontal bar in the footer up toward the stem and securely tying it to the vertical reinforcement of the panel. Landphair and Klatt (1979) recommend that the vertical reinforcement and the footer reinforcement overlap a distance equal to 20 bar diameters. For example, the required overlap of wall and footer reinforcement using a No. 4 vertical bar would be 10 in.

Brick Columns and Piers

Columns and piers are freestanding masonry constructions found in landscape elements such as arbors, pergolas, and bollards. Pilasters are integrated into masonry walls. Columns serve primarily as vertical supports. Piers and pilasters must provide lateral support, as well. Pier-and-panel walls use structural piers to support relatively thin brick wall panels that span from pier to pier.

In the landscape, masonry columns provide adequate support for vertical loads without internal reinforcing. Piers and pilasters require additional reinforcing to resist lateral forces. Foundations for brick piers and pilasters are typically reinforced cast-in-place concrete.

Foundations must extend to recommended structural depths or to the local frost depth, whichever is greater. Like walls, the topmost surface of columns, piers, and pilasters must be capped for water resistance.

Freestanding Wall Moisture Protection

The life span of a masonry wall is determined in part by its resistance to moisture penetration. The design of any wall must take into consideration the climate of the area in which it is to be built and the level of exposure to moisture. The various methods for protecting freestanding walls against moisture penetration include the following:

- Placement of wall capstones on the top course of concrete block, brick, and stone walls
- Use of drainage-type walls (e.g., cavity and veneer walls) and inclusion of clean cavities between wall wythes
- Use of weep holes, flashing, and waterstops
- Use of tooled mortar joints with a concave or V-shape
- Use of joint sealants
- Use of proven silicone water-repellant surface treatment (Certain compositions can also provide protection from acid rain.)

Figure 14.62 Configurations for solid brick columns.
Source: Hopper, Landscape Architectural Graphic Standards. Copyright 2007, John Wiley & Sons, Inc.

Overview of Caps and Copings

Caps and copings serve a visual function and provide weather resistance and drainage. Copings are typically composed of brick, stone, concrete, or tile. Brick copings using standard shapes should be sloped to encourage drainage. A variety of special shapes are available that facilitate drainage. Water penetration occurs primarily in the joints, not through the masonry material, so it may be advisable to use larger units of stone or precast concrete that are specifically shaped for drainage and offer fewer joints.

- Copings and caps prevent water from entering the inner wall from above by shedding water to the sides, where it is thrown clear of the wall, usually by means of a drip edge.
- Anchor coping as necessary. If the coping material is different from the wall material, compare their thermal and moisture expansion characteristics and make provisions for different movement.
- In general, through-wall flashing should be used immediately under the coping of walls. However, this decision depends on several factors, including the type of coping used, the number of joints used, and the climatic conditions of the area (whether there is high or low precipitation and the number of freezing and thawing cycles).

Wall Drainage

Drainage is a key concern in the design of any exterior masonry wall. A vertical section of aggregate immediately behind a retaining condition allows water to drain, diminishing the buildup of hydrostatic pressure. A filter fabric should be placed between the soil and the gravel to prevent the clogging of the aggregate's air voids. Footing drains, usually of tile or perforated plastic, are placed at the wall's footing. A water-permeable filter fabric should be placed over footing drains to prevent their sedimentation and clogging, as well.

Weep holes are openings, or voids, in the brick wall whose purpose is the venting and dispersion of any water that finds its way into the

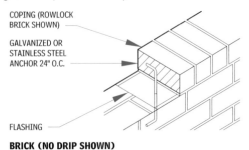

Figure 14.63 Rowlock brick coping.
Source: Hopper, Landscape Architectural Graphic Standards. Copyright 2007, John Wiley & Sons, Inc.

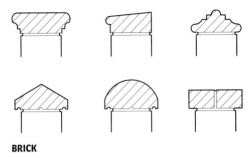

BRICK

Figure 14.64a Typical brick copings.

TERRA-COTTA

Figure 14.64b Typical terra-cotta copings.

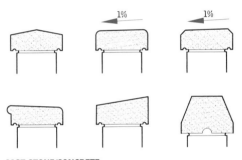

CAST STONE/CONCRETE

Figure 14.64c Typical cast stone or concrete copings.
Source: Hopper, Landscape Architectural Graphic Standards.Copyright 2007, John Wiley & Sons, Inc.

wall. To be effective, weep holes must be adequately sloped in section and must "daylight" slightly above finished grade on the nonretaining face of the wall. A weep hole can be as simple and reliable as an open, (nonmortared) head joint between bricks. A small plastic pipe may be inserted into the mortar joints.

Practices to Avoid

- Air entrainment has the detrimental effect of reducing the bond between mortar and masonry units or reinforcement. The use of air-entraining Portland cements (types IA, IIA, or IIIA) and air-entrained lime (types SA and NA) for masonry mortar and grout may not be appropriate. Two different air-entraining agents should not be used in the same mortar or grout. Air-entraining admixtures should not be used in structural masonry. Building codes mandate lower allowable flexural tension stresses if air-entrained cements or lime are used in mortar.

- Avoid risking damage to your eyes, always wear protective goggles when cutting masonry units with a brick set or mason's hammer.
- Do not mix more mortar than you can use in less than two hours. Keep mixing it periodically with the trowel to keep portions from hardening.
- Do not allow mortar to dry out; keep covered in hot weather.
- Do not adjust or move a masonry unit once the mortar has begun to set.

Stone Walls

Description

Stone masonry provides either an integral or an applied wall finish in various patterns, colors, textures, and grains. The most common stone masonry walls are 4- or 8-in. cavity or veneer walls. Less common is the 18-in.-thick, double-faced solid dry-laid free stone wall with masonry bonding.

Dry-laid stone walls are generally constructed of either irregular-shaped or squared stone. Walls of squared stone are skillfully pieced together with smaller chips and flint stones fitted between the larger course stones. This interlocking arrangement results in a very stable condition. The core of the wall is packed with small stones or chips to render the required weight for stability. Longer bonding stones are turned transversely to serve as ties through the wall. For walls constructed of more rounded rubble stone, a batter is recommended of

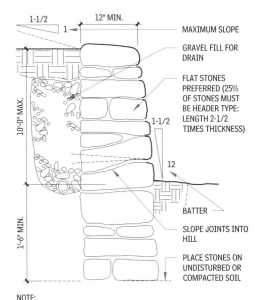

NOTE:
STAGGER VERTICAL JOINTS FROM COURSE TO COURSE 6" MIN. HORIZONTALLY. THE THICKNESS OF THE WALL AT ANY POINT SHOULD NOT BE LESS THAN HALF THE DISTANCE FROM THAT POINT TO THE TOP OF THE WALL

Figure 14.65a   Typical stone wall detail
Source: Hopper, Landscape Architectural Graphic Standards. Copyright 2007, John Wiley & Sons, Inc.

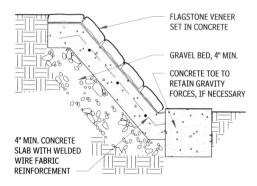

Figure 14.65b Typical stone bank wall detail.
Source: Hopper, Landscape Architectural Graphic Standards. Copyright 2007, John Wiley & Sons, Inc.

generally 1-½ in. per 12 in. of wall height. A "batter" is a slight slope on the face of the wall that recedes from wall bottom to top.

The foundation of a free stone wall is constructed to be horizontal, but the top of the wall is sloped to follow the lay of the land. The traditional free stone wall was laid "dry," that is with no mortar between the joints. Free stone walls use either a random rubble or a coursed rubble stone pattern. Random rubble has no apparent coursing; coursed rubble has relatively continuous courses and horizontal bed joints.

Cavity and veneer stone walls typically use random rubble (no apparent coursing), coursed rubble (continuous horizontal bed joints), or coursed ashlar patterns (cut-faced stone with ranged coursing and broken bond). The stone used is more dressed relative to the rubble wall stone.

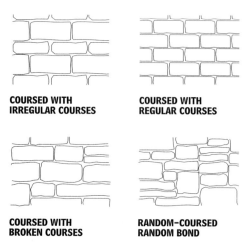

Figure 14.66a Typical stone wall patterns

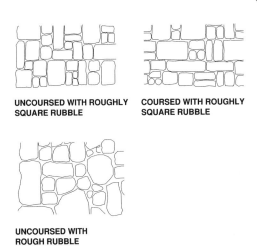

UNCOURSED WITH ROUGHLY SQUARE RUBBLE

COURSED WITH ROUGHLY SQUARE RUBBLE

UNCOURSED WITH ROUGH RUBBLE

Figure 14.66b Typical stone wall patterns (continued)
Source: Hopper, Landscape Architectural Graphic Standards.Copyright 2007, John Wiley & Sons, Inc.

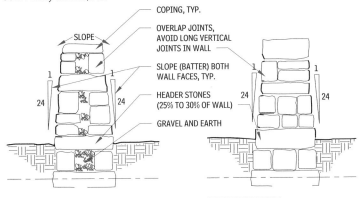

DOUBLE TIER WALL

SINGLE TIER WALL

Figure 14.67 Typical single and double tier wall details.
Source: Hopper, Landscape Architectural Graphic Standards.Copyright 2007, John Wiley & Sons, Inc.

As with the solid wall, the pointing of the veneer wall can also be recessed to give the appearance of a "dry" wall. The typical facing joint for an ashlar wall is $3/8$ to $3/4$ in. wide. Some types of stone, such as sandstone, are especially porous or light-colored, and care must be taken in the detailing of the wall to avoid the use of corrosive metal ties and mortars that stain the stone face.

Assessing Site Conditions

There are many different types of stone and picking a type that blends well with the existing site is a first step. The second step is finding a supply of stone to build the wall. If there is a large quantity of stone or old stone walls on site, the wall may be constructed from this collected stone.

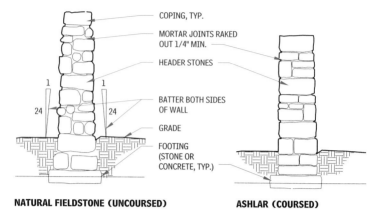

NATURAL FIELDSTONE (UNCOURSED)   **ASHLAR (COURSED)**

Figure 14.68   Typical stone wall details with deeply raked mortar joints.
Source: Hopper, Landscape Architectural Graphic Standards. Copyright 2007,
John Wiley & Sons, Inc.

If the stone needs to be purchased, a stone supplier or quarry can supply the stone, but the quantity to build the wall will need to be calculated.

To calculate the quantity of stone needed for a dry laid or mortared stone wall, multiply the length of the wall (in feet) times the overall height of the wall (from bottom of base to top of wall, in feet) times the width of the wall (in feet) which will give you the volume of stone required in cubic feet. Suppliers that sell stone by volume will usually use cubic yards as a measure, which will require that you take your cubic foot total and divide by 27, to calculate your volume in cubic yards (there are 27 cubic ft in one cubic yard). If the stone is being sold by weight, a ton of stone will be approximately 14 to 16 cubic ft, depending on the density of the stone chosen.

The calculation for the quantity of stone for a veneer wall is based on the thickness of the veneer stone and square feet of wall face. A 4-in.-thick veneer stone will cover approximately 40 square ft per ton and a 6-in.-thick veneer stone will cover approximately 30 square ft per ton. For thin stone veneers ranging in thickness from 1 to 2 in., the stone will cover approximately 60 to 70 square ft per ton.

Acceptable Practices

Dry Laid Stone Walls

A freestanding dry laid stone wall is built a bit like a puzzle. Typically, the different stones will be segregated by shape and purpose:

- Corner stones are fairly flat and require two good faces to create a good right angle corner;

- Tie stones are long enough to be placed perpendicular to the face and extend through the entire wall helping to hold it together;
- Risers that are large enough to extend up through several smaller courses of stone, provide visual interest by breaking up long expanses of wall;
- Capstones are fairly flat stones that are large enough to cover the entire top of the wall.

The line of the wall should be excavated slightly wider than the width of the wall. Because a dry laid stone wall has the ability to move, it isn't necessary to excavate down to the frost line. After the level trench is dug, the subgrade should be compacted. A layer of stone can help set the first course of stone firmly in place. Stakes and a string line should be set to keep the wall properly aligned as it is being constructed.

A dry laid stone wall is usually set wider at the base and the wall tapers toward the top. The wall should be built from the ends or corners toward the middle. As the ends are built, the string line can be supported by the end stones to help guide the middle stones into place at the right height.

Mortared Stone Walls

Mortared stone walls are basically built using the same techniques as a dry laid wall, except that the voids between the stones are filled with mortar. This bonds the individual stones together creating a wall that is more monolithic. This allows walls to be built higher and without the taper of the dry laid stone walls. The base of the wall should extend down to the frost line.

Veneered Stone Walls

Veneered stone walls are constructed by using thin layers of flat stone that are attached onto a structural concrete or concrete block wall. The structural wall is constructed first, including wall ties that will be used to aid in attaching the stone to the wall. The stones are mortared up against the structural wall and the wall ties are mortared into the stone joints. An alternative to wall ties, a metal lath can be attached to the structural wall with a thin scratch coat of mortar troweled over the lath.

The stones are laid starting at the corners and bottom of the wall and continue toward the middle and top attaching to the wall with $3/8$ to $3/4$ in.-thick mortar. The backs of the stones themselves should be troweled with approximately $1/2$ in. of mortar before they are pressed into mortar bed.

Joints should be fairly uniform in thickness ranging from $3/8$ to $1/2$ in. Wide joints are susceptible to shrinkage cracking.

▶ Keep absorptive structural wall and/or scratch coat as well as absorptive stones moist so that they do not absorb water from the mortar.

Practices to Avoid

- Avoid rushing, building a rock wall is an art and takes time, patience and skill.
- Avoid building thin rock walls, they will not be stable or long lasting.
- Avoid long horizontal joints and break all vertical joints.
- Avoid placing stones on end, it is best to place them as they would naturally lie.
- For stone veneer walls, avoid moving or tapping the stones once they are set in place.

Gabion Walls

Description

Gabion walls are constructed with large rectangular steel wire mesh baskets that are filled with stone. Used for hundreds of years in Europe, it is being used more extensively in the United States as a low cost alternative to other wall solutions.

Although gabion walls can be designed to be built higher, they are generally best suited for walls 18 ft or less. To achieve the required structural stability the base of the wall becomes wider as the height increases.

Assessing Site Conditions

Gabion walls are well suited where conditions require a flexible and permeable retaining alternative. They are used effectively to control erosion along river, shore and water channels, as retaining structures for roads and railroads and along mountainous highways to trap falling rock.

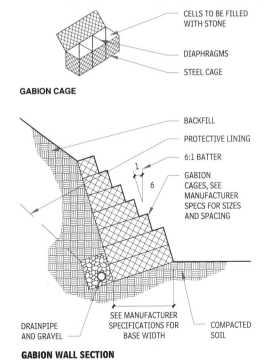

Figure 14.69 Typical gabion wall section.

Source: Hopper, Landscape Architectural Graphic Standards. Copyright 2007, John Wiley & Sons, Inc.

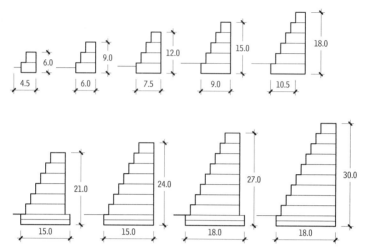

Figure 14.70 Diagram showing the typical relationship of wall height to the width of the base.
Source: Terra Aqua Gabions Inc.

Acceptable Practices

The gabion retaining walls can be placed directly on a compacted soil base. For increased load distribution that will minimize differential settling and for increase drainage capability, a base layer of well compacted graduated stone, from ½ to 1-½ in. can be used.

Figure 14.71 Typical installation along a water channel.
Source: Terra Aqua Gabions Inc.

The gabion baskets are filled with clean, hard stone with the objective of creating the minimum amount of void space with the maximum amount of weight. Round stone is less likely to damage the wire of the baskets than sharply angled stone. The gabion baskets are filled and compacted in three 12-in. lifts.

The Federal Highway Administration has set the following size criteria for the stone fill for gabions:

- 6-in. sieve—100% passing;
- 3-in. sieve—75-100% passing;
- Number 200 sieve—0-25% passing.

Gabion retaining walls depend on their weight for stability. They can be constructed with a setback to achieve greater stability. Where required, the width of the gabion wall can be increased to resist the retained soils lateral pressures. The gabion walls can also be constructed with a batter by preparing the base of the wall at the required angle.

Gabion walls can be constructed with a straight wall face or with a wall face that is stepped back each tier. For a straight wall face, the wall should be constructed with a 6–10 degree batter. For a stepped wall face, each tier should be stepped back horizontally between 1 ft to 1-½ ft for every 3-ft vertical change in height.

For maximum resistance to lateral pressure, the gabion baskets should be placed with their long dimension perpendicular to the face of the

Figure 14.72   A view showing the range of different stone sizes and stepped back tiers.
Source: Terra Aqua Gabions Inc.

wall. When places with the long dimension are parallel to the wall face, the vertical seams between the baskets should be offset.

A geotextile filter fabric should be used behind the wall to prevent the soil that is being retained from migrating into the stone filled gabions and filling the voids. If a crushed stone backfill is used to reduce the hydrostatic pressure exerted on the wall, then the geotextile should be placed between the crushed stone backfill and the soil. The voids in the stone of the gabion wall must allow water to freely pass through the wall.

Practices to Avoid

- Poor compaction can lead to shifting and movement that can compromise the structural integrity of the wall. The backfill behind a gabion retaining wall must be compacted in 6 to 9-in. lifts to a minimum of 95% standard Proctor.
- To prevent loss of retained soil, a geotextile filter fabric should be installed to prevent soil from migrating and filling the voids of the gabion stone filled baskets.

Figure 14.73 Crushed stone backfill should be compacted behind the gabion wall in 6 to 9-in. lifts. Note the geotextile fabric separating the retained soil from the crushed stone and gabion wall, preventing the filling of the void spaces between the stones.
Source: Terra Aqua Gabions Inc.

Figure 14.74 When used to protect against erosion of water channels, a gabion apron is installed at the base to prevent scouring from undermining the wall.
Source: Terra Aqua Gabions Inc.

Wood Retaining Walls

Description

Wood, or landscape timbers, is most typically used in the construction of retaining walls, versus freestanding walls. Recycled plastic wood is not generally a suitable alternative for landscape walls due to its relatively high initial cost, low structural capacity, and tendency to bend.

There are three typical types of wood retaining walls:

- Horizontal timber wall;
- Timber wall with vertical posts;
- Timber crib wall.

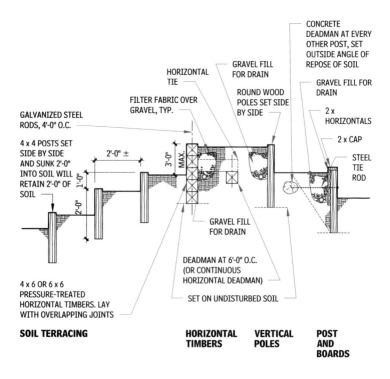

Figure 14.75   Various timber retaining wall sections.
Source: Hopper, Landscape Architectural Graphic Standards.Copyright 2007, John Wiley & Sons, Inc.

Assessing Site Conditions

Two major site condition elements that affect the design and construction of a wood retaining wall are the soil that it is being built upon and drainage:

- It is important that the retaining wall is built upon a stable base. Generally, gravel and sand soils make for a better foundation material than soils that are high in organic material, clays or silt. Soil borings or test pits can be used to determine the type of subsurface material present. For wood wall construction, it is typical to use a compacted granular base for drainage and stability. If the site is not well drained, incorporating a perforated pipe in the gravel base to carry water away to an outlet on-site away from the wall is typically used.

- Water pressure (hydrostatic) can build behind a wall and saturated soils can become very heavy exerting sufficient force on the wall to cause it to fail. Therefore, provision needs to be made to provide proper drainage behind the wall to relieve any hydrostatic pressure that may develop. This is particularly critical in retaining walls that are at the bottom of a slope. The additional water flowing down the slope toward the wall creates a greater surcharge behind a wall than when the high side of the retaining wall is relatively flat. If the site allows, it is always advisable to create a swale a few feet back and running parallel to the wall, to allow water from the slope to be diverted away from the back of the wall toward a stabilized outlet. In this case, the soil should slope away from the back of the wall toward the swale.

If the height of the retaining wall is significant (over 4 to 6 ft), consideration should be given to terracing the change in elevation with two or more walls of lesser height. Although this requires more horizontal distance, the walls can be structurally easier to build and aesthetically provide a more interesting look, with room for vegetation between the walls to soften their effect and resulting in an overall less imposing structure.

Acceptable Practices

Wood and Fasteners

Wood timbers for retaining walls are generally 4 x 6, 6 x 6 or 8 x 8 in. and come in 8- or 10-ft lengths. Any wood for retaining walls must be pressure treated and designated for "Ground Contact". This information will be marked with ink or on a tag that is stapled to each piece of lumber. Fasteners must be compatible with the pressure treated wood that is being used.

(See section on "Pressure Treated Wood")

Horizontal Timber Retaining Wall

A horizontal timber retaining wall starts with the trenching for the first timber to a depth that will allow for a 6 to 12 in. base of $3/8$ to $3/4$-in. diameter well rounded, washed stone or bank run gravel and the top of the first timber row to be set at finished grade (one full tie below grade). This may require some additional excavation into the soil that is to be retained to allow some room to work. After the trench is dug, line the trench with enough filter fabric to accommodate the drainage stone and be overlapped at all seams a minimum of 6 in. If the soil is not well drained, the addition of a 4-in. perforated pipe in the stone base to carry water away from the base of the stone should be considered. The stone can then be spread and compacted.

A mason's string line is used to set the first row perfectly level in every direction and at the correct height. The drainage stone is added or removed as needed to set the timbers correctly. After setting the first row, the geotextile should be wrapped and overlapped around the stone to prevent migration of the soil into the stone voids that would negatively impact affect its drainage function. The first row of timbers is the most critical, affecting the strength and stability of the entire wall.

After the first row of timbers is set, successive rows can be added on top. When laying the upper rows of ties it is important to stagger the joints. Typically, this is done by cutting a tie in half and placing it on a full length tie below. With some thought, it is possible to cut the ties to a length that the resulting piece left over can be used somewhere in the construction and not be wasted (to stagger the next row or as a deadman). For walls taller than 3 ft, a batter is employed by setting each row edge back $1/2$ in. from the face of the row below to give the wall additional stability.

▶ The ends of landscape ties sometimes are not cut perfectly square and can result in gaps in the wall. Ends that do not fit together square should be field cut (the cut end treated with a compatible preservative) and fit together tightly to close any gaps.

Each row of ties should be attached to the row below with spikes or steel reinforcing bars. Spikes should be $3/8$ by 10 in. (for a 6 by 6 in. tie) with four spikes per tie, starting at approximately 6 in. from the ends of each tie. They are easier to drive if the holes are pre-drilled. Steel reinforcing bars should be #3 bars set through pre-drilled hole and driven into the ground below. The reinforcing bars should fit tight into the pre-drilled holes. For taller walls, this may only be practical for the first two or three rows, with the others above joined together with spikes.

For wood retaining walls greater than 2 or 3 ft in height, deadmen are installed to give the wall greater stability. A deadman is a tie that is set back perpendicular to the wall face with a "T" on the side where the soil is being retained. This will require some excavation back into the soil that is to be retained. After the soil behind the wall is backfilled, the pressure of the retained soil on the deadmen help keep the wall from overturning. A typical installation might have a deadman at the end of every 8 ft landscape tie. The deadman might consist of a 5-ft-long cut tie with a 3-ft-long "T" (totaling 8 ft which would use 1 tie without any waste). The deadman should extend out from the face of the wall by an inch or so, which provides more stability and minimizes absorption of water into the end grain which can result in splitting. Each deadman should be attached to the tie below and to the "T" with two ³/₈ in. spikes. Deadmen nearer the top of the wall tend to be longer and extend into the retained soil a greater distance than the deadmen installed in the lower rows. Deadmen are typically installed every second or third row. Deadmen do not generally extend to the top two rows, as not to interfere with any planting that may be considered. Whatever pattern the deadmen are placed in, they are not just a structural element but also aesthetically contribute to breaking up the monotony of large expanses of vertical wall faces.

For wood retaining walls greater than 3 or 4 ft in height, extra measures for drainage may need to be used. As some water is free to pass through the spaces between the wood members or percolate down to the stone drainage layer, taller walls will need provision to relieve any hydrostatic pressure that may build and affect the stability of the wall. Two typical approaches are to use weep holes or a drainage composite sheet.

Weep holes drilled through the wood every 3 to 4 ft, lined with 1- to 1-¹/₂ in. pvc pipe pitched slightly toward the front of the wall, with the pipe fitted into a cubic foot of drainage stone surrounded by a geotextile fabric on the retained soil side of the wall, is the typical detail used.

Drainage composite sheets are made of a high strength plastic core with a layer of geotextile fabric on either side. Placed vertically up against the inside of the wall, it provides continuous drainage away from the face of the wall and down to the base, where the water will percolate through the stone drainage base and/or be carried away by a perforated pipe. The geotextile fabric prevents the soil from clogging the plastic core and any water flows freeing to the base.

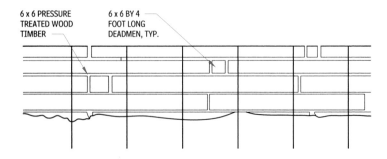

6 x 6 PRESSURE
TREATED WOOD
TIMBER

6 x 6 BY 4
FOOT LONG
DEADMEN, TYP.

Figure 14.76 Alternative anchoring approach using vertical steel reinforcing bars driven through the landscape ties and into the subgrade. Pre-drilling holes slightly smaller than the diameter of the spikes makes driving them easier and minimizes the chances of having the wood split. For higher retaining walls the upper rows of timbers may need to be spiked to the ones below that are anchored with the reinforcing bars.

Soil should be backfilled and compacted in 12-in. lifts as the wall is being built. Waiting to backfill after the wall is completed will not allow the soil to be compacted properly.

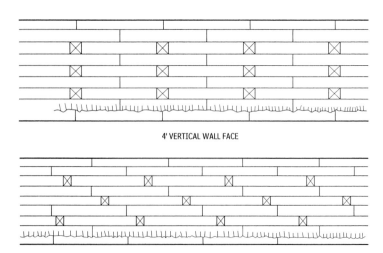

4' VERTICAL WALL FACE

4' VERTICAL WALL FACE

Figure 14.77 Different header configurations for a typical 4-ft-high wall. Deadmen every second row align vertically in the top example; deadmen every third row are staggered in the bottom example.
Source: www.sustland.umn.edu/implement/timber.htm.

Timber Wall With Vertical Posts

Timber walls can be built with horizontal or vertical boards, supported by vertical posts. The vertical posts are placed in the ground so that at least half of the total length of the post (which should equal the height of the wall) is embedded in the ground approximately every 4 ft. (For example, if a wall is to be 3 ft tall, 3 ft of the post should be embedded in the ground, with 3 ft of the post extending above ground to support the wall boards.).

If vertical retaining boards are used, they should extend 1 ft below finished grade and they will need a horizontal back board to connect them. For horizontal retaining boards, they should extend at least one board width below finished grade. The retaining boards are attached to the posts with 16 d nails (compatible with the wood preservative). Retaining boards are typically 2 by 6 in. pressure treated lumber.

Deadmen are used for stability in much the same way as they are for a horizontal timber retaining wall. However, rather than having a wood member extend perpendicular to the wall face, the deadman timber is connected to the upper portion of the wall by a tie rod that is bolted to the face of the wall and the deadman. The tie rod and deadman are tilted slightly back for extra stability.

Provisions for drainage are similar to a horizontal timber retaining wall, with geotextile wrapped stone placed along the base (with a perforated pipe if soil is not well-drained) or with regularly spaced weep holes.

The top of the wall should be capped with a piece of pressure treated lumber that will protectively extend over the post ends and retaining boards.

Timber Crib Wall

Timber crib walls of pressure treated lumber are constructed by interlocking stretchers (longitudinal members) with headers (transverse members) to form vertical bins or cribs that are then backfilled with coarse granular stone. The connection between the headers and stretchers are made by the interlocking shapes in the wood, although sometimes they are pinned or spiked. The construction is very much like that of a log cabin. The timber crib wall is basically a flexible wall system that can move to adjust to different pressures and forces. The wall stability is dependent upon the weight of the material that fills the crib cells.

The timber crib walls are generally constructed with a minimum width of 4 ft and as a rule of thumb, a width that is one half the wall height. The walls can be constructed vertical or typically in the case of taller walls with a batter of 1:4 to 1:6 (1 ft horizontal for every 4 or 6 ft vertical offset tilting back into the slope). The batter is achieved by constructing the wall on a base with the appropriate slope to equal the desired batter. They can be constructed on a stone base course, or for taller timber crib walls, the wall may be set on a reinforced concrete base.

The crib cells should be filled with stone in layers and compacted. The backfill behind the crib wall should be compacted in layers as the wall is constructed. Drainage should be provided for taller walls or where the soil is not well-drained in a similar manner to a horizontal timber wall with washed stone, a geotextile fabric and a perforated pipe if necessary.

Live timber crib walls are being used for streambank and slope stabilization. Timber crib walls have live branch cuttings (cut when the plants are dormant) approximately 6 ft long placed into the wall and extending out a foot or so from the face of the wall as the stone is being placed into the crib cells. The cuttings need to be long enough so that their ends extend beyond the width of the crib wall and into the retained soil behind. The cuttings will sprout in the spring and the roots that develop will help, along with the crib wall, to stabilize the streambank or slope.

Figure 14.78 Timber crib wall seen from above with open crib cells waiting to be filled with stone and compacted.
Source: Maccaferri Ltd.

Figure 14.79 Timber crib wall with the crib cells backfilled near the top of the wall.
Source: Maccaferri Ltd.

Practices to Avoid

- Avoid rushing or taking shortcuts when establishing the base of a wood retaining wall. It is one of the most critical steps in the construction process and has a direct effect on the structural integrity and longevity of the entire wall.
- Avoid backfilling all at one time after the wood retaining wall is complete. Instead backfill as the wall is built compacting in 12-in. layers with a hand tamper. The top 6 to 12 in. can be lightly compacted if the area behind the wall is to be planted.
- Avoid not compensating for additional loads on a wall that could cause it to lean or fail. Evaluate whether there will be additional loads placed near the top of the wall and compensate by adding additional deadmen, increasing the length of the deadmen and/or building the wall with a batter to ensure stability. It is far less costly to make adjustments during construction than it is after the project is finished and a problem develops.

Figure 14.80 Front face of crib wall showing backfilled stone, stretchers and headers.
Source: Maccaferri Ltd.

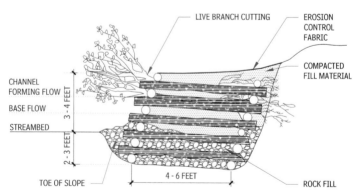

Figure 14.81 Live timber crib wall incorporating live branch cuttings for streambank stabilization.
Source: www.dnr.state.oh.us/water/pubs/fs_st/stfs17/tabid/4172/Default.aspx

Figure 14.82   Timber crib wall incorporating planting provides a great deal of visual interest and contrast with the crib stone.
Source: Maccaferri Ltd

References

ALSO IN THIS BOOK:

- Concrete
- Pressure Treated Wood
- Wood

OTHER RESOURCES:

- Harlow C. Landphair and Fred Klatt, Jr. 1988, Landscape Architecture Construction. New York: Elsevier.
- Hopper, Landscape Architectural Graphic Standards.Copyright 2007, John Wiley & Sons, Inc.

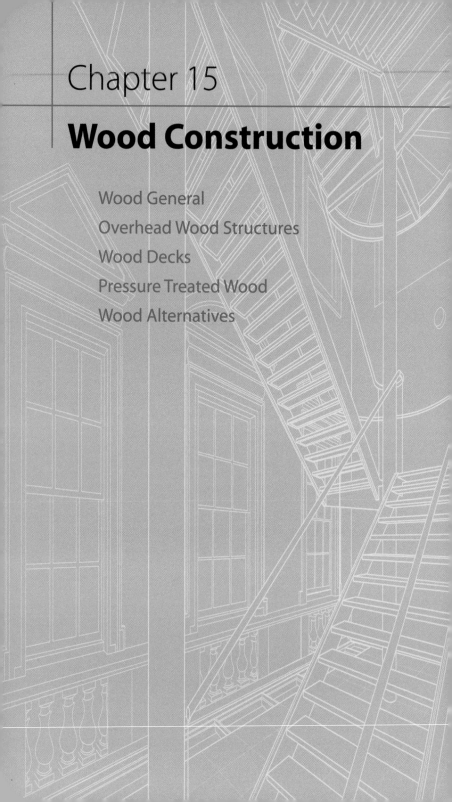

Chapter 15

Wood Construction

Wood General

Description

The primary factors influencing the properties of lumber include soil type, growth conditions, and natural calamities or periods of stress. Other influences include the location and orientation of the wood within the log, the presence of naturally occurring conditions including knots (where branches were located), checks, splitting, sap deposits, and proximity of the wood to the bark layer.

Assessing Site Conditions

Once cut, wood begins to discharge moisture, and if the drying is uncontrolled, splitting around the end grain or distortions within the board often occur.

Cupping.   Cupping occurs when the two flat faces of a board dry at different rates. Cupping may be seen as the profile of the board's end grain curving in from the sides, creating a cupped form on the faces. Prevalence for cupping is higher in boards with a flat grain than in those with vertical grain. Boards tend to cup away from the bark side of the wood; and when used for decking, the term "bark side up" refers to the laying of the decking boards with the growth rings facing down and with the convex side up, preventing the board from entrapping water. Live loads on the deck will tend to flatten the boards and reduce the mounding that can occur in the "bark side up" orientation.

Bowing, crooking, twisting.   These distortions occur along the length of the board. Bowing constitutes a single curving of its face (widest dimension) plane. Crooking is observed by looking down the face plane to find the board curving on itself at the edge (narrowest) dimension. Twisting is a combination of curves in different directions. All major structural members need to be true and free of distortions.

These distortions to the lumber most frequently occur during an accelerated and uneven drying process. Wood is best seasoned either by the air-drying (AD) or kiln-drying (KD) process. Drying time varies according to species, lumber thickness, and the moisture content of wood and air. Wood is sold with a range of moisture content from less than 15% to more than 19%. Optimum moisture content of lumber for stability in a structure is 12%. Once dried, wood, due to moisture absorption, is still susceptible to variations in size. As a general rule,

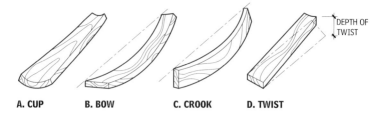

DEPTH OF
TWIST

A. CUP   **B. BOW**   **C. CROOK**   **D. TWIST**

Figure 15.1   Distortions commonly found in board lumber.
Source: Hopper, Landscape Architectural Graphic Standards.Copyright 2007,
John Wiley & Sons, Inc.

wood expands as it gains, and shrinks as it loses, moisture. The degree
of change depends on the amount of moisture absorbed, the species
of wood, and the cut of the grain.

Acceptable Practices

Overview of Sizing and Surfacing

Lumber comes in standardized thicknesses, widths, and lengths, and can
be custom-milled to meet any nonstandardized dimensions. The "nominal dimension" is the actual thickness and width of the wood after being
"rough cut" at the sawmill. The terms "surfaced" or "dressed" refer to the
wood members after they have been finish planed, where ¼ in. of surface material per side is removed. A designation of (S4S) means "surfaced
four sides"; a designation of (S2S), two sides. The term "2 x 4" refers to a surfaced member, and is smaller in cross-sectional area than a 2-in. by
4-in. piece of rough lumber. Its actual measurements when dry and surfaced on four sides will be 1½ in. by 3½ in. Structural lumber is commonly
available in members that are nominally 2 to 4 in. thick, and in "timbers,"
lumber greater than 5 in. in thickness. The thinnest standardized dressed
thickness for lumber is ½ in. and increasing in thickness to ¾ in., ⁵⁄₄ in.,
1½ in., and 3½ in. and greater. If the size of a required member exceeds
the limits of a log, several members can be glue-laminated together to
create the desired dimensions.

Overview of Grading Systems

Because lumber characteristics vary according to species, size of
members, and by intended use, a grading system has been established to make various designations reasonably uniform throughout the country. Lumber grading takes place at the sawmills, and in
the United States is supervised by one of 10 agencies accredited by
the American Lumber Standard Committee (ALSC), which is also

responsible for writing the standards used for lumber milling and grading.

All dressed softwood lumber, treated or untreated, and glulams receive a lumber grade stamp. The stamp, applied to the wood members by an approved grading or inspection agency is mandatory, required by building codes throughout the country for all lumber used for structural purposes. The lumber-graded mark uses standardized symbols to list five pieces of information: grade designation (quality), species identification, the maximum moisture content at the time of surfacing, the grading agency responsible for the inspection, and the mill identification. These symbols are used nationwide and are required to be visible for confirmation at the job site.

Lumber is graded by visual inspection to assess strength and/or appearance and is based on the frequency, size, quality, and location of knots; cross grain; and any natural decay, splits, wanes, or milling flaws.

Overview of Grade Designation

Lumber grades are divided into four performance standards: light framing; structural light framing; structural joists and planks; and those designated for use as studs, vertical members used in load-bearing walls. These can be further broken down into grade names, which are designations based on quality variation. For example, in the light framing category are the following grades: construction, standard and utility, with construction being the highest and utility being the lowest. These divisions are predominantly based on appearance since all qualify for the use of light framing. The quality of wood is designated by use in the grade stamp and is labeled by number (such as #2), by name (e.g., Stud) or by abbreviation (e.g., STAND, for standard).

Several species are available in appearance as well as structural grades. The factors inspected for appearance grade include grain orientation, presence of heart or sapwoods, quantity, size and quality of knots and other natural or manufacturing flaws. The designations include tight knot and clear.

Overview of Species Identification

The species symbol states the species of tree the wood was milled from, and is indicated by names (e.g., redwood), abbreviation (e.g., D Fir, for Douglas) or symbol (e.g., PP, for Ponderosa pine). Some symbols designate a combination of species, which have similar mechanical properties, such as SPF, for Spruce-pine fir. In addition, symbols indicate moisture content and grading agency/mill designation.

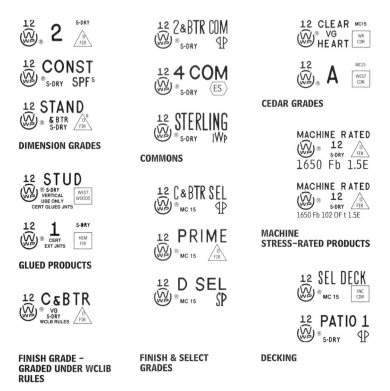

Figure 15.2 Typical grade stamps.
Source: Hopper, Landscape Architectural Graphic Standards.Copyright 2007,
John Wiley & Sons, Inc.

Moisture content. Moisture content is important in evaluating how much shrinkage, and potentially distortion, can be expected from the board. The amount of moisture is shown as either an abbreviation or as a number. The symbol S-GRN (for surfaced green) indicates that the board was milled with a moisture content above 19%, and it is cut slightly oversized so that when dried to a 19% moisture content it will have the same dimensions as S-DRY (surfaced dry) planed at 19% or less.

Grading agency/mill designation. This is a certification symbol that identifies the agency (NELMA, for example) that supervised the grading. The mill symbol is designated by name or number (e.g., 38), to identify the mill where the lumber was cut.

Solid lumber used for engineered components and glulams are graded mechanically and designated as MSR, for machine stress rated. The members are inspected both mechanically and visually. The stamps indicate the species, assign one of four grades (construction, standard, utility, and stud), and give two stress test measurements. The

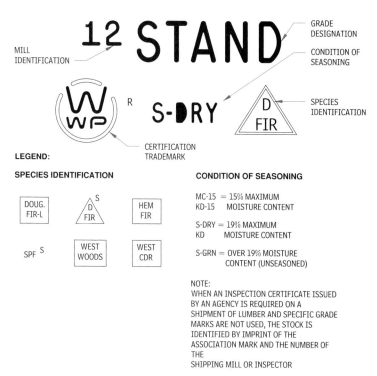

Figure 15.3 Interpreting grade marks.
Source: Hopper, Landscape Architectural Graphic Standards. Copyright 2007,
John Wiley & Sons, Inc.

fiber stress bending (Fb) figure is a measure of tensile and compressive forces; and the modulus of elasticity (E) figure indicates how much deflection will occur under certain loads.

Overview of Connectors and Adhesives

Mechanical Connectors

Wood connectors can be divided into five primary groups by use: concrete, caps and bases, hangers, straps and ties, miscellaneous and options. The standard connectors are available with galvanized coatings and in stainless steel.

Concrete Connectors

The concrete connectors are designed to attach wood members to concrete walls, footings, or slabs. Concrete connectors can be divided into two groups, retrofit or embedded

- *Retrofit* bolts are inserted into a predrilled hole and bonded to the concrete structure using expansion bolts, epoxy adhesives, or non-shrink cementitious grouts;

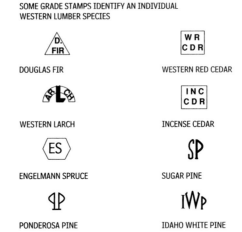

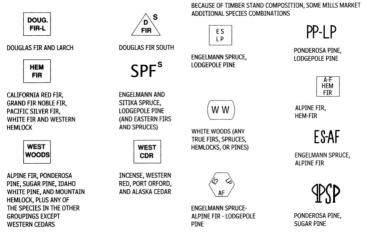

Figure 15.4 Species identification stamps.
Source: Hopper, Landscape Architectural Graphic Standards.Copyright 2007,
John Wiley & Sons, Inc.

- *Embedded* anchor bolts and hold-downs are set in place during the concrete pour, and the layout must be precise. The threaded end of the anchor bolt extends out from the concrete and receives the wood member or metal connector. Hold-downs are not bolts but consist of brackets, hurricane ties, or strap connections.

Post Caps and Bases

With base anchors, which are available for retrofit and new construction, the anchor is epoxied or expansion-bolted to a concrete footing

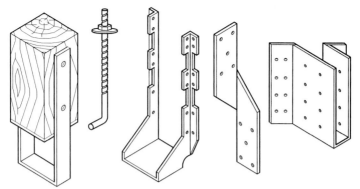

Figure 15.5 Metal connectors for wood. from left to right: Post Anchor; "J" Anchor Bolt; Joist Hanger; Joist to Beam Connector; and Face Mount Connector for Two Horizontal Members.
Source: Hopper, Landscape Architectural Graphic Standards. Copyright 2007, John Wiley & Sons, Inc.

or embedded into the concrete pour. The anchors are available as fixed or adjustable, and are designed to receive standard dimensioned wood posts. The caps are designed to sit on top of a post or column and provide a seat to receive a horizontal member (beam or joist). Each connection is pre-bored to receive carriage bolts and/or screws or nails to secure the post or horizontal member.

Hangers
Hangers can be divided into face mount and top flange types. Both are designed to connect a horizontal member (beam or joist) with another horizontal member (beam). The face mount is connected into the face of the supporting member, while the top flange is attached to the top of the supporting member, bending 90 degrees down the face to receive the supported member (other angles can be specified). They rely on nails, screws, or bolts to form the connection.

Straps and Ties
Straps and ties are used to form a mechanical link between two wood members, eliminating toe or end nailing and increasing the rigidity of the joint, especially in areas prone to seismic activity. Included in this category are seismic and hurricane ties, framing anchors, strap ties, and others.

Miscellaneous and Hanger Options
The miscellaneous category includes a variety of bases, fence brackets, header hangers, twist straps (to attach a joist seated on a beam), wall bracing, bridging, and others. The hanger options category includes hangers designed to receive multiple members (joists or rafters) with

preset angles. Also included in this category are custom hangers and connectors, where a steel plate is cut and bent and holes are predrilled based on a CAD drawing submitted by the designer to form a custom hanger.

Overview of Coatings for Fasteners and Connectors

Exterior fasteners and connectors are available in stainless steel or galvanized carbon steel. Galvanized coatings are applied by electroplating, mechanical plating, chemical treating, or hot dipping (molten zinc). The hot-dipping method provides the coating with the thickest profile, and research has shown it provides the best longevity and resistance to corrosion. However, in situations where salt is airborne, or in marine applications, stainless steel is a better choice than hot-dipped galvanized fasteners or connectors.

Adhesives

When gluing laminated beams or attaching wood members, adhesives can provide a strong connection more easily and effectively than mechanical fasteners.

Glues based on resorcinol-formaldehyde and phenol-resorcinol-formaldehyde are all formulated for exterior applications. Resorcinol and resorcinol-formaldehyde glues are ideal for bonding high-density hardwoods such as oak. Phenol-resorcinol-formaldehydes are commonly used to structurally bond softwoods.

All resorcinol glues require closely mated surfaces for effective bonding with hardwoods, requiring clamping pressures as high as 250 psi, and softwoods 100 to 125 psi. These pressures force the glue over the wood surface and into the wood cell structure. The optimum strength is achieved in woods with a moisture content between 6 and 12%.

Epoxies are among the most versatile and expensive of the adhesives. They have multiple applications, including anchoring concrete and masonry fasteners and restoring rotting wood. Evidence has shown that structural epoxy bonds in members subject to prolonged outdoor exposure and water saturation can deteriorate rapidly; however, some early research suggests priming with a 2% solution of polyethyleneamine may improve exterior performance.

Polyurethane foam adhesives offer many benefits, and many can bond either wet or frozen, treated and untreated lumber. These adhesives are nontoxic, waterproof, and temperature-tolerant. The glue, once cured, is waterproof; and because curing is triggered by moisture, it will activate on wood with a moisture content of up to 25%.

Climate and Natural Factors

Moisture penetration and the associated damage caused by fungi, mold, and insects is the most common cause of wood failure. This usually is the result of inappropriate detailing and joinery, which can defeat even the effects of pressure-treated wood. An understanding of the materials, combined with a fundamental knowledge of construction detailing, is critical to the successful design of lasting wood structures in the landscape.

It is essential to drain away all water from the wood structure. Slope finish grades away from the post connections and provides positive drainage within the structure for decks, stairs, and landings. All deck railings, fence caps, and horizontal surfaces should be pitched to drain and direct water away from joints and exposed end grain.

Some woods are naturally resistant to attack by fungi and insects, such as cedar and redwood, others need to be treated with a preservative for exterior applications (see section on Pressure Treated Wood). Both cedar and redwood should be treated with a water repellent sealer. They can also be treated with sealers that will help them retain their bright, non-weathered appearance if desired. They both have their own grading systems that are largely based on aesthetic appearance. Because of strength and cost considerations, when used for deck boards, they are usually combined with pressure treated wood for the less visible structural members.

For railing and trim applications, Select Tight Knot or #1 grade Cedar are high quality (and expensive) choices. Cedar #2 graded is the most common grade to use for deck applications. For deckboards, WRCLA Architect Knotty and WRCLA Custom Knotty (the least expensive) are the most common grades of cedar used (designations are from the Western Red Cedar Lumber Association). The clear grades are the most expensive and not generally used for exterior decking. Cedar can be used with hot dip galvanized, aluminum or stainless steel fasteners and connectors.

There are many grades of redwood, separated into two major classes, architectural and garden grade. Garden grade redwood is not suitable for deck components but can be used for fences, planters and trellises. Clear heart and select heart are the premium grades of architectural redwood. Construction heart is less expensive with the wood containing some knots and defects. Redwood can be used with hot dip galvanized or stainless steel fasteners and connectors, with pre-drilling of holes near the end of boards recommended to avoid splitting.

▶ Strict standards protecting old growth redwood forests limit its availability. Cedar is more widely available but old growth forests still require protection. With either wood, it is important to specify and purchase only wood that has been certified by the Forest Stewardship Council to ensure that it has been responsibly harvested.

Overview of Structural Considerations

Wood structures must resist the stresses of tensile, compressive, and lateral forces acting upon them. These three forces are accounted for in the design process when selecting, sizing, placing, and connecting wood members. The process of structurally composing routinely encountered fences, gates, decks, arbors, and gazebos is relatively straightforward. The standard charts and tables for the sizing and spacing of the wood members can be found later in this chapter under the section on *Wood Decks*. For larger decks, small pavilions, and bridges, the applied forces may be more significant and complex, requiring the consultation of a structural engineer.

Loads on a structure can be calculated as dead or live loads. The dead load is the weight of the materials composing it. The live loads are all nonpermanent objects that will use, or bear, on the structure.

Span and height tables are often used as the most expedient method to size structural members. These tables come from several agencies, including the United States Department of Agriculture (USDA). When using the listed maximum spans, the wood member must be without flaws, including checks and knots, since any structural flaws may compromise the calculations. Structural engineers typically include a safety factor, often 15%, and it is common practice to choose spans below the capable maximum. The tables are typically based on maximum loads of 50 pounds per square foot (psf), which include a live load of 40 pounds (psf) and dead load of 10 pounds (psf).

The process of sizing most structures is carried out from top to bottom. With a deck or pedestrian bridge, this begins with the deck boards and moves down through the joists to the beams, posts, and footings. The working process appears to be linear, but it is, in fact, a circular one. After the initial design of the structure, the look may not be satisfying and can be changed by revisiting the spacing, spans, and material dimensions of the wood members.

Practices to Avoid

Problems common to wood fall into six categories, which are identified below, along with guidelines for avoidance:

- *Splitting and cracking.* This problem common to wood members can be avoided by using properly dried materials. Ensure that all nailing is located a sufficient distance from the end of the board, and provide adequate support to alleviate bounce that stresses the lumber. Select materials with consistent grain and minimal imperfections.

- *Wood decay.* Decay in exterior applications is often the result of trapped moisture. Adequate air circulation will extend the life of the structure, particularly in shaded areas that receive little sun. Contact with the ground should be avoided whenever possible, and if unavoidable, treated material should be used. Details that impede drainage or entrap water should be redesigned.

- *Sagging members.* Beams, joists, rafters, and decking should be adequately supported, as shown in the span charts in the article on *Wood Decks*. Joist blocking stiffens the framing structure increasing rigidity. All framing material should be set with the natural curve, viewed across the length of each member, facing up to resist the tendency to sag under loading.

- *Joint separation.* Avoid toe nailing wherever possible, and use mechanical hangers, slice plates, and anchors for wood-to-concrete/steel or wood-to-wood connections. In wood-to-wood connections, wood joints such as dovetails, mortise, and tenon, and scarf joints resist separation better than butt joints.

- *Fastener failure.* Use only galvanized, stainless-steel, or epoxy-coated fasteners for exterior connections. Properly size the fasteners; stagger them as needed to prevent rocking of the attached member; and space them so the loads are sufficiently distributed.

- *Finish failure.* Preparation of wood surfaces is critical to finish performance. Material should be dry and clean, and the temperature during application should not exceed the manufacturer's recommendations. Locating the wood structure so that it is sheltered from winds, abrasive materials, and extended sun exposure can all extend the life of a finish.

Overhead Wood Structures

Description

Overhead structures are used to provide scale and weather protection, and often to mark an important function or event in the landscape, such as a passageway, lookout, or center of activity.

Following is a brief summary:

- Pergola—Parallel columns supporting an open roof of beams and cross members, used to delineate a space or passage;
- Arbor—Columns supporting an open roof structure, generally simpler and more rustic in design than a pergola, and typically used to support vines for shade;
- Trellis—A horizontal overhead or vertical plane of open latticework, usually for the purpose of training vines.

Wood is economical and aesthetically compatible with many landscape settings, as a result of its natural appearance. It is also easy to work with from a construction standpoint. Wood has been used in the design of landscape structures for centuries, with countless precedents, both rustic and refined.

As the design of a structure moves from concept to detail, the landscape architect will need to check with local planning and building departments to obtain their design guidelines and requirements for coverage, height, and construction. Many municipalities require a structural engineer to confirm the sizing of wood members and attachment details, as well as the footing design to ensure structural integrity.

Assessing Site Conditions

Overhead structures have wide-ranging application in the landscape and can take many forms. They are particularly useful in areas where planting trees is not an option, such as over underground utility lines or on top of a building structure, if weight and soil depth are limited. In general, such overhead structures serve one or a combination of the following functions:

- Solar radiation and wind are two weather variables that can be manipulated by the design of the landscape to modify the microclimate.

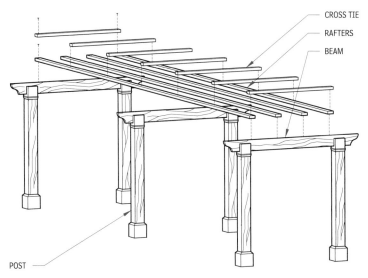

CROSS TIE

RAFTERS

BEAM

POST

Figure 15.6 Elements of arbors and pergolas.
Source: Hopper, Landscape Architectural Graphic Standards. Copyright 2007, John Wiley & Sons, Inc.

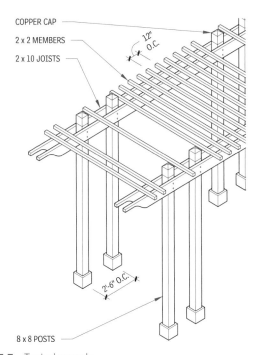

COPPER CAP

2 x 2 MEMBERS

2 x 10 JOISTS

12" O.C.

2'-6" O.C.

8 x 8 POSTS

Figure 15.7 Typical pergola.
Source: Hopper, Landscape Architectural Graphic Standards. Copyright 2007, John Wiley & Sons, Inc.

- Energy usage related to the selected material—the amount of energy required to produce and transport those materials and the amount required for maintenance over the course of the structure's lifetime.

The effect on the microclimate, material usage, and energy usage all play a role in the sustainable design of an overhead structure.

Acceptable Practices

The primary elements of arbors and pergolas are posts, beams, rafters, and cross-members. The most efficiently milled lumber sizes should be used, such as two 2 by 8 joists versus one 4 by 8 joist. A number of other elements, such as brackets, braces, railings, and seating, are often employed as well. The beams are oriented either parallel or perpendicular to the post alignment. Note the inset sandwich beams, notched rafters, and cross ties in the accompanying figures.

Overhead structures on roofs or structures can add an important vertical element to a design when other options are limited. Complemented with wood screens they provide both horizontal and vertical definition of the space and protection from strong sun and winds.

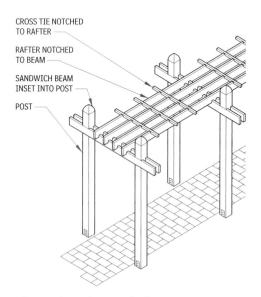

CROSS TIE NOTCHED
TO RAFTER

RAFTER NOTCHED
TO BEAM

SANDWICH BEAM
INSET INTO POST

POST

Figure 15.8 Beam oriented perpendicular to posts.
Source: Hopper, Landscape Architectural Graphic Standards. Copyright 2007, John Wiley & Sons, Inc.

Figure 15.9   The framework for wood overhead structures braced during the early stages of construction.
Source: Photo courtesy of Mark K. Morrison, FASLA, RLA, GRP.

Doing so increases thermal comfort and decreases energy usage. In designing an overhead structure, methods for modifying exposure to sun and wind include the addition of deciduous vines for summer shade/winter sun, the extension of an overhang to promote shade in summer but allow winter sun to enter, or the positioning of a canopy to collect and direct breezes for cooling, ventilation, and wind protection. Structures with solid overhead panels or canopies can provide shelter from rain as well as sun;

- Overhead structures can be used effectively to define or enclose passageways and to direct circulation through a site. A structure can take the form of a simple overhead plane supported by columns, or use a combination of vertical and horizontal elements to create a stronger sense of enclosure;

- Structures also can be used to mark a special destination or center of activity, such as a gathering place, a contemplative seating area, a bandstand, or a focal point in the landscape. The complexity of the structure should be appropriate to its setting and function.

Overhead structures can be used to increase thermal comfort and decrease energy usage in an area. When designed properly, they can do a great deal to contribute to sustainability. Other sustainability-related factors to be considered include:

- The content of the materials used in construction, the materials required during maintenance, and the potential for reuse of materials after the structure has reached the end of its useful life;

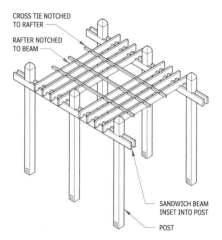

CROSS TIE NOTCHED
TO RAFTER

RAFTER NOTCHED
TO BEAM

SANDWICH BEAM
INSET INTO POST

POST

Figure 15.10 Beam oriented parallel to posts.
Source: Hopper, Landscape Architectural Graphic Standards.Copyright 2007,
John Wiley & Sons, Inc.

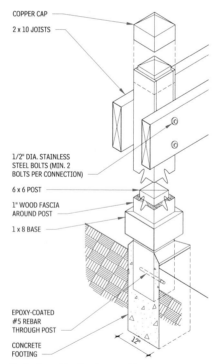

COPPER CAP

2 x 10 JOISTS

1/2" DIA. STAINLESS
STEEL BOLTS (MIN. 2
BOLTS PER CONNECTION)

6 x 6 POST

1" WOOD FASCIA
AROUND POST

1 x 8 BASE

EPOXY-COATED
#5 REBAR
THROUGH POST

CONCRETE
FOOTING

12"

Figure 15.11 Typical post to footing and beam to post connection, with
base trim. The decorative base trim can be used to hide post to footing connectors that are better unseen. Beam to post connections are best made
with bolt connections.
Source: Hopper, Landscape Architectural Graphic Standards.Copyright 2007,
John Wiley & Sons, Inc.

Figure 15.12 Rooftop pergola with the beams sandwiched around the posts and bolted through. Additional filtered sun screening and sense of vertical enclosure is provided by 2 x 4 cross ties laid flat.
Source: Photo courtesy of Mark K. Morrison, FASLA, RLA, GRP.

Practices to Avoid

- Avoid premature deterioration of the wood overhead structure by choosing a type of wood that will resist decay and require a level of maintenance that the structure is likely to receive.
- Avoid staining and rust by using an appropriate fastener or bracket (hot dipped galvanized or stainless for example) that is compatible with the wood type.
- Avoid water damaging the end grains of the wood posts. Protect the top of the posts with a cap and elevate the bottom of the post off the ground with an anchor. The post base can be trimmed to hide the anchor.

Wood Decks

Description

When designing a deck, the sizing of members is calculated from the top down, in reverse of the actual building process. The spacing of the structural members is determined by the span of the members above, thus a top-down process makes sense. For the designer, the process becomes somewhat circular, as aesthetic decisions may require dimensional changes of the members and necessary recalculations.

Assessing Site Conditions

Overview of Foundation

The structural integrity of a deck begins with the foundation, and unlike a house with a continuous perimeter concrete foundation, deck foundations are typically footings that receive concentrated loads at specific isolated points. To create a stable structure, the framing must transfer the combined live and dead loads through the joists, beams, and posts to the footing and into the ground.

If the loads are equally distributed, one can determine the footprint of the footing by dividing the total load on all the footings by the number of footings. Then divide the load on each footing by the bearing capacity of the soil.

The concrete footing must sit below the point at which soil freezes in winter, to prevent frost heave. In areas prone to frost heave or with poor drainage, additional drainage material such as drain rock can be placed below the footings. For additional strength, a grid of rebar can be embedded into the footing.

Acceptable Practices

Overview of Piers and Posts

Concrete piers, used in lieu of a wood post, are required by code in many parts of the country, as they are not susceptible to insect infestations, are decay-proof, and very strong. The pier is typically poured on top of a spread footing with reinforcing bars to tie the two together.

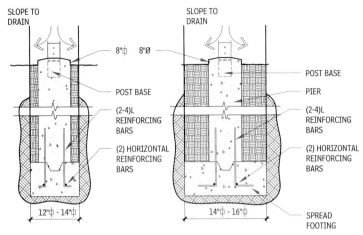

SLOPE TO DRAIN

8"⌀ 8"Ø

POST BASE

(2-4)L REINFORCING BARS

(2) HORIZONTAL REINFORCING BARS

12"⌀ - 14"⌀

SLOPE TO DRAIN

POST BASE

PIER

(2-4)L REINFORCING BARS

(2) HORIZONTAL REINFORCING BARS

14"⌀ - 16"⌀

SPREAD FOOTING

Figure 15.13 Typical square footing and pier (left) and round footing and pier (right).
Source: Hopper, Landscape Architectural Graphic Standards. Copyright 2007, John Wiley & Sons, Inc.

A galvanized steel post anchor can be embedded into the top of the pier to receive a post or beam or can be attached to a "J" bolt that is embedded in the concrete footing. The post anchor separates the end grain of the post from the concrete surface and creates a $\frac{1}{2}$-in. to an inch air gap below the post that ensures good ventilation below the end grain of the wood post. The top of the concrete pier should be

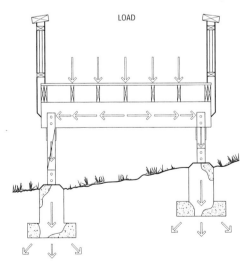

LOAD

Figure 15.14 The transfer of loads through the decking structure to the joist, the beams to the post and then through the footing and into the subgrade.
Source: Hopper, Landscape Architectural Graphic Standards. Copyright 2007, John Wiley & Sons, Inc.

Figure 15.15 Post anchor components with anchor bolt to be set into concrete footing. The large hole in the base of the anchor along with the multi-hole plate that fits over the hole allows for some flexibility in adjusting the post anchor around the embedded bolt. Holes in the sides of the post anchor are for nailing the post after deck framework has been completed.

pitched away from the post base, reducing any water buildup that could infiltrate the end grain.

The intermediate wood posts transfers the load from the beam and joists to the pier or footing. If the finished elevation of the deck is less than 1 to 2 feet from grade, the concrete piers typically extend up above grade to receive the beam, eliminating the wood post. If a wood post is used, a 4 by 4 one is often adequate to transfer the loads; however, many designers specify larger 6 by 6 posts, and double-notch the post on either side to provide a $1\frac{1}{2}$-in. seat that will receive a sandwich beam. In this method a $2\frac{1}{2}$-in. tongue is left on the post that protrudes up through the beam and through which the beam and post can be bolted together

The post need not be one solid member, especially if it is greater than 8 in. in either dimension, but can be fabricated using standard 2x dimensional lumber. A 6 by 8 post can be fabricated from three pieces of 2 by 8, glued and laminated.

Overview of Beams

The beams are intermediate structural members, transferring the loads from the joists or decking to the post or pier. Typical sizes are solid

Figure 15.16 The wood post sits on the inverted "U" plate to keep the end grain off the top of the concrete footing. The lock washer and nut can be tightened after the deck framework has been completed. The front panel of the post anchor can then be folded up and nailed to the post.

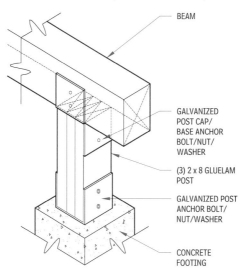

BEAM

GALVANIZED
POST CAP/
BASE ANCHOR
BOLT/NUT/
WASHER

(3) 2 x 8 GLUELAM
POST

GALVANIZED POST
ANCHOR BOLT/
NUT/WASHER

CONCRETE
FOOTING

Figure 15.17 Large posts can be expensive and are not always readily available. An alternative is a glue laminated or mechanically fastened "built-up" post.

4 by 6 or 4 by 8, or they can be fabricated of 2x material. Nailing the boards face to face, a common mistake, promotes premature material decay. In fabricating a built-up beam, spacers made of treated lumber or plywood are glued between the two or more pieces of 2x material, creating a void for water to pass through and to allow air circulation between the members.

The best method for supporting the beam is to rest it on top of the post, which uses the post to provide the best compressive resistance. It is important that the width of the beam be equal to or greater than the post, so water doesn't flow down the face of the beam and into the end grain of the post. This method does raise the profile of the deck, and if this is functionally or aesthetically unacceptable, the beams can be bolted to the side of the post. Side bolting places much of the shear stress on the fasteners, and the fasteners must be appropriately sized to resist the pressures. Notching the post and bolting it to the beam is an alternative solution.

A ledger supports the same loads as a beam, but instead of resting on posts or piers, it is mechanically attached to an existing structure. A 2x or 4 x member is connected to the existing rim joists with lag bolts or to the foundation wall with expansion bolts.

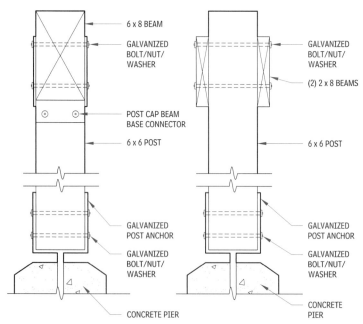

Figure 15.18 Typical beam on post detail (left) and typical beam bolted to the side of post detail (right).
Source: Hopper, Landscape Architectural Graphic Standards. Copyright 2007, John Wiley & Sons, Inc.

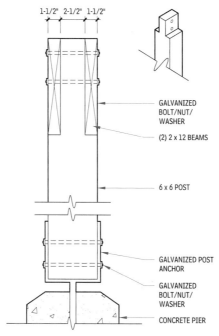

1-1/2" 2-1/2" 1-1/2"

GALVANIZED
BOLT/NUT/
WASHER

(2) 2 x 12 BEAMS

6 x 6 POST

GALVANIZED POST
ANCHOR

GALVANIZED
BOLT/NUT/
WASHER

CONCRETE PIER

Figure 15.19 Typical notched beam method relieves stress on fasteners.
Source: Hopper, Landscape Architectural Graphic Standards.Copyright 2007,
John Wiley & Sons, Inc.

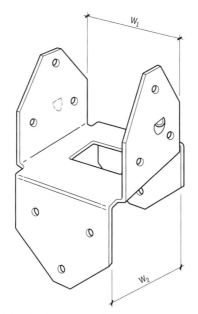

W_1

W_2

Figure 15.20 Galvanized connector for beam to post connection.
Source: Simpson Strong Tie.

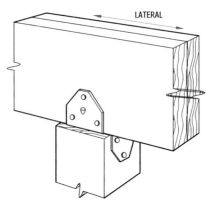

Figure 15.21 Diagram of galvanized connector showing how beam connects to post.
Source: Simpson Strong Tie.

To eliminate a toenail connection, joist hangers should be nailed to the ledger to receive the joists. The ledger should receive a Z-flashing strip tucked under the wall siding, running 90 degrees out over the top and 90 degrees down the face of the ledger, to prevent water from penetrating the rim joist or sill.

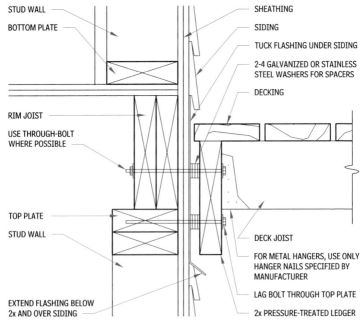

Figure 15.22 Spacers are set between the ledger and the flashing to allow air to circulate and water to pass.
Source: Hopper, Landscape Architectural Graphic Standards.Copyright 2007, John Wiley & Sons, Inc.

Overview of Joists

The joist, used in the platform method, transfers the live and dead loads of the decking to the beams. They are positioned perpendicular to the beam and can be set either on top of the beams or hung flush with the top of the beam with joist hangers. The first method elevates the joist, increasing the profile of the deck by the vertical dimension of the joist lying above the beam. The connectors used in this application are hurricane ties, twist straps that connect the joist to the beam to resist uplift by wind pressure. When set flush with the beam, a joist hanger is employed. The spacing of the joists is determined by the span capability, which is determined by the dimension of the decking board thickness.

Joists can span long distances in relationship to their vertical dimension, but the twisting or curving is a potential problem. To counter this tendency, solid wood blocking, the same dimension as the joists, or

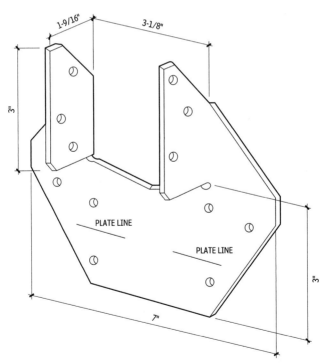

Figure 15.23   Diagram of a hurricane tie where the 7-in.-wide plate is attached to the face of the beam and a double joist running perpendicular to the beam passes through the 3-⅛-in.-wide space. Nail holes are provided for easy attachment to the wood members.
Source: Simpson Strong Tie.

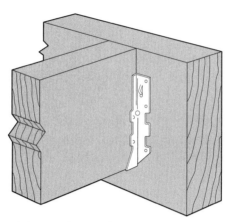

Figure 15.24 A diagram showing the joist hanger and flush attachment of the joist to beam.
Source: Simpson Strong Tie.

metal bridging is placed between the joists at the midpoint of the spans and nailed to each member to resist lateral movement and deformation.

In orienting both beams and joists, the members are designed to orient vertically to the cross section's longitudinal axis. All board lumber has a "crook," a bend that is counter to the greatest dimension. In some members, this is obvious; in others, it may be more difficult to

Figure 15.25 Joist hangers attaching the joists to the beams.

Figure 15.26 Wood blocking between the joists stiffens the framework to prevent movement and deformation. Joist hangers are used to connect the joists to the beams.

see. When the joists are placed, it's important to orient the "crowned" side up. This allows the weight of the structure to provide a counter-resistance that will straighten the crown, instead of increasing pressure on the natural curve as it would if the member were placed crown side down.

Overview of Decking

The decking provides a usable surface on which to stand and walk and transfers loads to the joists or beams. The span is determined by the spacing of the joists below and is calculated to the size and span capabilities of the decking material. The optimal decking material choices include $5/4$ by 6 or 2 by 4 or 2 by 6 and should be no greater than 6 in. in width due to a propensity to warp in wider boards. In some public structures, thicker material such as 2 or 3 in. is used in the plank-and-beam method. A gap of $1/8$ to $1/4$ in. should be maintained between the decking boards to allow proper drainage, depending on their moisture content and subsequent shrinking.

As the most exposed material, decking takes the most abuse over time and thus is often the first material to deteriorate. Frequent applications of preservative treatments will extend the life span of the decking material. When possible, butt joints in the decking should be

Figure 15.27 Deck boards should be laid with staggered joints with the fasteners of the non-joint deck board lined up consistently with the line of fasteners of the board joints at the joist. There should be a slight gap between the end joints to allow water to drain past the end grains of the boards. The use of a double joist allows the screws to be installed away from the edge of the wood and still leave a gap between the ends of the deck boards.

Figure 15.28 There is a slight gap between deck boards to allow for any expansion. Too large a gap will widen as the wood shrinks. Notice the curved end grain of the boards, indicating that they've been installed correctly with the "bark side up".

avoided, or the double-joist system used, to prevent trapped moisture between the end grains.

Another cause of deck failure is the migration of water through the nail holes, particularly when the nails lose their withdrawal resistance and pop up. These openings leave a clear path for water to penetrate below the effective treatment penetration zone, causing the material to degrade from the inside out. The rate of withdrawal among smooth shank nails is quite high in areas of heavy foot traffic, so spiral-groove or ring-shank nails or screws are recommended for attaching decking boards in these conditions. The length of the connecting mechanism will also affect withdrawal, and the fastener should be 3 in. (10d) or greater when securing 1-in.-thick decking and $3\frac{1}{2}$ in. (16d) or greater for $1\frac{1}{2}$-in. boards. If edge nailing can't be avoided, all holes should be predrilled to minimize splitting at the ends of the boards.

In deck construction where the elevation is greater than 5 ft in height, bracing (diagonal cross members) should be used to resist racking and possible structural failure. If the length of the bracing is 8 ft or less, 2 by 4's are usually adequate; for longer unsupported lengths, 2 by 6's are recommended. All connections should be to the main framing with a minimum of $\frac{3}{8}$-in.-diameter bolts used for fastening.

For decks sited on sloping lots requiring long posts, the need for bracing is critical. Bracing can take a number of forms, including Y-type bracing, sufficient for standard post-to-beam connections, and allowing easy access below the deck. When the structure is designed with long beam spans or tall posts, X-cross bracing can be installed at alternate bays, although some decks may require bracing at every bay for structural support. If the post height exceeds 14 ft, two X-braces or K-braces, one on top of the other, might be required, and an engineer should be consulted.

Overview of Stairs

Most decks contain at least some stairs, and in many cases the stairs are a feature, equal in visual impact to the decking. If the stairs include more than two risers (vertical steps), most codes require at least one railing at the side of the run. All risers and treads (horizontal steps) should be of a consistent dimension within any run, and preferably within the whole design. The material for the treads should not be less than $\frac{5}{4}$ in., and 2x stock is the most common. Thinner material, typically $\frac{3}{4}$ in., can be used for the risers, to prevent tripping and for aesthetic effect.

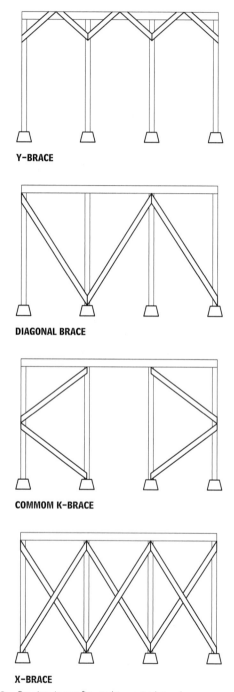

Y-BRACE

DIAGONAL BRACE

COMMOM K-BRACE

X-BRACE

Figure 15.29 Bracing is configured to resist lateral sway.
Source: Hopper, Landscape Architectural Graphic Standards.Copyright 2007,
John Wiley & Sons, Inc.

Figure 15.30   Diagonal bracing bolted through posts.

The tread and riser boards are supported by a stringer that is fabricated from a large board, often a treated 2 by 12 or 2 by 14 that has been cut to form a stepped pattern supporting the tread and riser boards. The number of stringers required depends on the width of the stairs; however, if fewer than three are used, sagging can occur even on a stair with a width as short as 2 ft 6 in. Joist hangers or other metal connectors can be employed to connect the upper stringer end to the joist or blocking. The lower stringer end should rest on a concrete beam foundation or footings.

Overview of Railings

The design of deck railings can be very complex, ranging from those with ornate features such as turned ballustrades and finials to plain railings designed as very simple and functional elements.

Most local building codes regulate railing heights and maximum ballustrade openings and should be consulted. Generally, openings between ballustrades or pickets should be no greater than 4 in., and a 42-in. railing height is required if the deck is greater than 30 in.

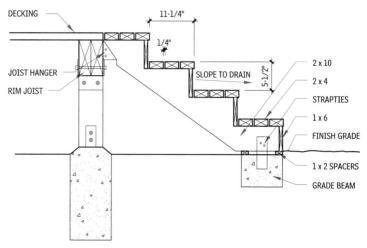

Figure 15.31 Stair stringer connected to a ledger with a joist hanger at the upper end, and to a lower joist that also supports a landing between stair runs.
Source: Hopper, Landscape Architectural Graphic Standards.Copyright 2007, John Wiley & Sons, Inc.

(check local building codes) above finished grade. Posts are often extended up through the decking as vertical supports for the top, bottom, and mid-rails since the full length of the posts is used to resist the rail load. When used to support the rails, the post spacing should not exceed 6 feet, as the rails transfer the dead loads of the

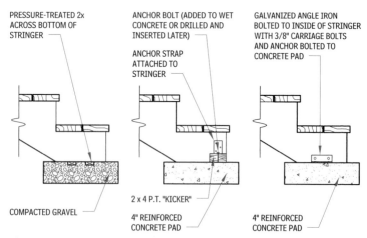

Figure 15.32 Options for resting the stringer at grade. The option on the left is the least permanent and is prone to settlement. The middle option provides a good connection, and the layout of connections allows some flexibility. The option on the right provides a good connection and, with a retrofit bolt, can be installed after the pad is poured, allowing the greatest flexibility.
Source: Hopper, Landscape Architectural Graphic Standards.Copyright 2007, John Wiley & Sons, Inc.

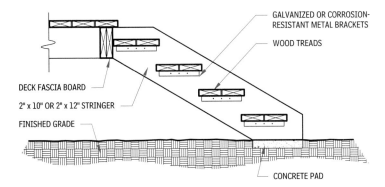

WOOD DECK STAIRS WITH METAL BRACKETS

Figure 15.33 Wood deck stairs with metal brackets supporting the treads instead of cutting the stringer to the tread and riser pattern.
Source: Hopper, Landscape Architectural Graphic Standards. Copyright 2007, John Wiley & Sons, Inc.

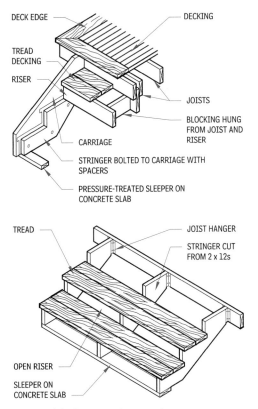

Figure 15.34 Wood deck stairs stringer options.
Source: Hopper, Landscape Architectural Graphic Standards. Copyright 2007, John Wiley & Sons, Inc.

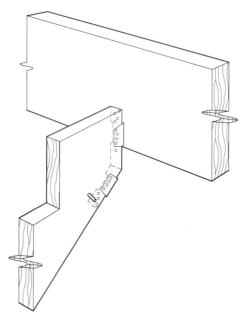

Figure 15.35 Diagram showing the use of metal stringer attachment to make the connection to the joist or ledger.
Source: Simpson Strong Tie.

Figure 15.36 Attached to the stringer are a 2 by 6 used as a riser and two 2 by 6s are used for the treads creating an overhang past the riser.

Figure 15.37 Viewed from underneath, these stairs are supported by intermediate stringers to prevent the tread from sagging.

ballustrades and rails to the posts. If the posts can't be extended through the decking, the rail posts can be bolted to the beams or joist framing.

▶ A rail cap prevents water from penetrating the end grain of the posts. The rail cap should be angled to shed water away from the decking.

Overview of Decking Spans

Recommended lumber dimensions for decking include ⁵⁄₄ by 6 radius-edged boards, 2 by 4 and 2 by 6. Looking at a single decking member, the span of the board is the distance from joist to joist or from bearing point to bearing point. Deck span tables are consulted. Once decking material span and its equivalent joist spacing are selected, the joist size and span can be determined.

Overview of Joist Spans

The span of a joist, the distance between the two bearing points of the beams, is also the beam spacing. Standard joist sizes range from 2 by 6s to 2 by 10s. The standard joist spacings are 16, 24, and 32 in., and should be matched as closely as possible to the chosen decking spans. Once the joist size, spacing, and species have been selected, the joist span and equivalent beam spacing will be indicated.

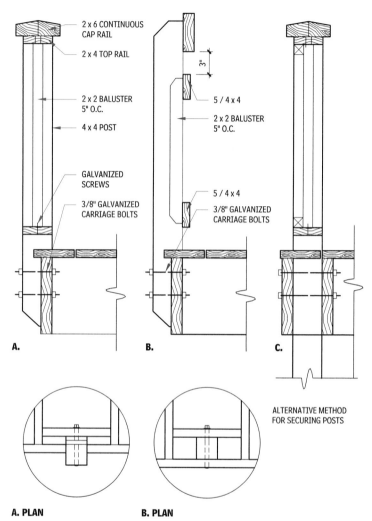

Figure 15.38 There are a number of options for connecting the rail to the deck. In system C, the rails can be attached to posts extending up through the decking or to post extensions attached to the beam or rim joists. *Source*: Hopper, Landscape Architectural Graphic Standards. Copyright 2007, John Wiley & Sons, Inc.

Overview of Beam Spans

With the beam spacing in hand, size and span of a beam can be chosen. The span of the beam will be its length between the two bearing points of the posts. Standard beam sizes range from 4 by 6 to 6 by 12. Built-up beams may require further calculations since they vary in deflection and in their capability to resist forces. If the design calls for closely spaced beams, two members laid parallel without internal

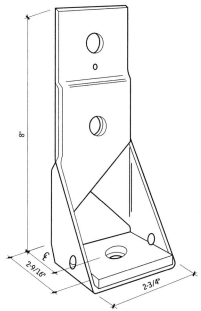

Figure 15.39   Metal connector for railing post to deck detail. The double hole side is bolted to the joist, the single hole side receives a bolt that passes through both the post and beam.
Source: Simpson Strong Tie.

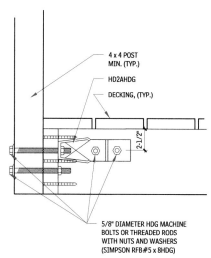

Figure 15.40   Diagram showing how the metal connector is bolted to the joist and connects to the post by the bolt passing through both the post and beam. The metal connector helps resist the force of people leaning on the top of the rail, which could tend to pull the rail away from the beam.
Source: Simpson Strong Tie.

Figure 15.41   Simple railing with balustrades, posts are bolted to the beam, lattice prevents large animals from getting under the deck. The 2 by 2 (1-$\frac{1}{2}$ by 1-$\frac{1}{2}$ in. actual size) balustrades are spaced 5 in. on center, leaving a 3-$\frac{1}{2}$-in. space between them.

Figure 15.42   Railing post is notched to fit over beam and bolted to the beam. Deck boards are notched to fit around post. Bolts attaching the post to the beam are vertically offset to minimize the chance of the post cracking along the vertical grain.

Figure 15.43 Bottom of rail is screwed to the post and balustrades are screwed to the bottom of the rail from the bottom. The screw heads are hidden from view and the joints appear clean and neat.

Figure 15.44 Top of rail consists of two parts, a 2 by 4 that is screwed to the post and a 1 by 6 top plate that is centered and screwed to the 2 by 4 leaving a 1-in. overhang on each side, cut on an angle to meet the post. Post is fitted with a cap to protect the end grain of the rail post.

Table 15.1 Recommended Decking Live Loads

Source: Hopper, Landscape Architectural Graphic Standards. Copyright 2007,
John Wiley & Sons, Inc.

Material	Load (Lb/ft)
Residential decks, light traffic	40
Public decks, heavy traffic	80–100
Pedestrian bridges	100
Vehicular bridges, light traffic	200–300

Table 15.2 Maximum Spans for Decking

Source: Hopper, Landscape Architectural Graphic Standards. Copyright 2007,
John Wiley & Sons, Inc.

Species Group	Decking Material	Recommended Span (In.)
Douglas—fir	Red (5/4 radius-edge decking)	16
Southern pine		
Hem—fir		
Southern pine—fir	2 x 4	24
Ponderosa pine		
Redwood		
Western cedar	2 x 6	24

Table 15.3 Maximum Span for Joists

Source: Hopper, Landscape Architectural Graphic Standards. Copyright 2007,
John Wiley & Sons, Inc.

Species Group	Decking Material	Recommended Span 12′	16′	24′
Douglas—fir	2 x 6	10′–4″	9′–7″	7′–10″
Southern pine	2 x 8	13′–8″	12′–7″	10′–4″
	2 x 10	17′–5″	15′–11″	12′–11″
	2 x 12	20′–0″	17′–10″	14′–7″
Hem—fir	2 x 6	9′–2″	8′–5″	7′–1″
Southern pine—fir	2 x 8	12′–1″	11′–1″	9′–4″
	2 x 10	15′–4″	14′–3″	11′–8″
	2 x 12	18′–8″	17′–10″	13′–6″
Ponderosa pine	2 x 6	8′–10″	7′–11″	6′–7″
Redwood	2 x 8	11′–8″	10′–4″	8′–5″
Western cedar	2 x 10	14′–10″	13′–2″	10′–7″
	2 x 12	17′–9″	17′–10″	12′–7″

Table 15.4 Maximum Spans for Beams: 40lb/Ft Design Load

Source: Hopper, Landscape Architectural Graphic Standards. Copyright 2007, John Wiley & Sons, Inc.

Species Group	Beam Material	Beam Spacing								
		4′	5′	6′	7′	8′	9′	10′	11′	12′
Douglas—fir	4 x 6	7′	7′	6′						
Southern pine	4 x 8	10′	9′	8′	7′	7′	6′	6′	6′	
	4 x 10	12′	11′	10′	9′	8′	8′	7′	7′	7′
	4 x 12	14′	13′	11′	11′	10′	9′	9′	8′	8′
	6 x 10	15′	13′	12′	12′	11′	10′	9′	9′	8′
	6 x 12	16′	16′	15′	13′	12′	12′	11′	10′	10′
Hem—fir,	4 x 6	7′	6′							
Southern pine—fir	4 x 8	8′	7′	6′	6′					
	4 x 10	11′	10′	9′	8′	7′	7′	6′	6′	
	4 x 12	13′	12′	10′	10′	9′	9′	8′	8′	7′
	6 x 10	12′	12′	11′	10′	10′	9′	9′	8′	8′
	6 x 12	15′	13′	12′	12′	11′	11′	10′	9′	9′
Ponderosa—pine	4 x 6	6′								
Redwood	4 x 8	8′	7′	6′	6′					
Western cedar	4 x 10	10′	9′	8′	8′	7′	7′	6′	6′	6′
	4 x 12	12′	11′	10′	9′	9′	8′	8′	7′	7′
	6 x 10	12′	12′	11′	10′	9′	9′	8′	8′	8′
	6 x 12	15′	13′	12′	11′	11′	10′	9′	8′	8′

blocking, the members act independently and should be calculated using the dimensions of the single member. For example, two 2 by 10 beams sandwiched to posts have the span capacity of a single 2 by 10. A built-up beam will always have less strength and resistance than a solid member of a similar size.

Overview of Post Sizes

The final wood calculation for the structure uses a derivation of the load and a chosen height to determine the size in cross section of the post. The load, known as the tributary load, is a figure for square area calculated by multiplying the beam spacing by the post spacing. The post height is measured from the footing attachment to the post beam connection. The tributary load area and the chosen post

Table 15.5 Maximum Post Heights: 40lb/Ft Design Load

Source: Hopper, Landscape Architectural Graphic Standards.Copyright 2007, John Wiley & Sons, Inc.

Species Group	Post Material	Post Load Area = Beam Spacing X Post Spacing (Ft)								
		36	48	60	72	84	96	108	120	132
Douglas—fir	4 x 4	12′	12′	11′	10′	9′	8′	8′	7′	7′
Southern pine	4 x 6	14′	14′	13′	12′	11′	10′	10′	9′	9′
	6 x 6 (#1)	17′	17′	17′	17′	17′	17′	16′	16′	16′
	6 x 6 (#2)	17′	17′	17′	17′	17′	16′	14′	14′	12′
Hem—fir	4 x 4	12′	12′	10′	10′	9′	9′	8′	8′	7′
Southern pine—fir	4 x 6	14′	14′	12′	12′	11′	11′	10′	9′	9′
	6 x 6 (#1)	17′	17′	17′	17′	16′	14′	14′	12′	12′
	6 x 6 (#2)	17′	17′	17′	16′	15′	13′	12′	11′	11′
Ponderosa pine	4 x 4	12′	10′	9′	8′	8′	7′	7′	6′	5′
Redwood	4 x 6	14′	13′	12′	11′	10′	9′	8′	8′	7′
Western cedar	6 x 6 (#1)	17′	17′	16′	14′	14′	12′	12′	12′	12′
	6 x 6 (#2)	17′	16′	16′	13′	12′	12′	12′	7′	

height can be located on the table "Maximum Post Heights: 40 lb/ft Design Load," to give the size of post required in cross-sectional dimension. The choice of posts should be made on appearance as well as structural integrity. A tall 4 by 4 post may look thin in comparison to a large deck, and increasing the size may provide a more pleasing proportional relationship.

Overview of Footing Sizes

The size of a concrete spread footing is calculated using the bearing pressure of the soils and the amount of tributary load each footing will be required to support. The bearing capacity (pounds per square foot, psf) of the soils is available at the local building department. If the deck is uniformly loaded, the total area of deck in square feet multiplied by the loads, typically 50 pounds psf for combined dead and live loads, divided by the number of posts, will provide the tributary loads to be carried by each post and its footing.

To determine the size of the footing, divide the load on the footing by the soil-bearing capacity. For example, to determine a footing to support a post carrying an individual load of 2000 psf with a soil-bearing capacity of 1500 psf, divide 2000 psf by 1500 psf, which equals 1.33, or 192 square in. For a square footing, this is equal to about $13^3/_4$ in. per side, thus a 14-in. by 14-in. footing will work.

Practices to Avoid

A common problem to be avoided when attaching the decking to the joists is nailing close to the end grain of the decking boards. The nails should be set no less than $^3/_4$ in. from the edge. If a pattern requires the decking to change directions at particular points, or if joints line up in a running pattern, a double-joist system can be employed. Instead of using one joist, which provides only $^3/_4$ in. of bearing and forces the nail to be driven at the edge of the decking board, a double joist can be added to provide increased bearing, proper drainage, and air ventilation to the decking end grain. This prevents water being trapped by the joist below in the single-joist method.

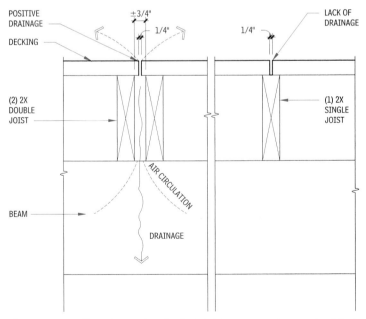

Figure 15.45 The advantages of a double joist system where ends of deck board meet.
Source: "Wood in the Landscape" Daniel Winterbottom, Wiley.

Avoid installing wood in the wrong orientation. Beams and joists should be installed "crown" side up to better resist the loads they will need to carry. Deck boards should be installed with the "bark" side up to avoid cupping which can trap water on the deck board leading to premature deterioration. On some boards the crown and bark side are easy to identify, on others, not so easy. If the bark side is not easily identified on one end of the deck board, look on the other end, usually one end will clearly have a grain pattern that can be identified.

▶ **It is helpful to identify and mark the crown side and bark side of the lumber before construction starts. During construction, it is easy to forget to check, and one or two deck boards placed bark side down will become very obvious over time, requiring replacement after the deck has been completed.**

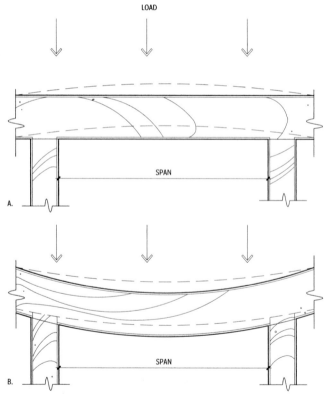

Figure 15.46 The crown side should be oriented up toward the top of the deck (A) to provide greater resistance to the loads place upon it. If reversed, (B) the structural members will tend to sag.
Source: "Wood in the Landscape" Daniel Winterbottom, Wiley.

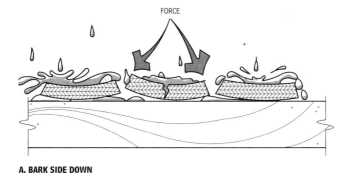

A. BARK SIDE DOWN

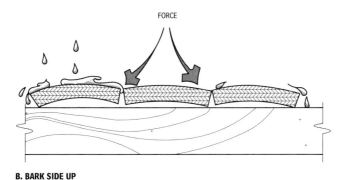

B. BARK SIDE UP

Figure 15.47   When the bark side is oriented down, the boards cup up and can trap water. With the bark side up, the boards will shed water to the sides. *Source:* "Wood in the Landscape" Daniel Winterbottom, Wiley.

Figure 15.48   An example of most of the deck boards being installed with the bark side down, instead of up. These deck boards will cup over time and hold water which will lead to premature deterioration.

Pressure Treated Wood

Description

Wood that will be used outdoors exposed to the elements or in contact with the ground is subject to attack and decay by fungi and insects. Other than species that are naturally resistant, like cedar or redwood, wood that will be used in an exterior application needs to be treated with a preservative.

Pressure treating lumber is the most effective way to extend the useful life of wood for exterior uses. The process involves placing the wood in a large tank that is filled with the liquid preservative and placed under high pressure to force the preservative deep into the wood fibers. The tank is drained, the wood removed and the remaining preservative can be re-used.

▶ Wood preservatives are classified as water based or oil based, depending on the carrier's composition.

For many years, almost all pressure treated lumber used chromated copper arsenate (CCA) as a preservative. Public concern related to the use of arsenic in CCA led the industry to voluntarily transition to alternative preservatives. The use of CCA treated lumber is highly restricted and is no longer available for residential use. Several alternative preservatives have been developed that are less toxic but are still effective in resisting decay from fungi and insect attack.

In response, several pressure treatment preservatives have been developed that do not contain arsenic including ACQ, Copper Azole and Borates. Water-based preservatives like ACQ and Copper Azole, bind with the wood fibers and are resistant to leaching. They can generally be painted or stained. They can increase corrosion in fasteners and metal hardware, so those need to be galvanized or made of stainless steel. Borates do not become fixed in the wood and can leach out if exposed to rain or contact with the ground.

▶ As testing and research continue it is expected that these preservative treatments will evolve and change over time. The most recent data should always be consulted before specifying a pressure treated wood for a project.

There are several species of wood that can be effectively pressure treated, some are more locally available than others. Wood preservatives penetrate sapwood easier than heartwood. The readily available southern yellow pine is the most widely used because it has a higher percentage of sapwood and a cell structure that allows the preservative to penetrate uniformly and deeply into the wood. Wood that has higher percentages of heartwood, like Douglas Fir, are more difficult to penetrate and the preservative often needs modification to be effective or slits cut into the wood (incising) to get the preservative to penetrate deeper.

Assessing Site Conditions

Pressure treated wood is used for a wide variety of outdoor projects including utility poles, bridges, foundations, decks, overhead structures, docks and marine bulkheads.

Varying conditions of exterior wood use require an applicable level of preservative to resist the negative impact of the elements. Wood that will be in contact with the ground is more likely to be subjected to greater decay than wood that will be used above ground. Wood under more extreme conditions will require even higher levels of preservative.

The level of preservative treatment is measured by the pounds of preservative retained by a cubic foot of wood after pressure treatment (see Table 15.6).

▶ ***Retention levels may vary for other types of preservatives. Check their end use category to be sure the wood being used or specified matches the project. End use categories are marked on tags stapled to the end of the lumber. They will specify whether the lumber is appropriate for above ground use or for ground contact., the preservative used, the retention level and AWPA U1, indicating the wood has been treated in accordance with AWPA specifications.**

To make the new preservatives more effective, the level of copper is increased. Copper is toxic to insects and fungi that can cause decay and deterioration. This accounts for wood members that are treated with the newer preservatives being more expensive than wood that had been treated with the less expensive CCA. Choosing wood treated to the appropriate level of retention for an end use is most economical.

▶ **Even projects that use naturally resistant woods or composites for deckboards for example, use pressure treated wood for structural members because of their strength and ability to resist deterioration.**

Table 15.6 American Wood Preservation Association Standards

Code	Preservative Name	UC1,2	UC3B	UC4A	UC4B
ACC	Acid Copper Chromate	0.25	0.25	0.50	--
ACQ	Alkaline Copper Quaternary (Types B,C,D)	0.15	0.15	0.40	0.60
ACZA	Ammoniacal Copper Zinc Arsenate	0.25	0.25	0.40	0.60
CA-B	Copper Azole, Type B	0.10	0.10	0.21	0.31
CA-C	Copper Azole, Type C	0.060	0.060	0.15	0.31
CuN-W	Waterborne Copper Naphthenate	0.070	0.070	0.11	—
CX-A	Copper HDO	0.206	0.206	—	—
EL2	DCOI- Imidicloprid-Stabilizer	0.019	0.019	—	—
PTI	Propiconazole- Tebuconazole- Imidicloprid	0.013	0.018	—	—
PTI	PTI plus Stabilizer	0.013	0.013	—	—
SBX	Inorganic Boron (Formosan termites)	0.28	—	—	—
SBX	Inorganic Boron (non-Formosan termites)	0.17	—	—	—

Use Category	Brief Description
UC1	Interior Dry
UC2	Interior Damp
UC3A	Exterior Above Ground, Coated with Rapid Water Runoff
UC3B	Exterior Above Ground, Uncoated or Poor Water Runoff
UC4A	Ground Contact, General Use
UC4B	Ground Contact, Heavy Duty
UC4 C	Ground Contact, Extreme Duty
UC5A	Marine Contact, Northern Waters (Salt or Brackish Waters)
UC5B	Marine Contact, Central Waters (Salt or Brackish Waters)
UC5 C	Marine Use, Southern Waters (Salt or Brackish Waters)
UCFA	Interior Above-Ground Fire Protection
UCFB	Exterior Above-Ground Fire Protection

Acceptable Practices

Water Based Wood Preservatives

Other than the restrictive use of CCA, most commercial and residential projects use one of the following water based pressure treatment preservatives:

- ACQ (alkaline copper quaternary) is the most common water-based preservative. There are several slightly different compound variations, ACQ-A (discontinued), ACQ-B (penetrates hard to treat woods, has a dark greenish brown color that fades to a light brown), ACQ-C (ranges in color from a dark to light greenish brown) and ACQ-D. ACQ-D is the most common of the variations, except on the west coast where harder to penetrate woods are used, and imparts a light brown color to the wood. Lumber treated with ACQ is commonly used for landscape ties, fences, posts, decking and marine pilings. It can be painted or stained.
- MCQ (Micronized Copper Quaternary) uses microscopic copper particles that bond with the wood cells without the use of a solvent. The process allows wood to keep much of its natural color. It can be painted and stained, even with light colored stains. It is recognized as having a reduced impact on the environment and human health than other wood preservative treatments.
- Copper Azole (CBA) is a water based preservative with copper that has two different compound variations, CBA-A (which contains boric acid) and CA-B (which does not contain boric acid). CA-B contains more copper and is more widely used than CBA-A. With the addition of ammonia, it can effectively penetrate wood that is inherently more difficult to treat, such as Douglas Fir. It imparts a light brown color to the wood that can be painted or stained. Lumber treated with copper azole is commonly used for structural lumber, fence posts, decking, utility poles, fresh water or land pilings as well as shingles, siding, plywood and other building materials.
- Ammoniacal copper zinc arsenate (ACZA) contains copper, zinc, and arsenic. It is used to treat poles, piling, and timbers and is able to penetrate more difficult woods to treat, such as Douglas Fir, and therefore is very commonly used on the west coast. Treated wood can be painted or stained.
- Borate preservatives are dissolved in water and can provide good penetration. However, they do not bind with the wood fibers, and remain water soluble in the wood. Because it will readily leach out, borate treated wood should not be used where it will be subjected to rainwater or ground contact. It is very often used in interior applications. Treated wood can be painted or stained. Borates have a low

toxicity and are naturally occurring in the environment. The most common is Disodium Octoborate Tetrahydrate (DOT).

▶ The lumber pressure treated with these preservatives is often sold under a variety of different brand names.

Oil Type Wood Preservatives

Oil type preservatives are not used where they will be in frequent contact by humans. They are generally used for utility poles, railroad ties and pilings where their water repellant characteristics can prevent checking and splitting. The following are commonly used oil type preservatives:

Creosote, made from coal tar, is not actually dissolved in oil, but has the characteristics of an oil type preservative. It is widely used in railroad ties, utility poles, pilings, marine applications and wood bridge members. It is very dark brown or black and is difficult to stain or paint.

Pentachlorophenol is effective against fungi and insects but not as good for salt water applications. It is commonly used for utility poles, wood bridge members, laminated beams, wood foundations. It can be dissolved in light oils (giving the wood a light brown color) or heavier oils (which will give the wood a darker brown closer to creosote). As the heavier oils provide a more effective resistance to decay and deterioration, the lighter color penta treated wood is generally used for above ground applications and the darker penta treated wood for contact with the ground. It is difficult to stain or paint.

Copper naphthenate dissolves a mixture of napthenic acids and copper salts in oil. The color of the wood varies from light brown to dark green depending on the type of oil. It is difficult to paint or stain unless using a light oil. It is commonly used for utility poles, fence posts, earth retaining walls and wood bridges as well as to treat the ends of field cuts of pressure treated wood.

Preservatives Not Currently Available

Some preservatives are currently no longer commercially available. They are listed here for reference:

- Ammoniacal copper arsenate (ACA)
- Acid copper chromate (ACC)
- Ammoniacal copper citrate
- Copper dimethyldithiocarbamate (CDDC)

Finishing

Although preservatives protect wood against decay from fungi and insects, it does not protect against weathering and moisture damage that can cause warping and cracking. A protective seal coat can slow drying and shrinking and repel water. The protective coating must be compatible with the type of pressure treated wood that it is being used to protect. Manufacturer's directions should be followed regarding how soon a protective coating can be applied, although it can usually be applied as soon as the project is completed.

Most pressure treated woods can be stained or painted successfully. Generally, the pressure treated wood should dry before the application of paints or stains. The drying time may vary because of geographical climate differences; follow the manufacturer's directions for the proper timing before these products are applied.

▶ For existing wood treated with CCA, treating it with a penetrating oil finish or painting can reduce exposure to the CCA.

▶ Wood cuts of pressure treated lumber in the field leave exposed untreated ends. Treat all cuts by brushing with the readily available preservative copper naphthenate.

Fasteners

As always, metal corrosion is an important consideration when choosing fasteners and connectors that will be used with pressure treated wood. In the past, hot dipped galvanized or stainless fasteners and connectors have been recommended, largely based on their ability to resist corrosive environmental conditions. With the higher levels of copper in the pressure treated wood preservatives being used today, corrosion of metal fasteners and connectors from the wood itself is a factor to consider.

The potential for corrosion caused by the galvanic reaction between wood treated with the higher levels of copper and the dissimilar metals of fasteners and connectors that will be used is great. As is the concern involving the galvanic reaction between dissimilar metal fasteners and hardware that are in contact with each other. Careful consideration needs to be given to these concerns during the specifying phase as well as during construction.

Hot dip galvanizing is a process of applying a protective coating of zinc over bare steel. The thicker the zinc coating the more protection against corrosion. The designations related to the galvanized coating thickness (in accordance with ASTM A653) are G-60, G-90 and G-185. Each manufacturer of pressure treated wood will have their own requirements, however, generally, galvanized fasteners and connectors with a minimum of a G-90 rating are required, and a G-185 rating recommended for the highest level of galvanized protection.

▶ **Electroplated galvanized metal has a relatively thinner layer of zinc protection and is not generally considered acceptable for exterior applications.**

Stainless steel fasteners and connectors can be used with pressured treated wood. Not all stainless steel fasteners and connectors are the same. Type 304 and type 316 stainless steel have proven to be compatible with the newer preservatives being used with wood. If the preservative retention of the wood exceeds the level for ground contact, it is recommended to use stainless steel rather than hot dip galvanized fasteners and connectors. If the wood is to be subjected to higher corrosive conditions, such as contact with salt water or areas around swimming pools, type 316 stainless steel has a chemical structure that will provide increased resistance to corrosion in these environments.

▶ **Direct contact between galvanized metal and stainless steel will result in accelerated corrosion of the zinc coating. To avoid the galvanic reaction between dissimilar metals that can lead to corrosion of fasteners and connectors, stainless steel fasteners should only be used with stainless steel connectors.**

Aluminum corrodes very quickly in contact with wood treated with copper based preservatives. Any flashing material and related fasteners should be copper or hot dip galvanized.

There are also proprietary fasteners and connectors available for use with pressure treated wood, and the manufacturers of each should be consulted to ensure that compatible products are being specified and used.

Finishes

After several months of exposure to the weather, pressure treated wood will begin to change color and may exhibit some checking and cracking, particularly to wood that is in a horizontal position. To protect against the deteriorating effects of weather, a water repellent sealer or penetrating semi-transparent stain can be used on most types of pressure treated wood. Paint is another alternative that can be an effective coating if matched to the preservative if the wood is prepped properly and the paint applied in accordance with the manufacturer's instructions. Most manufacturers recommend a drying time before application, which may vary from weeks to months dependent on the climatic conditions of the area. Projects built with wood that is kiln dried after pressure treatment (KDAT) are not subject to the same waiting period. Products are also available to restore wood to its original pre-weathered color.

▶ Paint and solid color stains are not recommended for fully exposed decks.

Whatever finish is chosen, regular maintenance will require a re-application every year or two. Proper preparation of the wood is important, and the product manufacturer's instructions should be followed for a successful application.

Practices to Avoid

- Avoid direct contact with pressure treated wood. Use gloves when handling and use a mask and eye protection when cutting;
- Do not eat after working with pressure treated lumber until your hands have been washed;
- Do not burn pressure treated wood;
- Do not use pressure treated wood for any projects that will be used in direct contact with food or food preparation (this does not mean picnic tables where food is served but not prepared);
- Do not use pressure treated wood for interior projects unless it is specifically designated for that purpose;
- Do not use standard carbon steel products in direct contact with pressure treated wood.

Wood Alternatives

Description

There are several types of wood alternatives available ranging from virgin vinyl, to recycled plastics to combination wood-plastic composites. They are available as solid and hollow. The most popular wood alternative is currently the wood-plastic composite, a combination of recycled wood and plastic.

These wood alternatives do not have the same structural strength and are almost always installed onto traditional treated wood structural members. Because they lack the same structural strength as wood, the structural supports need to be spaced closer than if traditional treated wood is being used and may not meet requirements for handrails.

Assessing Site Conditions

The composition of a wood-plastic alternative and how that might relate to its purpose in the project should be given consideration. The wood fibers contained in these composites can stain and discolor from food or grease spills. They do absorb water and can hold dirt which leaves them susceptible to some decay, mold and mildew. All natural wood alternatives require cleaning with compatible cleaning solutions several times throughout the year. Stains should be cleaned as soon as possible, especially on wood-plastic composites.

All plastic deck lumber is generally made from virgin polyvinyl chloride (PVC) or recycled high density polyethylene (HDPE). Containing no organic material at all, it does not absorb moisture or stain. It can be easily cleaned with soap and water and any mildew can be scrubbed off with any cleaner containing bleach. It has a much smoother surface than wood or wood-plastic composites and as a result might be a bit slippery. Therefore, it may not be the best choice around a pool or other area that is likely to be wet.

Acceptable Practices

As wood alternatives do not have the structural strength of wood, they are almost always attached to a naturally resistant or pressure treated wood framework. Attaching the different types of wood alternatives involves the use of special fasteners and techniques.

Wood alternative lumber can be cut with a circular saw. A carbide-tipped blade with 18 to 24 teeth per inch is recommended (less teeth reduces friction and prevents the blade from getting gummed up). Any small cuts, like around posts, can be made with a jigsaw. Sharp edges can be rounded or beveled with a belt sander or carbide-tipped router bit.

Fasteners made specifically for use with wood alternative lumber should be used and manufacturers often recommend specific fasteners that are compatible with their product. It is best to install fasteners perpendicular to the board and a minimum of 1 in. from the ends to prevent splitting. For decks, it may be best to install a double joist wherever the ends of deck boards will meet. Some material may bump up slightly around each screw hole (sometimes called "mushrooming"). There are some screws specially designed to prevent this, for other screws, pre-drilling the holes will prevent this from happening. The screws should be set flush or slightly below the face of the lumber.

Wood alternatives containing plastics will expand and contract with temperature change, both in width and length. Therefore, a slight gap should be left between boards as well as where ends of boards join to allow for some movement. Plastics will also lose some rigidity in extreme heat and deck boards could sag. To minimize any sagging, joists should be spaced between 12 to 16 in. on center, even if recommendations or local building codes allow for greater spans.

▶ Crowned or bowed wood alternative lumber can be pulled straight and screwed into placed, just like regular wood lumber.

Practices to Avoid

Avoid disappointment by understanding that wood alternative lumber, although requiring less regular maintenance, is not maintenance free:

- Wood fibers in wood-plastic composites can absorb grease and stain
- Wood fibers can hold moisture and mildew can develop
- Wood fibers at the surface may discolor or decay

All wood alternatives require regular washing, need to have stains cleaned up quickly and address mildew issues if they should arise.

▶ Not all wood alternative products are created equal. Some are made with higher quality materials than others, and the higher quality products exhibit less problems than their lesser quality counterparts. Be aware of the materials being incorporated into the lumber and their quality.

References

OTHER RESOURCES:

- American Wood Preservation Association
- Daniel M. Winterbottom. Wood In The Landscape, Hoboken, NJ: John Wiley & Sons, 2000.
- Hopper, Landscape Architectural Graphic Standards. Copyright 2007, John Wiley & Sons, Inc.

Index